Chicano and Chicana

Literature

THE MEXICAN AMERICAN EXPERIENCE

Adela de la Torre, EDITOR

Other books in the series:

Chicano and Chicana Literature

Otra voz del pueblo

Charles M. Tatum

The University of Arizona Press   Tucson

The University of Arizona Press
© 2006 The Arizona Board of Regents
All rights reserved

This book is printed on acid-free, archival-quality paper.
Manufactured in the United States of America

11   10   09   08   07   06   6   5   4   3   2   1

Library of Congress Cataloging-in-Publication Data

Tatum, Charles M.
Chicano and Chicana literature : otra voz del pueblo /
Charles M. Tatum.
p. cm. — (The Mexican American experience)
Includes index.
ISBN-13: 978-0-8165-2427-3 (pbk. : alk. paper)
ISBN-10: 0-8165-2427-0 (pbk. : alk. paper)
1. American literature—Mexican American authors—
History and criticism. 2. Mexican Americans—Intellectual
life. 3. Mexican Americans in literature. I. Title. II. Series.
PS153.M4T38 2006
810.9'86872—dc22

                                        2006013503

Publication of this book is made possible in part by the
proceeds of a permanent endowment created with the
assistance of a Challenge Grant from the National
Endowment for the Humanities, a federal agency.

CONTENTS

■ ILLUSTRATIONS

Chicano and Chicana

Literature

Introduction

Why study Chicana/o literature? One plausible answer would be that it is a very important part of U.S. literature. Another would be that we live in an increasingly diverse and interdependent society, and a broadly educated citizenry should be familiar with Americans unlike themselves in order to function effectively and harmoniously in the social, political, commercial, and educational realms of the twenty-first century. Americans of all ethnic, racial, and national backgrounds should be knowledgeable about and respectful of one another's cultures, of which literature is a vital part. According to the latest census, Hispanics (especially Americans of Mexican descent) have become the largest minority group in the United States. It is therefore compelling that we study the literature of this rapidly growing segment of the U.S. population.

This book has been carefully written with a reader in mind who is interested in an introduction to Chicana/o literature. It may also serve as a guide for teachers who include Chicana/o literary material in their courses. This is not a book that purports to break new scholarly ground or to advance a particular or original theoretical or critical approach. A reader who already has substantial familiarity with Chicana/o literature will find this book covers familiar ground.

▊ Terms

In the chapters that follow, I use a variety of terms to describe ethnicity or national origin, including *Anglo*, *Hispanic*, *Latino*, *Mexican*, *Mexican national*, *American of Mexican descent*, *Mexican American*, *Mexican origin*, and *Spanish speaking*. In addition, as you are most likely aware, Spanish nouns carry grammatical feminine (*a*) or masculine (*o*) endings. In describing groups of people, I frequently use a form analogous to *s/he* in English (for example, *mestiza/o*, *tejana/o*, and *Chicana/o*).

Because these terms can be confusing, I offer a brief explanation of how I use them in this book. *Anglo* is the abbreviated form of *Anglo Saxon* and is often used as the equivalent of *white*. *Hispanic* and *Latino* are broadly inclusive terms that generally refer to U.S. citizens and noncitizens of Mexican, Central American, or South American origin. *Mexican* and *Mexican national* are synonymous terms that refer to a person who has retained her or his Mexican citizenship and may reside in Mexico, be temporarily in the United States, or even be a noncitizen resident of the United States. *American of Mexican descent*, *Mexican American*, and *Mexican origin* are also synonymous, and I use them interchangeably in this book to refer to a U.S. citizen whose parents (or only one parent) are of Mexican descent. This individual may be a naturalized U.S. citizen, a first-generation citizen, or a citizen whose family roots extend as far back as the sixteenth century. *Mestiza/o* refers to an individual of mixed Indian and European ancestry (for example, Yaqui and Spanish). *Tejana/o*, *nuevomexicana/o* (or *neomexicana/o*), and *california/o* refer to a Mexican-origin person from, respectively, Texas, New Mexico, and California.

Chicana/o is a very special term that deserves a detailed explanation. Most scholars agree that the term is an abbreviated form derived from *mexicano* (Mexican), which is in turn derived from the Meshica Indians who, according to Mexican legend, founded Tenochtitlán (the present site of Mexico City) sometime before the fifteenth century. From the late nineteenth century until about the mid-1960s, some Mexican Americans used the term as a derogatory label for Mexican Indian or mestiza/o immigrants who had recently arrived from Mexico and were thought to be socially and culturally deficient, less educated, and even racially inferior. Mexican Americans who had been the victims of Anglo racism and discrimination from the mid-nineteenth century forward and who had begun to assimilate into U.S. society used the term in order to disassociate themselves from recently arrived immigrants as a way of maintaining their status as equals or near equals to Anglos in the larger society. This practice of racism and exclusivity among assimilated ethnic groups has been a common phenomenon throughout U.S. history. For example, the Irish who had begun assimilating into the dominant U.S. society by the late nineteenth century referred to more recent immigrants from Ireland as "shanty Irish."

The connotation of *Chicana/o* changed dramatically in the mid-1960s, at least for Chicana/o cultural and political activists who adopted the term as a source of pride and began to use it in a positive sense to identify themselves as descendants of Mexican Indians. In the same way, black activists adopted the term *Afro-American* (today, *African American*) to associate themselves with their cultural and ethnic origins in Africa. Many former 1960s cultural and political activists continue to identify themselves today as Chicana/o, and the term still persists, particularly among high school and college students who prefer it to *Mexican American*, *Hispanic*, *Latina/o*, or other similar terms. *Chicana/o* is the preferred term when referring to cultural practices such as literature, music, and art.

I use the combined term *Chicana/o* (and the plural *Chicanas/os*) as a noun and an adjective throughout this book. It is increasingly preferred over the term *Chicano/a*, which was formerly much more common. The principal reason for the reversal of the masculine and the feminine forms is to confront and move beyond the vestiges of a patriarchal culture toward greater equality between women and men. Historically, Spanish grammar has used the masculine form to designate men and women together (for example, *mexicanos* can designate either Mexican men alone or both Mexican men and women). About thirty years ago, the combined term *Chicano/a* began to be used in recognition of the importance of women; however, always putting the masculine *o* before the feminine *a* implied the superiority of men and the patriarchal nature of their relationship to women. The use of the feminine form in first position (that is, *Chicana/o*) is at least grammatically and symbolically a way of questioning and subverting this patriarchal relationship and affirming the equality between women and men. It is in this spirit that I use *Chicana/o* (*Chicanas/os*) where I am describing both women and men. I will use *Chicano* to designate the male writer, historical figure, or other person, and *Chicana* to designate a woman writer, historical figure, or other person.

I use the term *Southwest* throughout this book to encompass the states of Texas, New Mexico, Arizona, Colorado, Nevada, and California. These states, or at least parts of them, were Mexico's northern territories until the mid-nineteenth century, when they became U.S. territories and later states.

▮ Shaping the Canon of Chicana/o Literature

The word *canon* may not be familiar to all readers. It is commonly used to describe a body of music, art, literature, or other cultural form that over time has been designated as worthy of preserving and passing on to succeeding generations. A canon consists of the "classics" of, for example, symphonic music, opera, art, and literature that are thought to have somehow "stood the test of time" because of their inherent aesthetic worth and because they express and reflect "universal values."

For example, the ancient Greek poet Homer's *The Iliad* and *The Odyssey* are considered classics of world literature. Similarly, Shakespeare's plays and Milton's *Paradise Lost* are classics of English literature and are considered part of the canon of English literature. Every country has its own canon, or classics, of national literature (for example, Emile Zola and Marcel Proust belong to the French canon; Miguel de Cervantes to the Spanish canon; James Joyce to the Irish canon; Gabriel García Márquez to the Colombian canon).

Rarely discussed and even more infrequently questioned is the essential question of who gets to define what "universal values" are and what works reflect these values over time. In other words, who has been privileged to designate the "classics" and the particular canon they comprise? Who is privileged to add or omit works from a canon? We tend to take for granted that an exclusive group of very wise and intelligent men—women have historically been excluded from influencing literary canons—decided long ago and then periodically reconsidered over many generations what literary works merit inclusion in literary histories, bibliographies, anthologies, high school and college literature courses, topics for scholarly study, and the like. However, when we begin to question the assumptions on which these choices are made, we begin to discover that canon formation is very much influenced by social standing, gender, ethnicity, class, education, economic power, and other forms of status.

Let us briefly consider a limited aspect of the canon of U.S. literature. Up until about thirty years ago, standard anthologies used in high school and college courses typically included very few women or ethnic and racial minority writers (that is, Chicana/o, African American, Native American, and Asian American). With the wholesale reevaluation of social norms and political practices that took place in the 1960s, women and underrepresented minority students, teachers, professors, scholars, and others began to demand that voices historically excluded from the U.S. literary canon be represented. As a consequence, anthologies used today in high school and college U.S. literature courses contain many more women and minority authors. Further, we have discovered that these works so long excluded from the canon of U.S. literature are every bit as "universal" as other works that have historically been included. As a result of this process of reevaluation, Chicana/o literature is in the process of becoming a part of the canon of U.S. literature.

Another related and equally important question is, Who decides what literary works and authors should be included in the Chicana/o canon? The answer to this question is both vexing and fascinating. In addition, it provides us with an excellent illustration of how literary canons are established in the first place. Let me draw on my own work on Chicana/o literature to illuminate a possible answer to the question. In the late 1970s, I began working on a book that I wanted to serve as an overview of Chicana/o literature from its origins in the sixteenth century through the latter part of the twentieth century. I was very soon faced with the dilemma of what works and authors I should include in my study. To a great extent I relied on the work of Chicana/o scholars who, like myself, had begun identifying and systematically studying the literature that had been published from the sixteenth century to contemporary times. But I still faced the dilemma of what authors and works to include and how much attention to give each. I ultimately made decisions assisted in part by the length limits on the book and a publisher's deadline. Subsequent scholarly studies and very significant literary recovery efforts have rendered my book somewhat out of date. The current book, written some twenty years after the publication of my first book, includes dozens of writers who have been discovered, as well as writers who have either continued to publish or have begun publishing, during this period. I have had to reevaluate my own thoughts on the Chicana/o literary canon by questioning my own assumptions and limited vision that guided me twenty years ago.

Shaping the Canon through Recovery Projects

The ongoing process of shaping the Chicana/o literary canon has been informed and influenced over the past century by the efforts of numerous scholars who have discovered, recovered, and published both orally transmitted and written literary texts. Scholars committed to recovering the literary past work much like archaeologists who conduct field research in order to collect artifacts to learn more about civilizations and cultures, although their methods may be different. Chicana/o literary archaeologists have employed some of the following methods: interviews with individuals who have preserved the memory of oral traditions that have been passed on from generation to generation; systematic examination of public and private family libraries and archives in search of both published and unpublished manuscripts; and careful scrutiny of collections of old newspapers in search of literary nuggets such as poems and short stories by little-known and sometimes anonymous authors. Much of this literary archaeological work is tedious, frustrating, and time-consuming and may take years before yielding results.

We are indebted to many scholars who have done their part in recovering and bringing to our attention the foundations of the Chicana/o literary heritage and who have thereby helped shape its canon. A few pre-1960s examples are Aurelio E. Espinosa, Arturo L. Campa, Juan B. Rael, Aurora Lucero-White, and Elaine K. Miller; they interviewed hundreds of rural and urban dwellers throughout the Southwest and painstakingly began to piece together important pieces of oral and written traditions that in many cases can be traced back to the Iberian peninsula and, later, Mexico. More recently scholars including Doris Meyer, Raymond Paredes, Genaro Padilla, Rosaura Sánchez, Beatriz Pita, Clara Lomas, Gabriel Meléndez, Nicolás Kanellos, Luis Leal, Francisco Lomelí, Erlinda Gonzales-Berry, Teresa Márquez, and Tey Diana Rebolledo have contributed many works to the Chicana/o literary canon.

Recovering the U.S. Hispanic Literary Heritage Project

The single most important effort to recover the Chicana/o literary heritage and at the same time help to shape its canon is the Recovering the U.S. Hispanic Literary Heritage project (http://Benito.arte.uh.edu/Recovery/recovery.html), a broad-based group of scholars and editors (including some of the scholars mentioned in the previous paragraph) who in the 1990s developed strategies to recover and preserve the literary heritage of all U.S. Hispanic groups (such as Cuban Americans, Puerto Rican Americans, and Dominican Americans, as well as Chicanas/os). Nicolás Kanellos, a distinguished scholar and professor at the University of Houston and founder of Arte Público Press (see figure 1), assembled an advisory board that has met periodically since 1991 to guide the project in its recovery efforts and especially its publication of scholarly studies and original literary manuscripts. In addition to these important tasks, members of the advisory board and other scholars have engaged in a lively debate about what guidelines and criteria should be used to help develop the canon of the U.S. Hispanic literary past. In general, these scholars have been very strong advocates for inclusiveness in terms of the criteria, categories, and

■ 1. Nicolás Kanellos

definitions of what constitutes literature worthy of recovering, preserving, and publishing. Incorporated into the recovery project's guidelines is the concept that literature should not be defined narrowly to include only established genres—that is, poetry, novels, short stories, drama, and essays—to the exclusion of literary practices and discourses that women, for example, have historically cultivated (such as personal anecdotes and tales, diaries, letters, prayers, or recipes). The recovery project conferences and publications will have a very strong influence on defining and shaping the Chicana/o canon well into the twenty-first century.

■ Language

Up until about the end of the nineteenth century most Chicana/o writers published their works in Spanish, either because it was their only language or because it was their first, or dominant, language. Many writers who were fluent bilinguals and equally comfortable in both languages preferred Spanish because, among other reasons, it was the language of most of their readers. During the twentieth century, as Americans of Mexican descent began to assimilate more rapidly into mainstream Anglo society and to become progressively less fluent in Spanish, most writers for whom English was now their dominant language naturally wrote in English. From about 1965 forward, contemporary Chicana/o poets, playwrights, novelists, short story writers, and essayists have published primarily in English, but there have been notable exceptions among the writers whose works I discuss in subsequent chapters. I have not separated out the authors who have written all or at least some of their works in Spanish (for example, Miguel Méndez, Rolando Hinojosa, Alicia Gaspar de Alba, Erlinda Gonzales-Berry, Alejandro Morales, Aristeo Brito, Margarita Cota Cárdenas, Lucha Corpi, or Tomás Rivera), but instead I have discussed their works as representative of certain themes and trends. Wherever appropriate, I indicate that a work was originally published in Spanish.

▮ Organization of the Book

This book is organized into seven chapters, each of which is divided into shorter sections. At the end of each chapter are discussion questions intended to help you focus on the chapter's content and relate it to other material in the book. Suggested readings are also listed at the end of each chapter for those of you who would like to gain a more in-depth knowledge of different aspects of Chicana/o literature.

Chapter 1 is an overview of some of the most important theoretical and critical approaches employed by scholars over the past forty years to analyze and better understand Chicana/o literature. Chapter 2 reviews Chicana/o history and the parallel development of its literature from the sixteenth century to about 1965. Chapter 3 focuses on the Chicano Movement and the flowering of Chicana/o literature during the 1960s and early 1970s. Chapter 4 discusses some major themes in contemporary autobiography and memoirs, and chapter 5 does the same for contemporary narrative fiction. Chapter 6 focuses on major trends and themes in theater, and chapter 7 on contemporary poetry. A short conclusion is followed by a comprehensive bibliography of the primary and secondary works cited and referred to in the book.

■ Suggested Readings

Acuña, Rodolfo. 2000. *Occupied America: A History of Chicanos.* New York: Longman.

Bruce-Novoa, Juan. 1990. *RetroSpace: Collected Essays on Chicano Literature.* Houston: Arte Público Press.

Kanellos, Nicolás. 1994. *The Hispanic Almanac.* Detroit: Visible Ink.

Leal, Luis, and Pepe Barrón. 1982. Chicano Literature: An Overview. In *Three American Literatures: Essays on Chicano, Native American, and Asian American Literature for Teachers of American Literature,* ed. Houston A. Baker, 9–32. New York: Modern Language Association of America.

Paredes, Raymond A. 1982. The Evolution of Chicano Literature. In *Three American Literatures: Essays on Chicano, Native American, and Asian American Literature for Teachers of American Literature,* ed. Houston A. Baker, 33–79. New York: Modern Language Association of America.

Rosales, F. Arturo. 1996. *Chicano! The History of the Mexican American Civil Rights Movement.* Houston: Arte Público Press.

Shirley, Carl R., and Paula W. Shirley. 1988. *Understanding Chicano Literature.* Columbia: University of South Carolina Press.

Tatum, Charles M. 1982. *Chicano Literature.* Boston: G. K. Hall & Co.

Zimmerman, Marc. 1992. *U.S. Latino Literature: An Essay and Annotated Bibliography.* Chicago: MARCH/Abrazo Press.

Approaches to the Interpretation
of Chicana/o Literature

In this chapter, I discuss the development of multiple and varied approaches to the interpretation of Chicana/o literature over the past thirty years that coincide with the surge in the publication of literary texts themselves. Many of the approaches I describe originated in Europe or the developing world (for example, Latin America and India), or are homegrown in the United States. Chicana/o literary scholars have played a major role in drawing upon and adapting at least some of these approaches to the particular socioeconomic, cultural, and historical circumstances in which the production of literary texts is embedded. With some notable exceptions, these scholars have tended to avoid highly abstract theoretical approaches to literature in favor of those that deal with the particularities of the Chicana/o experience in the United States from the mid-nineteenth century forward. As a consequence, some approaches have left a lasting impact on the ways we view Chicana/o literature whereas others have been abandoned.

I have divided the chapter according to theoretical or critical categories and have provided examples of scholars whose works are representative of different approaches, but in doing so I do not mean to imply that these scholars have relied on a single approach to the exclusion of others. The very nature of scholarly inquiry in any field of study (for example, literature, microbiology, physics) requires that scholars continue to explore new theories and test the validity of those theories they prefer. Just as various theoretical and critical approaches have developed over the past few decades, Chicana/o scholars themselves have continued to evolve and adapt in their consideration and interpretation of literary texts. Some scholars have experimented with various approaches and have taken on different ones while shedding old ones.

◼ 1970s Theoretical and Critical Approaches

The Chicano Movement of the 1960s and particularly its impact on university campuses throughout the Southwest were key to development of at least two early critical approaches to Chicana/o literature that are closely related and often confused: the cultural-nationalist (also referred to as nationalist and culturalist) and the dialectical-historical approaches.

In 1977, Joseph Sommers, an ideologically progressive scholar and authority on contemporary Mexican literature, published the first overview of Chicana/o criticism based on his analysis of several Chicana/o scholars' literary studies published since the mid-1960s. In 1979, Sommers coedited a book, *Modern Chicano Writers*, with Tomás Ybarra-Frausto. This book brought together many important studies by Chicana/o scholars. In a shortened version of his 1977 essay "From the Critical Premise to the Product," Sommers provides a contrastive model of how to apply several critical approaches to a single work, namely, Tomás Rivera's highly regarded 1971 novel, ... *Y no se lo tragó la tierra* (... And the Earth Did Not Part). Sommers preferred a dialectical-historical approach to analyzing and understanding Chicana/o literary texts. He considered this approach to be more dynamic and socially responsible than either formalist or cultural-nationalist criticism. In general, the historical-dialectical model evolved in the 1960s from a tradition of Marxist analysis of sociohistorical processes that originated in the nineteenth century. In applying this model to literature, the critic would approach a literary text as a cultural product embedded in a historical, social, economic, and political matrix; the critic would emphasize the politics of the text and would question to what extent the text was the product of the historical period in which it was written and to what extent the writer's beliefs and perspective had been influenced— even determined—by his or her social class, economic status, and other factors. The role of the critic is thus "to challenge both writer and reader to question the text for meaning and values . . . and to situate this meaning and these values in a broad cultural framework of social and historical analysis" (Sommers 1977, 62). From a dialectical-historical perspective, the critic would emphasize the relationships across time among class structures, social institutions, and literary forms and would focus on how a literary text constitutes Chicana/o cultural responses to the history that this ethnic minority has lived.

Juan Bruce-Novoa was in the mid-1970s already a rising star among

2. Juan Bruce-Novoa

Chicana/o critics (see figure 2); he would subsequently go on to have, through numerous articles, essays, and books, a major and lasting influence in shaping the new field of Chicana/o literary criticism. Bruce-Novoa is widely considered an extremely influential critic whose prolific scholarship has often been cited by Chicana/o and non-Chicana/o critics alike. He was instrumental in opening up and helping to define the canon of Chicana/o literature by bringing to our attention writers such as John Rechy, Cecile Piñeda, and Sheila Ortiz Taylor. His 1980 book *Chicano Authors: Inquiry by Interview* included extensive interviews with key Chicana/o writers. His 1982 book *Chicano Poetry: A Response to Chaos* has become a standard critical reference work for students and scholars of Chicana/o poetry.

In contrast to Sommers's dialectic-historical approach, Bruce-Novoa (1990, 160) believes that "the text itself, and not the critic's interpretation, remains the central point of the reading encounter, and that the critic's role is to lead readers back to the text better equipped to enjoy and understand the experience. The critic should never attempt to impose her or his own pre-established norms or expectations on either the text or the reader.

The Evolution of Theoretical and Critical Approaches

In 1979, the Chicano critic Ramón Saldívar (see figure 3) published the groundbreaking article "A Dialectic of Difference: Towards a Theory of the Chicano Novel." He would later more fully develop some of the ideas set forth in this article as a book, *Chicano Narrative: The Dialectics of Difference* (1990), that is today required reading in many graduate-level courses on Chicana/o literature across the United States. Saldívar was raised in Edinburgh, Texas, along the U.S.–Mexico border and completed his doctoral studies in English at Yale University. The Yale Department of English was in the 1970s home to a very distinguished group of literary scholars. Saldívar's 1979 essay and 1990 book reflect the strong influence that these scholars had on his development as a critic. Some of them, including Paul de Man, J. Hillis Miller, and Jacques Derrida, were largely responsible for importing poststructuralism from Europe and legitimizing it among scholars in the United States.

Poststructuralism is an enormously complex set of ideas about which much has been written. My brief overview of these ideas is necessarily superficial and general, but I have provided several excellent resources on poststructuralism in the "Suggested Readings" at the end of this chapter for those readers interested in a deeper understanding than I provide here.

Poststructuralism developed in

3. Ramón Saldívar

France in the 1960s. One of the most important strains of poststructuralism, and the first to reach the United States, was *deconstruction*, whose basic ideas are generally attributed to the French intellectual Jacques Derrida. Derrida questions our faith in language and objective analysis by arguing that both written and oral language are fundamentally unstable and unreliable modes of communication. He argues that both human perception and knowledge are fundamentally flawed and that we can have no reliable or genuine knowledge of ourselves or our identity. The literary critic who follows deconstruction argues that the instability of language "always undoes the apparent coherence of literary texts" (Bertens 2001, 145). Such a critic would deconstruct a literary text by carefully teasing out meanings that reveal the binary oppositions it contains (for example, good versus evil, truth versus falsehood, masculinity versus femininity, purity versus impurity); each opposition has both a center, or privileged, part and a peripheral part. Most of the time, the privileging of one concept over the other escapes readers' notice or is hidden within the literary text; the deconstructionist's task is to bring the terms and their privileging to our attention. Another important aspect of deconstructionism is that the interpretation of a literary text will never lead to a definitive or complete explanation of its meaning, because interpretations are in constant flux.

Poststructuralism in general and deconstruction in particular also had profound implications for the notion of logocentrism, an underpinning of

Western thought that has played an integral role in our intellectual tradition. Logocentrism is basically an unswerving belief in some ultimate and transcendental explanation of being (for example, God, the Idea, the Creator, Self, Substance, Matter) or of a concept of nationhood and national values (for example, Democracy, Independence, Family, Authority, Order) as well as identity (Woman, Man, Black, Indian, Chicana/o). Literary theorists often refer to these concepts as *metanarratives*; that is, concepts that explain everything and from which all other ideas originate. Poststructuralism questions the transcendental nature of these concepts, reinterpreting them as fictions shot through with nuances, contradictions, subtlety, and doubt. Derrida and others cast grave doubt upon the very notions of truth, reality, meaning, and knowledge (Eagleton 2003, 124).

Poststructuralism in general, and Paul de Man and J. Hillis Miller's version of French deconstruction in particular, were central to Ramón Saldívar's intellectual formation and led him to adopt some but not all of its basic ideas in developing his own theory of Chicana/o narrative. At the same time, he incorporated some of the concepts of dialectical-historical criticism. This artful and highly original interweaving of two seemingly disparate theories—dialectical-historical on one hand and poststructuralist on the other—in analyzing and interpreting Chicana/o literature established an excellent model for other critics to follow.

In his 1990 book, Saldívar seeks to "test the usefulness of new developments in literary theory" in an examination of "representative aspects of Mexican American narrative forms" such as the novel, short fiction, narrative poetry, and autobiography (Saldívar 1990, 3). In what is still one of the most ambitious and highly provocative book-length studies by a Chicana/o critic, Saldívar takes up the challenge of grappling with the complexities and nuances of various late twentieth-century intellectual currents, including poststructuralism, deconstruction, psychoanalysis, Marxist criticism, feminist theory, and "other nontraditional forms of literary analysis." His largely fulfilled purpose is to analyze key narrative works of Chicana/o literature that he characterizes as defining themselves in "opposition and resistance to mainstream social, historical, economic, and cultural modalities" (Saldívar 1990, 3). One of the strengths and enduring qualities of *Chicano Narrative* is Saldívar's grounding in what theorists refer to as "material reality"; that is, the lived experiences of Chicanas/os and the historical conditions under which they have struggled to survive against overwhelming socioeconomic odds and conditions of oppression since

1848. For Saldívar, history is not merely background or context, but rather the "decisive determinant of the form and content of the [Chicana/o] literature" (Saldívar 1990, 5).

Much less specific and easy to trace and define than the trends under the general label of poststructuralism is the elusive and very confusing term *postmodernism*. Postmodernism is generally viewed as encompassing poststructuralism, or at least sharing many of its intellectual trends. Many books and countless essays have been written about this paradigm in an attempt to pin it down conceptually and even historically. Marxist critics, for example, describe postmodernism in terms of the historical period and new economic order—the "commodification of cultural production"—that began in the late 1940s and early 1950s. They generally dismiss the phenomenon as ahistorical and even politically reactionary for its emphasis on the mass-production of commercial goods. Others see postmodernism as progressive because postmodernist works can constitute a force for resistance and change and be open to difference and a plurality of views, thereby allowing for diversity and difference, which should be particularly appealing to racial and ethnic minority theorists, critics, and writers. Others see postmodernism as being progressive and reactionary at the same time, while still others question whether the concept is at all meaningful. Some scholars use the term to describe 1960s U.S. countercultural opposition to "bourgeois" middle- and upper-class pretensions and values. Other scholars link it to the rise of popular and mass culture and the critique of "high" culture such as canonical works of art or literature.

Although there is little agreement on the characteristics, definition, or nature of postmodernism, it has generated a great deal of interest on the part of Chicana/o literary scholars, who tend to view it negatively. Most alarming to them is postmodernism's attack on the concept of subjectivity and its repudiation of representation, especially when a literary text is seen to refer only to itself and not to any concrete historical or material reality.

For example, the Chicana scholar Rosaura Sánchez is highly critical of some of postmodernism's more extreme advocates, who question the very validity of an ethnic minority literature or "discourse," as well as its historical or interpretative value. She observes that such an extreme view even questions the validity of a term like *Chicana/o* as being "essentialist" (Sánchez 1987, 1). Even more troubling for Sánchez and other Chicana/o scholars is the postmodernist rejection of what is referred to as a "fixed subject status." Postmodernism questions the very existence of subjectivity or the centrality of the individual—including, for example, the protagonist in a Chicana/o novel. The individual is no longer considered to be the source of knowledge, meaning, and history; the very status of the individual, or the subject, is placed in doubt. In place of the subject, the postmodernist posits "subject positions" or "subject identities."

Sánchez explains why the denial of the subject has profound implications not only for Chicana/o literature in general, but for Chicana feminism and feminist literary expression in particular: "The questioning and subsequent denial of the subject comes precisely at a moment in history when women and marginalized ethnic minorities are trying to assume their subject status to create a voice for themselves, to overturn the 'othering' to which they have been historically subjected" (Sánchez 1987, 6). Sánchez perceptively observes that a Chicana/o literary work can have postmodernist traits (for example, shifts in narrative perspective, fragmentation of time and space, parody, multiplicity of narrative levels), but the subjects of these works still continue "their way through the morass of poverty, exploitation, oppression, and ethnic discrimination," which would appear to violate—at least in the view of some theorists and critics—a postmodernist aesthetic (Sánchez 1987, 7). On the other hand, Sánchez is critical of Chicana/o writers and critics who impose one essentialist, or uniform, ethnic identity on their readers, thus failing to take into consideration gender and class differences and varied perspectives within the culture.

José David Saldívar, another prominent Chicana/o scholar (brother of Ramón Saldívar and Sonia Saldívar-Hull, a promising younger Chicana critic) shares Sánchez's wariness about the extremes of postmodernist theory and criticism. In a 1986 article, "Towards a Chicano Poetics: The Making of the Chicano Subject, 1969–82," Saldívar explicitly rejects the "erasure" of the Chicana/o subject by European and American "Eurocentric" postmodernists and poststructuralists. In this and subsequent literary studies, Saldívar in fact engages in the opposite exercise: to devise and describe the Chicana/o subject in border *corridos* and other narratives.

Jorge Mariscal, another Chicano critic who has recently published an anthology and a scholarly study on Chicanas/os in Vietnam (see chapter 5), traces how in the 1980s postmodernism became the dominant method for reading U.S. representations of the war and thereby displaced valuable feminist and other studies of both the war and writings about the war that emphasized the class and racial composition of combat units, the economic and emotional impact of the war on U.S. society in general and on Chicana/o communities in particular, and "the contradictions between U.S. democratic ideals and U.S. imperialist brutality." He laments the fact that in large measure Vietnam War studies and Chicana/o studies abandoned "an earlier insistence on material reality . . . and political engagement in general in order to accommodate themselves to the hegemony of postmodern and poststructuralist paradigms" (Mariscal 2000, 16).

In addition to Rosaura Sánchez, other Chicana feminist critics have also been sharply critical of what they view as some of the implications of poststructuralist and postmodernist theory as practiced in the United States by non-Chicana scholars. For example, Tey Diana Rebolledo perceives that postmodernist and postcolonial studies in the United States have profound ramifications for the study of Chicana literary texts. Like Sánchez, Saldívar, and Mariscal, she is especially concerned that these critical discourses consider the speaking subject (the voice of the author) to be "dead" at a time when it is just beginning to evolve among Chicana/o writers. Although Rebolledo does not go as far as to reject all contemporary critical theories, she does remind us that they should be used cautiously as Chicana feminist critics develop their own approaches to literary texts (Rebolledo 1995, 2).

The late Chicana writer Gloria Anzaldúa also deals with the sticky dilemma of subjectivity that poststructuralist theory presents for many minority literary and cultural critics. She deals with the question forthrightly by creating her own concept of multiple subjectivities, or plural selves, in her groundbreaking book *Borderlands/La frontera: The New Mestiza* (1987). Anzaldúa appropriates the notion of *mestizaje* (a concept associated historically with miscegenation, or the mixing of two distinct races, in this case Caucasian Spanish and Mexican Indian) in her self-identification as "the new mestiza," the embodiment of several subjectivities, a "plural" personality—woman, lesbian, feminist, cultural critic, Chicana, Mexican, white, Indian, working class, rural—that allows her to tolerate the subjective differences, ambiguities, and contradictions that characterize the formation of Chicana/o culture. Anzaldúa's concept of multiple or shifting subjectivities is perhaps unique among Chicana/o critics.

◼ Chicana Feminist Literary Critics

As I will discuss in greater detail in chapter 2, Chicana activists (including literary critics) confronted a number of issues during the years of the

Chicano Movement and afterwards. They often found themselves in a double bind as they struggled to gain positions of equality alongside their male counterparts and at the same time avoid being accused of disloyalty in their common cause of liberation. Chicanas found themselves struggling against both Anglo racism from without and patriarchy from within the Chicano Movement. Many males preferred that women in the movement continue to fill secondary and traditional roles as cooks, child-care providers, lovers, and the like, while Chicanos adhered tenaciously to their dominant roles as public spokesmen, decision makers, and political strategists. As the women grew progressively less tolerant of their subservient roles and began to assert their demands for equality, males and even other Chicana activists frequently accused them of "selling out" to Anglo feminism and ultimately to the very forces of oppression against which the movement was battling. A strong group of Chicana feminists began to coalesce and gain strength in the late 1960s and early 1970s.

Many of these first Chicana feminists whose primary interest was literature played an important role in defining Chicana feminism and in developing a new field of Chicana feminist theory and criticism. They struggled to come to grips with European and U.S. feminist literary theories. Chicana feminist scholars saw in these theories virtually no accommodation, understanding, or empathy for the historical, cultural, and socioeconomic particularities of Chicana/o literary expression. Issues of identity, racism, class, and difference that were important to Chicana literary scholars did not seem to fit within the agenda of European and U.S. feminist scholars. As a result, Chicana feminist theorists and critics since the late 1970s have developed their own very innovative and original approaches to Chicana/o literature. These feminist scholars include Cherríe Moraga, Tey Diana Rebolledo, Norma Alarcón, María Herrera-Sobek, and Rosaura Sánchez.

Cherríe Moraga's Realist Feminism, or "Theory in the Flesh"

In this section, I draw heavily on Chicana feminist critic Paula M. L. Moya's (2002) extremely interesting, well-informed, and perceptive study of what she identifies as Moraga's "realist feminism," a natural outgrowth of her status as a Chicana and a lesbian. Moya provides a careful and insightful analysis of Moraga's feminist thought developed in her writings in general and particularly in her mixed-genre book *Loving in the War Years*. She places Moraga at the forefront of the Chicana response to both

Chicano cultural nationalism and Anglo-American feminism. Moya explains that Moraga attained this position of respect based on two factors: first, the inherent strength of her writings; and second, the fact that her first works were published by feminist and not by Chicana/o presses, thereby avoiding a confrontation with publishers and editors who might have considered her disloyal to the Chicana/o cause for social justice.

Along with others, Moraga was frequently called upon in the 1980s by non-Chicana feminists to represent and speak about Chicana feminism. Moraga's feminist writings and public appearances were strongly indicative of her desire to build alliances with other women of color (that is, Native American, African American, and Asian American); her feminism is therefore best described as inclusive rather than exclusive.

Moya identifies five concepts as central to Moraga's theoretical approach: (1) the family as the primary instrument of socialization; (2) the need for theory to be grounded in one's emotional investment rather than being abstract and aloof; (3) the link between social location and experience (that is, race, ethnicity, sexual preference, class); (4) the body as a source of knowledge; and (5) the centrality of struggle to the formation of her political consciousness (Moya 2002, 144). Moraga identifies her feminist theory as "theory in the flesh," where the physical realities of women's lives—skin color, the land or concrete where they grew up, their sexual longings—all fuse to create a politic born of necessity. Moya comments that such a concrete theoretical position implies that the social facts of a woman's existence are relevant to the experiences she will have and that those experiences will necessarily inform her understanding of the world as well as her politics. Her social location, knowledge, and identity are mediated, or shaped, by her interpretation of her experience (Moya 2002, 144–45).

Tey Diana Rebolledo: A Feminist Critical Praxis

I have already mentioned Tey Diana Rebolledo's skepticism toward esoteric literary theories in general and poststructuralist and postmodernist literary theories in particular (see figure 4). She is also not impressed with critics who overuse jargon and sometimes confuse readers, especially readers not familiar with abstract and convoluted theoretical concepts and trends. In her 1995 book, *Women Singing in the Snow: A Cultural Analysis of Chicana Literature*, she presents her own alternative Chicana literary feminism, which is related to that of Moraga in the sense that it does not rely on theoretical or critical models from Europe, the United States, or develop-

4. Tey Diana Rebolledo (photo by Miguel Gandert)

ing countries. She applauds those theorists and critics who emphasize the historical and socioeconomic contexts surrounding the literary texts they analyze. Like Moraga, Rebolledo values theoretical models created by Chicana-feminists themselves. Rebolledo presents an eclectic and ever-evolving theoretical approach much like an excellent cook uses a recipe; rarely does such a cook follow a recipe rigidly like a blueprint but instead uses it only as a guide to be adapted, changed, fiddled with, and improved on. In like manner, the theoretical basis underlying a Chicana literary feminist critic's analysis of literary texts "is represented as a loose format around which things may be added or taken away" (Rebolledo 1995, 3). Rebolledo does not believe that Chicana feminist scholars can produce a pure (she uses the term *nativist*) theoretical model devoid of all influences from contemporary theory, but her guiding principle is that "theory must be appropriate to the literature, that the critic's biases need to be acknowledged" (Rebolledo 1995, 5). Her underlying thesis is that Chicana (and Chicano) literary critics need to be able to adapt, change, and be flexible and pragmatic in practicing their criticism of literary texts. There is no one right way, but rather several different approaches, each suitable for some writers and texts and not for others.

Other Chicana Feminist Approaches

Despite the well-founded caution and general skepticism with which Chicana critics view European and U.S. feminist theory and criticism, several Chicana critics have drawn on such theory and criticism, judiciously and creatively adapting them to better understand the expressive complexities that are characteristic of Chicana/o literature in general and Chicana literature in particular. I have identified three Chicana feminist critics who have been particularly successful in doing so—namely, Norma Alarcón,

María Herrera-Sobek, and Rosaura Sánchez—although I could have included many others.

NORMA ALARCÓN AND CONTEMPORARY FRENCH FEMINISM Contemporary French feminist criticism has several major variants revolving around the works of Julia Kristeva, Hélene Cixous, and Luce Irigaray. Although these variants do not present a uniform view of women authors and their literary texts, they seem united in being critical of much of U.S. feminist criticism. French feminist critics consider their U.S. counterparts to be superficial in that they analyze only the most obvious manifestations of women's oppression. French feminist critics, on the other hand, rely on the "deep structures" of culture and language hidden in the unconscious. Kristeva, Cixous, and Irigaray all posit an expression in literature and in other realms that they identify as *ecriture feminine*, or the expression of repressed femininity or writing "from the body." All three French feminist theorists speak of a space and a form of communication that exists between a mother and her infant before the infant begins to be exposed to language, particularly the male language of patriarchy that is identified as "symbolic" and "rational" as opposed to the nonrational, presymbolic expression embodied in writing from the body. A critic who accepts this basic tenet of French feminist criticism would focus her analysis of a woman's literary work on this prerational expression that comes directly from the writer's unconscious.

In general, French feminist criticism is criticized for isolating itself from ideological and political concerns that many Chicana feminists consider to be essential to a full understanding of patriarchy—such as the oppression and subjugation of women—as manifested in literary expression. Despite these reservations, Chicana critics such as Norma Alarcón have integrated certain aspects of contemporary French feminist theory into their own approaches to Chicana literary texts.

Norma Alarcón has found Kristeva's concept of the female speaking subject quite useful in analyzing Chicana literary texts. For example, in her study of several female narrators, she has revealed that some speak their subjectivity directly while others are bound by and speak through patriarchal symbolic language. Alarcón demonstrates how Chicana writers such as Sandra Cisneros, Ana Castillo, and Denise Chávez have their female speaking subjects or narrators look back to a transitional time when

5. María Herrera-Sobek
(photo by Stacey Keleher)

they are deciding whether or not to become a woman according to prescribed male patriarchal standards.

MARÍA HERRERA-SOBEK AND THE PRACTICE OF FEMINIST ARCHE-TYPAL CRITICISM María Herrera-Sobek (see figure 5) is perhaps unique among Chicana scholars in using what is referred to as *archetypal criticism* in her examination of Mexican and Chicana/o cultural expressions such as the *corrido*, a narrative ballad or folk song form found in Mexico and along the U.S.–Mexican border. The word *archetype* can be traced to the Greek philosopher Plato who uses the term in its basic Greek meaning (*arche*, "original," *typos*, "form"). Carl G. Jung, the Swiss psychologist, began to use archetypes in his own analytical psychology practice in the 1920s. Sixty years later feminist literary critics adapted Jung's concept of archetype to their examination of images and patterns in women's literature.

Herrera-Sobek applies feminist archetypal theory to the representation of women in corridos. In doing so, she defines feminist archetypal criticism "as a type of analysis that views archetypes as recurrent patterns in art, literature, film, songs, and other artistic endeavors depending on historical, political, and social forces for their formation" (Herrera-Sobek 1990, xiii). Unlike Jungian psychologists, who view archetypal images as being encased in the psyche at birth and revealing themselves throughout our lives, Herrera-Sobek considers archetypal images to be malleable, dynamic, and subject to each culture's particular historical circumstances. Gender and patriarchy are essential factors as a culture constructs these images and expresses them in literature, film, songs, and other forms of expression. Herrera-Sobek's position is that the crystallization of an archetype in a society is the result of a historical process, and that the archetypal images that an individual visual artist or literary author creates depend on her or his historical circumstances. The repeated or recurrent images that surface through artistic expression she identifies as archetypes.

Herrera-Sobek has identified four predominant components that she considers crucial to the construction of archetypal images in Mexican and Chicano culture: patriarchal ideology, the social class of the *corridista* (the composer of ballads) and his or her audience, Mexican history, and the Western literary tradition. Based on her examination of thousands of corridos from the nineteenth and twentieth centuries, she identifies four main types of recurrent images, or patterns, in which women appear: The Good and the Terrible Mother, the Mother Goddess, the Lover, and the Soldier.

As in the case of many other prominent Chicana/o scholars, Herrera-Sobek has by no means limited her analysis of literary texts to feminist archetypal criticism. Her extensive scholarly publications reflect, among other approaches, a broadly feminist criticism and an emphasis on cultural studies.

ROSAURA SÁNCHEZ AND CHICANA FEMINIST MATERIALIST CRITICISM

In an important 1987 article, "Postmodernism and Chicano Literature," Rosaura Sánchez challenges historians to approach the history of Chicanas/os using a "materialist" perspective. Her challenge to historians applies equally to literary critics. Sánchez points out that Chicana and non-Chicana historians from the 1960s forward have tended to focus exclusively, or at least primarily, on issues of gender and sexuality to the exclusion of the particular material circumstances such as class that determine women's status and struggles at any point along the historical continuum of Chicana history. She posits a much more comprehensive and complex set of socio-economic factors that should be considered for a more complete understanding of the history of Chicanas.

Sánchez grounds her approach on the concept that women form one biological but various sociological groups. She observes that feminist historians—and, by extension, feminist literary critics—who advocate that sex is a significant factor in determining self-identity tend to ignore the fact that not all women share the same positions in the world; instead their positions are differentiated by class, race, religion, and national origin. Although she does not deny that Chicanas share some of these and other factors in common, historians and literary critics should be aware of how such diversity affects the different material conditions among Chicanas. For example, a recently immigrated Chicana from rural Mexico is likely to be very different from a recently immigrated Chicana from Mexico City in terms of their respective values, attitudes, material wealth, education, observance of religious practices, and other factors. Third-generation, middle-class Chicanas whose parents are college-educated professionals will in turn be very different from first-generation, low-income Chicanas whose families may put pressure on their daughters to go into the job market after high school graduation to help support the family rather than continuing their studies in college. Literary critics who analyze and interpret literary texts must be aware of these factors in order to provide an accurate and nuanced understanding of, for example, a female protagonist in a novel.

■ Queer Theory

Queer theory is relatively new to literary scholarship in general and to Chicana/o scholarship in particular. Probably the first identified use of this unique approach to the study of culture—including literary texts—occurred in the early 1990s. It is generally considered to have grown out of gay/lesbian studies, which itself only came into existence as a defined area of study in the mid-1980s. Gay/lesbian studies in turn evolved from feminist studies and feminist theory from the 1960s on. Just as feminist scholars examine socially constructed notions of what constitutes femininity and how these notions have evolved over time, gay/lesbian scholars examine how homosexuality has been socially constructed and has changed throughout history. One of the principal tenets of gay/lesbian theory is to challenge the idea that heterosexuality is normative human behavior and homosexuality is a deviant behavior; this theory is thus highly critical of what scholars often refer to as *heteronormativity*.

Queer theory also questions the social construction of the categories of normative and deviant sexual behavior, but it is more expansive than gay/lesbian studies in challenging anything that falls into normative and deviant categories, with an emphasis on but not limited to sexual activities and identities. Like feminist theory and gay/lesbian studies, queer theory challenges the very notion that sexuality is an essentialist category. For example, what society defines as "male" and "female" is only in part biologically determined; the very nature of gender or sexuality is socially constructed.

The field of queer theory relative to Chicanas/os in general and Chicana/o literary studies in particular is only partially developed. Chicana lesbian literary studies are more advanced than gay literary studies due in part to the vigor of Chicana feminist studies, which began almost forty years ago as a response to the decidedly male-dominated Chicano Movement. The works of Norma Alarcón, Gloria Anzaldúa, Cherríe Moraga, and Rosaura Sánchez reflect to varying degrees a lesbian studies approach to literary texts. Mary Pat Brady, Alicia Gaspar de Alba, and Paula M. L. Moya have also made very important contributions to Chicana lesbian literary studies. Other scholars such as Emma Pérez have been instrumental in bringing a historian's perspective to lesbian studies.

■ 6. Yvonne Yarbro-Bejarano

Carla Trujillo's edited volume *Living Chicana Theory* (1998) includes some of these literary scholars as well as others such as Yvonne Yarbro-Bejarano (see figure 6) and Chela Sandoval.

Tomás Almaguer noted in 1993 that there were far more studies—literary and otherwise—on Chicana lesbians than on Chicano gay men. He observed that "unlike the writings on Chicana lesbianism [works on Chicano homosexuality] fail to discuss directly the cultural dissonance that Chicano homosexual men confront in reconciling their primary socialization into Chicano family life with the sexual norms of the dominant culture" (Almaguer 1993, 256). More than a decade later, Ralph E. Rodríguez has lamented the fact that this essential scholarship still has not been done (Rodríguez 2005, 35–36). Chicana/o queer theory is therefore still heavily skewed toward Chicana lesbianism.

■ Postcolonial Theory

Beginning in the 1920s and 1930s, African American writers began to define themselves on the basis of race and to express this emerging self-identity in literature under what has come to be known as the Harlem Renaissance. About the same time French-speaking Black writers from African and Caribbean colonies began to define themselves and their own literary expression as distinct from that of the dominant colonial powers, especially the United Kingdom, France, and Belgium. Soon after the end of World War II, many of the colonies began struggles for independence that culminated by the 1960s in the establishment of numerous new countries in Africa and the Caribbean as well as the founding of India and Pakistan. Writers and other artists from these former colonies became known as *postcolonialists* in the sense that their striving for cultural self-definition paralleled the political self-determination of their peoples.

An outgrowth of the colonies' cultural and political separation from the former colonial powers was the development of what has come to be known as postcolonial studies, an emerging and now vast field of cultural, political, and historical enquiry (Bertens 2001, 199–200). Postcolonial studies focuses not only on the power relationships between former colonial powers and former colonies but also on what is viewed as the aggressively expansionist imperialism of new colonizing powers and the system of values that supports such imperialist practices in the twenty-first century.

A significant group of Chicana/o historians, literary critics, and political scientists who emerged from the turbulent but intellectually formative period of the Chicano Movement began to view the relationship between the dominant Anglo society and the largely subjugated and economically and politically disenfranchised Chicana/o minority as one between the powerful center and an internal colony. This internal colony model was particularly popular among Chicana/o historians in the early 1970s. These historians reasoned that the collective experience of Americans of Mexican descent after 1848 was characterized by a massive loss of territory and a consequent loss of political and economic power that lasted more than one hundred years; in addition, the mechanisms of subjugation exercised by the Anglo-dominated center against the Chicana/o periphery had allowed an internal colony to exist within the nation. By the mid-1970s, Chicana/o historians began to question the appropriateness of the internal colony model as overly simplified and unable to accommodate factors such as race and class.

The idea of Chicanas/os as a colonized people did continue to appeal to literary critics, who saw the intersections of Chicana/o literature with the representations of colonial and postcolonial peoples across the continents and even within the United States. According to Chicano critic Rafael Pérez-Torres (1995), the advantage of considering Chicana/o literary criticism as a postcolonial discourse is that it serves to bridge the gap between it and other U.S. minority discourses (for example, Native American and African American) as well as Third World discourses (for example, many literatures on the African continent as well as in Latin America). He reasons that the analysis of Chicana/o literary discourse within the context of and in relationship to certain forms of literary expression elsewhere allows the reader to make historical connections and to understand more deeply that Chicana/o literature is not an isolated phenomenon. Pérez-Torres also believes that making such linkages allows critics and theorists to develop approaches to literary discourse that are not burdened by or dependent on dominant European or American theories such as poststructuralism (Pérez-Torres 1995).

■ Cultural Studies

Along with postcolonial studies, Chicana/o critics have incorporated cultural studies into the range of contemporary critical approaches they use to examine literary texts and other forms of cultural expression. Cultural studies, which is commonly thought to have originated at the University of Birmingham in England in 1964, began to emerge as a distinct academic discipline in U.S. universities in the 1980s and has become more widespread since that time.

It is difficult to define cultural studies precisely because its practitioners draw on several established disciplines, such as literary criticism, sociology, cultural anthropology, cultural geography, political science, economics, media studies, communication, and history; it is clearly interdisciplinary or, to use a more contemporary term, transdisciplinary. Cultural studies is different from many forms of literary study not only in that it is highly interdisciplinary but also because its proponents study many cultural objects (for example, film, music, magazines, comic books, radio, television) in addition to literary texts. Another difference is that they frequently reject the values assigned to forms of cultural expression defined as "high art" (for example, canonical literature, classical music, museum art) and "low art" (for example, detective fiction, rock music, graffiti). Literary texts are never examined as cultural objects separable from their conditions of production, distribution, and consumption.

The modes of inquiry employed in cultural studies criticism range from survey techniques, field interviews, and audience studies to textual analysis and especially institutional and ideological analyses. For example, a scholar of cultural studies who examines popular romances or comic books would include an examination of the practices of publishing companies, distribution networks, and bookstores in shaping and maintaining the rules of the romance or comic book genre as well as their packaging and promotion.

José David Saldívar has discussed both the advantages and limitations of cultural studies as applied to Chicana/o literary discourse. In the introduction to his 1997 book *Border Matters: Remapping American Cultural Studies*, he traces the evolution of cultural studies from the 1980s when U.S. academics begin to import British intellectuals' original concepts. Saldívar cites the founding documents on which the curriculum of British cultural studies at the University of Birmingham was based and emphasizes that *culture* was defined as a material, intellectual, and spiritual struggle and resistance rather than as an isolated and static phenomenon.

The practice of cultural studies at the University of Birmingham and elsewhere in Britain was not an isolated intellectual classroom exercise, but was characterized by active intervention in working-class social struggles. Saldívar expresses the fear that the dynamic nature and political edge of British cultural studies has become blunted through becoming institutionalized as just another interesting discipline in U.S. universities. He seeks to keep alive the dynamism and "political edge" of cultural studies by proposing a "remapping" of American cultural studies in an interdisciplinary articulation with border studies, itself a complex melding of various disciplinary perspectives that focus not only on the U.S.–Mexico border but on other international borders as well. The collection of essays in Saldívar's book is, in part, an answer to a question he asks in the introduction: "How do we tell other histories that are placed in local frames of awareness, on the one hand, and situated globally, geopolitically, on the other?" (Saldívar 1997, 12). Saldívar strives through the different strategies suggested in the essays to create "a new comparative area of intercultural studies" that draws on Chicana/o as well as Mexican writers and cultural critics whose focus is the U.S.–Mexico international border. His purpose is to suggest a historical and intercultural approach to what he calls "transborder" writing and cultural studies. This approach constitutes his "remapping" of American cultural studies.

Rosa Linda Fregoso and Angie Chabram draw on cultural studies to propose alternative representations of Chicana self-identity that contest and reject what they consider to be the gender-inflected cultural definition that emerged from the Chicano Movement of the 1960s and early 1970s. The two Chicana critics consider this identity problematic for several reasons: It was static, fixed, and one-dimensional; it was a collective identity and therefore failed to acknowledge historical differences and the multiplicity of Chicana/o cultural identities; and it proposed a "transcendental" Chicano subject that existed outside of time and was unaffected by changing historical processes. These critics draw on the cultural insights of Stuart Hall, one of the central intellectuals in the University of Birmingham cultural studies project. Hall conceives identity as a "production that is never complete," but a dynamic process in which representations are embodied in the forms and practices of culture (Fregoso and Chabram 1990, 205).

Perhaps the most ambitious project of any contemporary Chicana/o cultural critic and literary theorist is Chela Sandoval's book *Methodology of the Oppressed* (2000). In this very complex, brilliant, and densely textured study, she posits U.S. Third World feminism as the theoretical and critical conceptual underpinnings of her unique methodology whose aim is to empower us to understand, analyze, and act to correct social injustice in an increasingly bewildering, globalized world. Like other Chicana/o scholars, she is highly critical of the many pitfalls of the array of European and U.S. literary and cultural theories briefly discussed earlier in this chapter. At the same time, she engages some of the major trends of feminist, postcolonial, poststructuralist, cultural studies, and other theories of the past forty years, parts of which she finds compatible with U.S. Third World feminism. What she hopes will emerge from her selective melding of these theoretical currents is a unique theory and method of "oppositional consciousness" that is intellectually flexible enough to explain and confront some of the most powerful and corrosive socioeconomic and cultural forces of the twenty-first century.

Sandoval urges academicians of all theoretical persuasions to move beyond the endless and fruitless intellectual debates that have taken place over the past several decades within the confines of academia. She staunchly believes that if theory does not result in a change in behaviors and attitudes that has social justice as its highest aim, it is simply pontification and posturing among scholars. In the end, her methodology is intended as a broad and innovative mode of social analysis that allows us to understand the complexities of how the political, economic, and cultural forces that surround us dominate and subjugate women, people of color, gays and lesbians, and others.

Manuel Martín-Rodríguez and Reception Theory

Another contemporary approach to literary texts is what is commonly known as *reception theory* or *reader-response theory*. Underlying this approach is the tenet that meaning is not something that is contained within the text or can be extracted from it. Meaning is produced by the readers of a text who interact and work in conjunction with it. Readers of a text develop reading strategies and common interpretive conventions that bind them together in what are called "interpretive communities" (Macey 2000, 324). Manuel Martín-Rodríguez draws broadly on reception theory in his 2003 book *Life in Search of Readers: Reading (in) Chicano/a Literature*. His persuasively developed hypothesis is that Chicana/o literature has historically been defined as much by its readers as by its texts and authors. Adding substance to this hypothesis, he focuses on the development of pre-Chicana/o literature from the earliest colonial times through the Mexican American period, the rise of the Chicano Movement in the 1960s, and the combination of watershed political, social, and cultural forces since then that caused a basic redefinition of their cultural heritage by at least some sectors of the U.S. population of Mexican descent. Of particular interest is Martín-Rodríguez's knowledge and analysis of important historical trends and occurrences as well as other extra-literary factors that shaped Chicana/o writers, their texts, and particularly their audiences. His contention is that Chicana/o literature has throughout its history "manifested different characteristics based on who its intended readers were, what the material conditions of publication and distribution were like, the linguistic choices available for literary communication, and the geographical mobility of writers and readers" (Martín-Rodríguez 2003, 2). He also takes into consideration other factors including the class status of the literature's ideal readers, gender differences in access to both reading and writing literary texts, and the literary tastes that readers and writers acquired in Mexico or in other countries.

One of the most interesting aspects of *Life in Search of Readers* is its shift away from the patriarchal conception of society in general and literature in particular in the decades after the height of the Chicano Movement (see chapter 3). Up until about the mid-1970s, Chicana readers and writers were largely displaced and silenced by their male counterparts. And although there were notable exceptions, these exclusionary practices resulted in infrequent publication of literary texts by women. Martín-Rodríguez devotes a significant part of his book to the larger role played by Chicana writers from the 1980s forward, to how the readership for contemporary Chicana literature is created, and to how and why it is "gendered."

■ Discussion Questions

1. Discuss the double bind that many Chicanas found themselves in during and after the Chicano Movement.

2. How did this double bind manifest itself in Chicana feminist literary theory and criticism?

3. Discuss the major theoretical and critical trends in Chicana/o literary criticism from the mid-1960s through the 1970s.

4. What is your understanding of poststructuralism and postmodernism?

5. Discuss why some Chicana/o scholars, such as Rosaura Sánchez and Jorge Mariscal, are so critical of both poststructuralism and postmodernism.

6. Why is Ramón Saldívar's 1990 book *Chicano Narrative* such an important theoretical and critical study?

7. What distinguishes Chicana feminist critics such as Tey Diana Rebolledo from others such as Norma Alarcón?

8. Why is cultural studies a unique way of looking at a literary work?

■ Suggested Readings

Alarcón, Norma. 1988. Making *Familia* from Scratch: Split Subjectivities in the Work of Helena María Viramontes and Cherríe Moraga. In *Chicana Creativity and Criticism: Charting New Frontiers in American Literature*, eds. María Herrera-Sobek and Helena María Viramontes, 14–59. Houston: Arte Público Press.
——. 1989. Traddutora, Traditora: A Paradigmatic Figure of Chicana Feminism. *Cultural Critique* 5 (Fall): 57–87.
Aldama, Arturo J., and Naomi H. Quiñonez, eds. 2002. *Decolonial Voices: Chicana and Chicano Cultural Studies in the Twenty-First Century.* Bloomington: Indiana University Press.

Aldama, Frederick Luis. 2004. Cultural Studies in Today's Chicano/Latino Scholarship: Wishful Thinking, *Faltus Voci*, or Scientific Endeavor? *Aztlán* 29 (1): 193–218.

——. 2005. *Brown on Brown: Chicano/a Representations of Gender, Sexuality, and Ethnicity*. Austin: University of Texas Press.

Almaguer, Tomás. 1993. Chicano Men: A Cartography of Homosexual Identity and Behavior. In *The Lesbian and Gay Studies Reader*, eds. Henry Abelove, Michèle Aina Barale, and David M. Halperin, 255–73. New York: Routledge.

Anzaldúa, Gloria. 1987. *Borderlands/La frontera: The New Mestiza*. San Francisco: Spinsters/Aunt Lute.

Bertens, Hans. 2001. *Literary Theory: The Basics*. New York: Routledge.

Eagleton, Terry. 2003. *Literary Theory: An Introduction*. Minneapolis: University of Minnesota Press.

Fregoso, Rosa Linda, and Angie Chabram. 1990. Chicana/o Cultural Representations: Reframing Alternative Critical Discourses. *Cultural Studies* 4: 203–12.

Gaspar de Alba, Alicia, ed. 2003. *Velvet Barrios: Popular Culture and Chicana/o Sexualities*. New York: Palgrave Macmillan.

Groden, Michael, and Martin Kreiswirth, eds. 1994. *The Johns Hopkins Guide to Literary Theory and Criticism*. Baltimore: Johns Hopkins University Press.

Herrera-Sobek, María. 1990. *The Mexican Corrido: A Feminist Analysis*. Bloomington: Indiana University Press.

Mariscal, Jorge. 2000. Reading Chicano/a Writing about the American War in Vietnam. *Aztlán* 25 (2): 13–49.

Martín-Rodriguez, Manuel M. 2003. *Life in Search of Readers: Reading (in) Chicano/a Literature*. Albuquerque: University of New Mexico Press.

Moya, Paula M. L. 2002. *Learning from Experience: Minority Identities, Multicultural Struggles*. Berkeley: University of California Press.

Moya, Paula M. L., and Michael R. Hames-García, eds. 2000. *Reclaiming Identity: Realist Theory and the Predicament of Postmodernism*. Berkeley: University of California Press.

Pérez, Emma. 1999. *The Decolonial Imaginary: Writing Chicanas into History*. Bloomington: Indiana University Press.

Rebolledo, Tey Diana. 1995. *Women Singing in the Snow: A Cultural Analysis of Chicana Literature*. Tucson: University of Arizona Press.

Rodríguez, Ralph E. 2005. *Brown Gumshoes: Detective Fiction and the Search for Chicana/o Identity*. Austin: University of Texas Press.

Saldívar, José David. 1986. Towards a Chicano Poetics: The Making of the Chicano-Chicana Subject. *Confluencia* 1 (2): 10–17.

——. 1991. *The Dialectics of Our America: Genealogy, Cultural Critique, and Literary History*. Durham: Duke University Press.

——. 1997. *Border Matters: Remapping American Cultural Studies*. Berkeley: University of California Press.

Saldívar, Ramón. 1990. *Chicano Narrative: The Dialectics of Difference.* Madison: University of Wisconsin Press.

Saldívar-Hull, Sonia. 2000. *Feminism on the Border: Chicana Gender Politics and Literature.* Berkeley: University of California Press.

Sánchez, Rosaura. 1987. Postmodernism and Chicano Literature. *Aztlán* 18: 1–14.

Sandoval, Chela. 2000. *Methodology of the Oppressed.* Minneapolis: University of Minnesota Press.

Selden, Raman. 1997. *A Reader's Guide to Contemporary Literary Theory.* Lexington: University Press of Kentucky.

Sommers, Joseph. 1977. From the Critical Premise to the Product: Critical Modes and Their Application to a Chicano Literary Text. *New Scholar* 6: 51–80.

Sommers, Joseph, and Tomás Ybarra-Frausto, eds. 1979. *Modern Chicano Writers: A Collection of Critical Essays.* Englewood Cliffs, NJ: Prentice Hall.

Trujillo, Carla, ed. 1998. *Living Chicana Theory.* Berkeley: Third Woman Press.

2

The Origins and Evolution
of Chicana/o Literature

Any standard comprehensive history of a country's literature establishes the origins of that literature and then traces its evolution through contemporary times. In the case of many histories of U.S. literature, English-born writers such as John Smith, William Bradford, and Nathaniel Ward are commonly given as examples of early writers who helped to establish the origins of our national literature. U.S.–born writers come later, after the colonies declare their independence from Great Britain.

A full account of the origins and evolution of Chicana/o literature should include Spanish-born writers from as early as the sixteenth century through the beginning of the nineteenth century when Mexico gained its independence from Spain. A full account should also include U.S.–born Chicana/o writers who came into prominence after the middle of the nineteenth century, when Mexico's northern territories—today's U.S. Southwest—became a part of the United States. In recognition of these significant historical changes, I have divided the literature discussed in this chapter into two sections: the Spanish period (sixteenth century to 1848), and the Mexican American Period (1848 to the mid-1960s). The short period between Mexican Independence in 1821 and annexation of the U.S. Southwest in 1848, often referred to as the Mexican Period, is inconsequential in terms of literary production and therefore does not constitute a separate period in this chapter. I discuss the literature of the so-called Chicana/o period from the mid-1960s on in chapters 3 through 7.

The Spanish Period

By the time Christopher Columbus arrived on the shores of the Caribbean island of Hispaniola in 1492, there were already very highly developed native Indian societies throughout South America and Mexico, such as the Incas, the Mayas, and the Aztecs. By 1521, Hernán Cortés, a Spanish government official, and his small army of Spaniards and Mexican Indians conquered the center of the Aztec empire, Tenochtitlán, the site of present-day Mexico City. The Spanish quickly replaced Aztec military, social, and religious institutions with their own and then began four centuries of colonization and settlement of central Mexico as well as the far reaches of southern Mexico, the Yucatan Peninsula, and northern Mexico. This newly conquered territory became the Viceroyalty of New Spain, and its capital, Mexico City, served as the hub for the exploration and colonization of the rest of Mexico and later the Southwest.

The movement north into the southeastern region of the present-day United States began in the first part of the sixteenth century. Cuba was one of the staging areas from which Spanish expeditions set out to explore Florida, the entire Gulf Coast, and the Atlantic Coast as far north as North Carolina. A Spanish expedition founded St. Augustine, Florida, in 1565, the oldest Spanish settlement in the United States, and many other settlements in the southeastern United States after that.

The movement north into the southwestern region began shortly thereafter. The Spanish crown, through its representatives in the New World, was intent on acquiring material wealth—especially gold and silver—in the New World in order to finance its military campaigns in Europe. Numerous Spanish expeditions set out directly from Mexico City to explore the lands to the north. In 1540, Francisco Vásquez de Coronado, a band of mainly Mexican Indians, and four missionaries fruitlessly sought the fabled city of Cíbola, which was reputed to be built of gold. By 1546, the Spanish established the great silver mines in today's Mexican state of Zacatecas (Acuña 2000, 28–36). Using Mexican Indian slave labor, they became the most productive silver mines in Mexico, at one time providing up to a third of the Spanish crown's wealth in New Spain. But there was a great human cost to these and other Spanish enterprises. Demographers have estimated that the native population throughout Mexico declined precipitously from 1,700,000 in 1519 to 165,000 by 1800. Many Mexican Indians perished from the harsh conditions in Spanish mines and on plantations as well as from diseases imported by the Spaniards to which they had no natural immunity.

Spanish military personnel, Catholic Franciscan and Jesuit priests, and colonists established a string of presidios (forts), missions, and pueblos (towns and villages) in the northern Mexican states of Zacatecas, Durango, and Chihuahua. Their next step was to proceed farther north along inland routes to seek more mineral wealth. In 1598, Don Juan de Oñate, a prominent Zacatecan mine owner, came north with five hundred colonists to settle New Mexico, a vast expanse of territory. As in central and northern New Spain, the Oñate and other Spanish colonizing expeditions met with resistance from indigenous Indian tribes, but once they had overcome such resistance they imposed highly exploitative schemes condoned by Spanish authorities in Mexico City to expropriate Indian lands and establish a system of virtual slavery. The Spanish crown established Santa Fe as the capital of Nuevo México and achieved complete control over the territory by the end of the eighteenth century (Acuña 2000, 35). Parts of south Texas were not settled until the first decades of the eighteenth century with the establishment of missions in and around San Antonio that became the hub of further settlement and commerce extending as far east as Louisiana and as far west as El Paso.

Approximately 150 years after exploring and colonizing parts of New Mexico, the Spanish moved steadily northward from Sonora into southern Arizona and along the west coast of Mexico and California, repeating the process of establishing a chain of missions, presidios, and pueblos. Between 1769 and 1823, the Franciscans built a string of missions from Mexico as far north as San Francisco, including San Diego, Santa Barbara, San Luis Obispo, Santa Cruz, San Jose, and Santa Clara. Mexican and California Indians were forced into labor to cultivate the crops and build roads, churches, and other structures. In Arizona, the presidios of Tubac and Tucson were not founded until late in the eighteenth century.

New Spain, which by the early nineteenth century included all of Mexico and much of the U.S. Southwest, remained under the control of the Spanish crown until 1821, when Mexico became an independent nation. The Southwest briefly became Mexico's northern territories, but only until 1848 when this region was ceded to the United States at the conclusion of the Mexican War with the signing of the Treaty of Guadalupe Hidalgo.

◼ The Oral Tradition

As they explored and settled the U.S. Southwest, Spanish missionaries, military personnel, and colonists brought with them written civil and military documents, maps, and religious writings such as Bibles. And although some individuals probably also brought with them literary works popular in Spain and New Spain at the time, we have little evidence that these works survived. What is not in question, however, is that religious and secular poetry, songs, riddles, proverbs, folktales, and a few short dramatic religious plays did survive and were passed on orally from generation to generation for more than four centuries. Spanish and later Mexican and Mexican American inhabitants of the Southwest faithfully preserved some of these orally transmitted forms in their original versions, but they also adapted and created new ones to fit their changing circumstances and tastes.

Scholars interviewed Spanish-speaking inhabitants—especially ones in mountainous, isolated areas—during the first half of the twentieth century and published the transcriptions of their interviews. These scholars were intent on downplaying the Mexican and Mexican American contributions to the oral tradition, choosing instead to emphasize the parallels and similarities to Spanish peninsular forms. Nonetheless, they did set down in writing oral forms that were quickly disappearing as the Southwest became more urbanized.

Folktales, Riddles, and Proverbs

Scholars such as Juan B. Rael and Elaine K. Miller have collected and analyzed orally transmitted folktales, riddles, and proverbs, many of which were until about the 1950s part of a thriving storytelling tradition in rural areas such as northern New Mexico and southern Colorado. Although most of the tales that have survived have undergone many changes, their similarity to original peninsular Spanish versions of the sixteenth century attest to the continuous Spanish-Mexican presence in the Southwest for more than four hundred years.

Songs and Poetry

Spanish peninsular songs and poetry had taken firm root in the Spanish settlements in Mexico by the early 1600s, and they made a successful journey north to the mountains and river valleys of New Mexico and other areas later in the century. The most common forms found in areas of heavy Spanish colonization are the *décima*, the *canción*, the *romance*, and the corrido. The décima (which takes its name from its standard ten-line form), a song form popular in New Mexico during the nineteenth century, was sung on religious occasions; it was also adapted as a type of love song and as a political diatribe. The canción (song) is generally lyrical and frequently expresses love and affection toward a beloved or sadness and anger over unrequited love. The romance evolved from Spanish epic po-

7. Américo Paredes
(courtesy of Arte Público Press)

etry of the eleventh century. It is an easily memorized ballad form that individuals sang at home and in taverns to transmit news from one town to another (for example, births, marriages, singular achievements, tragedies). According to the eminent Chicano scholar Américo Paredes (1958; see figure 7), the romance was still strong in Spain when the Spanish conquerors arrived in Mexico in the sixteenth century. They brought with them a form of the romance called the romance corrido, and by the middle of the sixteenth century some Mexican Indian tribes were composing their own romance corridos. A ballad form that evolved from and is closely related to the romance is the corrido. The corrido becomes particularly important during the Mexican American period (discussed later in this chapter) when it often was used to express resistance to Anglo domination.

The Persistence of the Oral Tradition into the Twentieth Century

The Chicana scholar Tey Diana Rebolledo has studied transcribed oral histories of nuevomexicanas that were collected in the 1930s and 1940s under the auspices of the Federal Writers' Project (FWP), a governmental agency established by the Franklin Roosevelt administration to create jobs and promote public works. A trained corps of FWP employees traveled to urban neighborhoods as well as to remote rural areas throughout Texas, New Mexico, and Arizona to interview and transcribe both English- and Spanish-speaking Mexican Americans. Many of the oral histories came from people who were in their sixties or older, some of them from families of the earliest Spanish settlers (Rebolledo 1995, 13).

Rebolledo has not only uncovered hundreds of these oral histories, but also has brought to light a collection of oral folktales and personal recollections of real-life events told by women. She, like Rael, has found that some of the highly imaginative and descriptive tales are variants of Spanish peninsular tales, but more important, many others are of local origin. She comments that although many of these women could not read or write, their oral transmission of tales, personal histories, and the like left a heavy mark on the literary life of their time (Rebolledo 1995, 14).

Even today, Chicanas/os throughout the Southwest continue to collect and publish tales, personal histories, and other forms transmitted orally to them by their parents and grandparents and *los viejos* (the old ones). For example, Patricia Preciado Martin (see figure 8) has drawn on this rich oral tradition to publish several collections, including the

8. Patricia Preciado Martin (photo by Linda Kirkpatrick)

beautifully illustrated *Beloved Land: An Oral History of Mexican Americans in Southern Arizona* (2004). Nasario García has devoted many years to collecting and publishing oral histories, memories, tales, and the like from the nuevomexicanas/os of central and northern New Mexico. The oral tradition remains vital and vibrant even at the beginning of the twenty-first century and will continue to be so as more and more students of the past delve into this rich cultural heritage.

Early Written Poetry

The first surviving written poetry from what became the U.S. Southwest is Gaspar Pérez de Villagrá's epic history of New Mexico, *Historia de la Nueva México* (The History of New Mexico), published in Spain in 1610. Pérez de Villagrá accompanied Oñate on his expedition to New Mexico and soon thereafter composed his work. The poem's thirty-three cantos narrate in part how the Spanish entered and conquered New Mexico, the infamy and loneliness of the commanders and their soldiers, the tribulations of the first part of the trip, the founding of the first Spanish settlement at San Juan de los Caballeros, the exploration of lands bordering on the Rio Grande, and the siege of the Pueblo town of Acoma. Throughout the poem, Villagrá depicts the Indians as treacherous and marauding while emphasizing the Spaniards' positive qualities.

■ Spanish-Period Written Narrative Documents

We are fortunate that hundreds of written accounts (known in Spanish as *relaciones*), chronicles, short histories, reports, letters, announcements, memoirs, and diaries have survived from the Spanish period. Many of these narrative documents contain highly imaginative literary elements that convey the combination of fear, despair, wonder, tragedy, and excitement that their authors experienced in the sometimes inhospitable regions of the Southwest. They describe the extreme climatic conditions and difficult terrain, attacks from Native Americans who were defending themselves against what they considered to be invaders of their lands, and experiences of missionizing and Christianizing the Indians.

An excellent example of a relación is Alvar Núñez Cabeza de Vaca's *Los naufragios* (The Shipwrecked), his account of his eight-year trek through parts of Texas, New Mexico, and northwestern Mexico as he sought to return to New Spain after being shipwrecked along the Gulf Coast. This narrative work captures the range of emotions from despair to exhilaration that the author and a small band of men experienced during their trek. It is a moving story of human endurance and survival under very harsh conditions and at the same time it offers a unique perspective on how a small group of Spaniards found common ground with some indigenous peoples, who shared their food and medicinal plants with a hapless group of interlopers who stumbled onto their ancestral lands. Cabeza de Vaca's account is also important because it contains important ethnographic information about indigenous peoples as well as brief descriptions of varied flora and fauna ranging from coastal Texas to the high deserts of New Mexico. His account reads like a captivating adventure novel that succeeds in maintaining a high level of suspense and creates a rich texture of details while leaving much to the reader's imagination.

Fray Marcos de Niza's *Relación del descubrimiento de las siete ciudades* (Account of the Discovery of the Seven Cities) is a good example of how Spanish authors embellished the realities of what they encountered in the Southwest. While Fray Marcos is generally careful in the account of his expedition into New Mexico to distinguish between observation and hearsay, he seems to lose his good judgment as news of the fabled cities of Cíbola becomes more intense. While the whole narrative is of interest as an example of imaginative writing, it is his description of his supposed sighting of one of the seven cities of gold that stands out. Historians have documented that what he almost certainly saw from some distance was a simple Zuñi village that contained no gold or precious jewels.

Niza's work does illustrate the propensity of sixteenth-, seventeenth-, and eighteenth-century Spaniards to pepper their accounts of exploration with highly imaginative elements commonly associated with fiction. Other accounts of New Mexico expeditions are also interesting for the vivid descriptions their authors provide. These accounts include Francisco Vásquez de Coronado's expedition of 1540, the Chamuscado-Rodríguez expedition of 1581, the Espejo expedition of 1582, the Castaño de Sosa expedition of 1590, and the Morlete expedition of 1591.

During the last half of the eighteenth century, a period of intense Spanish exploration and colonization of California, many Spanish missionaries and military officials recorded, sometimes in careful detail, the events and impressions of expeditions and encounters with California's indigenous peoples. We are fortunate that so many of these written accounts have survived. The most highly imaginative accounts include those of Fray Junípero Serra, Francisco Palou, Gaspar de Portolá, Miguel Costansó, Juan Bautista de Anza, Fray Francisco Games, Fray Juan Díaz, and Fray Gerónimo Boscana.

Juan Bautista de Anza's accounts of the two expeditions he led in 1774 and 1775–76 are richly creative as he records the long marches and operations from the royal presidio of Tubac in southern Arizona to California. He cites landmarks, detailed directions, and the names of rivers and mountains, and describes different Indian groups encountered along the trek. Of particular interest are his lyrical descriptions of the natural beauty of mountain valleys, rivers, and especially the stunning land and water expanse of San Francisco Bay.

Fray Gerónimo Boscana's "Chinigchinich" (1831), is a favorable account of the origin, customs, and traditions of the Indians at the mission of San Juan Capistrano. Besides providing considerable ethnographic detail, Boscana includes a wonderfully imaginative summary of this people's story of the creation of the world. The title of his work comes from the super deity who, looking favorably upon the Indians, gave them rain, agriculture, and other gifts, and then commanded them to build a temple in his honor. Boscana focuses on the importance of astral bodies and the seasons in their mythology. He also tries to re-create the creation story in all its charm and fantasy. This part of "Chinigchinich" reads like the Greek account of the Gods on Mount Olympus.

■ Theater

Although there is no evidence of plays in written form until the nineteenth century, the first record of performed theater in the Spanish period is found in Gaspar Pérez de Villagrá's epic poem *Historia de la Nueva Mexico*. Pérez de Villagrá describes how on April 30, 1598, Don Juan de Oñate and his men paused among the trees on the banks of the Rio Grande somewhere near the present site of El Paso to witness the performance of a play written by a Captain Farfán, one of the members of the expedition. Pérez de Villagrá's account of the play is sketchy, but he does tell us that the soldiers themselves were the actors. There is almost nothing in the poem about Captain Farfán or the content of the work, but it is safe to surmise that it probably took the form of a religious thanksgiving.

Pérez de Villagrá includes a fuller reference to a second dramatic performance that occurred between July and September 1598 in the plaza of San Juan de los Caballeros, the first Spanish capital of New Mexico. Villagrá records the festivities surrounding the dedication of the church, which included the performance of the Spanish religious drama *Moros y cristianos* (Moors and Christians), which dates from at least the sixteenth century in Spain. This religious play, a reenactment of the routing of the Moorish troops by Christian troops late in the fifteenth century, was typically performed on horseback. The performance of this and other plays (some reenacting the Spanish defeat of the Aztecs in 1521) before the Pueblo Indians of New Mexico was a deliberate strategy used to warn them that acts of resistance to Spanish conquest and colonization would be futile and would bring disastrous consequences.

Religious dramas such as the traditional *autos sacramentales* (sacramental works), didactic religious plays based on Old and New Testament narratives and on popular Christian traditions, were performed from the sixteenth century forward to facilitate the conversion of indigenous peoples. The performance of *autos* was meant to imbue them with the rudiments of Christian history and religious doctrine (Gutiérrez 1993, 55–56). The same could be said for *Los reyes magos* (The Three Kings), perhaps the oldest of the Spanish medieval mystery plays. In the absence of a common language, Spanish officials and missionaries communicated with their Indian audiences through pantomime, mimicry, and the dramatized message made explicit in the performance of religious plays.

Not all plays written and performed during the Spanish period were religious. The best example of a secular play was *Los comanches*, a heroic drama written in the late 1700s. The play was based on a Spanish military campaign against the Comanche Indians between 1777 and 1779 under the command of Don Carlos Fernández. The defeat of the Indian forces forms the basis of the play. A later defeat in 1779 of another band of Comanches by Juan Bautista de Anza is also referred to. Don Carlos Fernández and Cuerno Verde, an Indian leader who was killed in 1779 by de Anza, are the main characters. It is not surprising that Cuerno Verde is characterized unsympathetically as an arrogant and brutal man who terrorizes the Spanish colonists with his band of renegades. Don Carlos, on the other hand, is characterized as man of deep Christian faith with a keen sense of justice.

The Mexican American Period

When Mexico declared its independence from Spain in 1821, the present-day states of Texas, New Mexico, Arizona, and California, and sections of Utah, Nevada, Colorado, Oklahoma, and Kansas became a part of this new nation's vast hinterland. Over the next thirty-three years this territory would become, in turn, part of the United States.

Texas was the first territory to become a part of the United States, a process that began with the arrival in 1821 of four hundred non-Hispanic Catholic families as part of an agreement signed between the United States and Mexico, which had just won its independence from Spain. The Anglo population grew to about 20,000 by 1830 and began to agitate for an independent republic. In 1836, Anglo and some Mexican Texans declared their independence from Mexico and established the Republic of Texas (also known as the Lone Star Republic). In 1845 the U.S. Congress ratified a treaty to annex Texas.

The expansionist war against Mexico began in all of its intensity shortly thereafter when Congress officially declared war on Mexico. U.S. troops invaded Mexico, and over the next three years bitter battles were fought on Mexican territory, including the invasion and occupation of Mexico City. The Mexican government reluctantly signed the Treaty of Guadalupe Hidalgo in February 1848, officially ending the war and ceding to the United States for a modest payment of fifteen million dollars much of its northern territories. In 1853, the Mexican government sold additional lands in southwestern New Mexico and southern Arizona to the United States under the provisions of the Gadsden Treaty.

The Denial of Civil and Constitutional Rights

The 1836 Texas constitution, the Treaty of Guadalupe Hidalgo, and the Gadsden Treaty all were supposed to protect the civil and constitutional rights of Mexicans in the newly acquired lands, but the historical record offers abundant examples of how these rights were routinely violated and how Anglo racism toward mestizo and Indian-origin Mexicans and Mexican Americans created a legacy of bitterness and conflict that has lasted to this day. Of the tens of thousands of Mexicans living in the newly acquired territories, only about three thousand took advantage of the Mexican government's offer to repatriate them to Mexico. The rest stayed and became U.S. citizens.

Due in large part to the refusal of Anglos to accept the majority of these new citizens as equals, U.S. officials at all levels of government often ignored treaty agreements that ostensibly gave Mexican Americans the same rights as all U.S. citizens under the Constitution. Anglo political, legal, and banking rings conspired with wealthy and ambitious Mexican Americans to deprive many communities in New Mexico and elsewhere in the Southwest of communal land grants. This corrupt transfer of lands intensified as land values rose with the dramatic increase in the Anglo population and with the increased economic importance of landownership for grazing livestock, farming, and mining.

The widespread loss of land was a grave injustice, but there were other more egregious racial crimes against the Mexican-origin population during the nineteenth century. For example, Texas Anglos commonly lynched Blacks, Mexicans, and Mexican Americans, a practice that increased significantly after the Civil War and continued until the end of the nineteenth century. In California and Arizona, Anglo vigilante groups also took the law into their own hands and hanged Mexicans and Mexican Americans. When they were tried in the criminal justice system, members of the Spanish-speaking population received poor legal representation and disproportionately long sentences.

Resistance to Injustice

The Mexican-origin population did not passively accept the loss of land and other injustices perpetrated against them from the mid-nineteenth century forward. For example, nuevomexicanos organized into bands of hooded nightriders known as Las Gorras Blancas [The White Hoods], who harassed Anglo land developers by destroying their fences and even derailing their supply trains. These bands in New Mexico and elsewhere in the Southwest have been thoroughly studied by contemporary Chicana/a historians, who have given them the name of "social bandits" because they often led the resistance against Anglo oppression. Some of the best-known social bandit leaders were Juan Nepomuceno Cortina and Joaquín Murieta. Cortina, a landowner in the Brownsville, Texas, area, frequently led raids against Anglo landowners and the officials who protected them. Murieta was a Mexican miner who came to California shortly after the 1848 gold rush. Like Cortina, he became the leader of a small guerrilla band that would target Anglos who had been identified for their mistreatment of Mexican and Mexican American miners and others.

Along with resisting economic and political domination, Mexican Americans in the Southwest actively struggled to maintain their culture, and as F. Arturo Rosales has pointed out, "The most crucial measure for resisting cultural domination for Southwest Mexicans was the maintenance of Spanish" (Rosales 1996, 17). And the most effective vehicle for maintaining Spanish was the Spanish-language press that thrived across the Southwest from the mid-nineteenth century through the first quarter of the twentieth century and formed part of a general Mexican American campaign to resist injustices and to preserve the unique identity of people of Mexican origin.

Los tejanos, a Spanish-language play written between 1841 and 1846, provides an excellent example of resistance to Anglo domination of the Southwest, not only through the use of Spanish but militarily as well. The play is based on a historical event, the defeat and capture of the Anglo Texas–Santa Fe expedition to New Mexico in 1841 by the soldiers of General Manuel Armijo. It focuses on the capture of General Hugh McLeod, who commanded the expeditionary force. The dramatic work is not entirely accurate historically, but it is possible that the author was trying to present in a patriotic way a composite picture of the New Mexican victory over the Texans, who were considered foreign invaders and a definite threat to the autonomy of Spanish-speaking New Mexico. The aggressors are Anglos and the defenders are Mexican, a fact that reflects the fear that the latter had of their expansionist neighbors.

The oral tradition rooted in the sixteenth-century Southwest also became a means of symbolic resistance. Américo Paredes and others have documented that the earlier romance corrido—by the nineteenth century it had come to be known simply as the corrido—underwent a period of decline in Mexico after the 1848 Mexican War but then enjoyed a period of renewed popularity from about 1875 to the beginning of the Mexican Revolution in 1910. Along both sides of the U.S.–Mexico border, the corrido became a popular form of expression among the Spanish-speaking population. This increase in popularity is related to the increased immigration of Anglos into Texas and the rest of the Southwest after 1848. Corridos began to be used to record in song the increasing number of incidents of social conflict arising from Anglo social and racial oppression of the Mexican American population. The corrido became a form of cultural resistance composed and sung in Spanish at a wide variety of public and private events. It clearly reflected the heightened tension associated with the intercultural conflict between Anglos and Americans of Mexican descent.

Paredes states that the most important and most popular of these border ballads was based on the historical events surrounding the life of Gregorio Cortez, a Texas Mexican rancher who lived with his family in central Texas at the beginning of the twentieth century. As narrated in "El Corrido de Gregorio Cortez" (The Ballad of Gregorio Cortez), a simple misunderstanding between Anglo lawmen and Gregorio and his brother leads to gunshots and the death of both Gregorio's brother and a deputy sheriff. Gregorio flees for his life and is pursued by a large Anglo posse. Due to his skill as a horseman and his familiarity with the terrain, he eludes his pursuers for several weeks until he is finally captured and jailed. *Corridistas* (balladeers) composed several versions of this story, but all highlight Gregorio Cortez's bravery, loyalty, gentleness as a husband and father, defiance of Anglo authorities, and victimization as a member of an oppressed group.

Corridos expressing intercultural conflict continued to be composed and sung until after World War II, but postwar corridos differ from the earlier corridos in important ways. In the pre–World War II period, the protagonist of a corrido was "invariably presented as a potent, larger-than-life hero who in a symbolic sense avenged the collective insults against his people," a pattern exemplified in "El Corrido de Gregorio Cortez" (Peña 1992–1996, 202). This hero is replaced in later corridos by a relatively weak character who is portrayed as a more-or-less helpless victim.

The shift in the role of the protagonist can be explained by the profound change in the socioeconomic circumstances of the Chicana/o population relative to the dominant society between 1900 and about 1950. Beginning during the Depression in the early 1930s, Mexican Americans along the U.S.–Mexico border moved by the thousands from rural settings and small villages to large urban centers such as Houston, San Antonio, El Paso, Phoenix, and Los Angeles.

Due in part to Mexican Americans' increasing dependence on labor opportunities found in manufacturing in cities and in part to the return to the United States after World War II of thousands of Chicano veterans who had fought valiantly in overseas war operations from 1940 to 1945, the expectations of the Chicana/o population changed. Urban Chicanos—especially veterans—expected more opportunities from the country they had defended and died for. Although they were more willing than before to assimilate into this society, they demanded that it be much more accommodating to them. At the same time, political organizations that advocated on behalf of Chicanas/os became stronger and more effective. Peña (1992–1996, 202) has suggested that these socioeconomic and political developments contributed in a very important way to a change in the role of the corrido from a form that uplifted a battered cultural image to one that rallied support for active political causes.

The corrido as a song form continues to thrive today along the U.S.–Mexico border, across the Southwest, and even in the Midwest and Northwest, where there are significant concentrations of Chicanas/os. It continues its legacy as a popular form of social resistance; there are countless recordings of corridos that deal with a wide range of social topics, ranging from racism to politics, intercultural and police violence, drugs and drug running, the plight of undocumented Mexican and Central American workers, poverty, and economic exploitation, among other topics.

Spanish-Language Newspapers as a Form of Cultural Resistance

The earliest known Spanish-language newspaper in the United States dates from 1808 with the founding of *El Misisipí* in New Orleans (Kanellos 1993, 107). In the Southwest and California, the earliest recorded newspapers were *La Gaceta de Texas* (The Texas Gazette) and *El Mexicano* (The Mexican), both founded in 1813 in San Antonio, and *El Crepúsculo de la Libertad* (The Dawn of Liberty), a broadside newspaper published in Santa Fe and later in Taos, New Mexico, in 1834 and 1835 (Meléndez 1997, 17). However, it was not until the mid-nineteenth century that Spanish-language newspapers began to proliferate across the Southwest and California, a development that can be attributed in large part to the passionate struggle of new U.S. citizens of Mexican descent against the Anglo threat of cultural erasure in an increasingly conflictive period.

Like most newspapers, Spanish-language newspapers provided a venue for advertising both Anglo- and Mexican American–owned businesses; announcements of cultural and social events; and local, regional, and national political news. The important commercial centers of Los Angeles and San Francisco supported dozens of periodicals between 1848 and the end of the nineteenth century (for example, *La Estrella de Los Angeles* (The Los Angeles Star), *El Clamor Público* (The Public Clamor), *La Crónica* (The Chronicle), *La República* (The Republic), and *La Voz del Nuevo Mundo* (The Voice of the New World) (Kanellos 1993, 111).

Many of these newspapers contained eloquent and passionate defenses of the Spanish language and cultural identity, civil liberties, and constitutional guarantees; in addition, editorials, essays, poems, and short fiction proliferated. The Spanish-language newspapers assumed an adversarial stance in the face of an English-language press that either misrepresented the Spanish-speaking population through caricature and negative stereotyping or simply ignored it. In short, these newspapers provided a vanguard of resistance against racism, discrimination, and domination by increasingly aggressive and economically and politically superior forces.

SPANISH-LANGUAGE NEWSPAPER POETRY Much of the early poetry in 1850s and 1860s newspapers is anonymous, but by the 1870s, several names begin to appear with increasing frequency in Spanish-language newspapers across the Southwest. The most common topics for poetry published in Spanish-language newspapers are patriotism, cultural pride, social protest, love and its powers, religion and spirituality, ethics and morality, and commemoration and eulogies.

Conscious of their status as second-class citizens, Chicanas/os used newspapers from 1848 through the 1950s to protest against the gross abuses of their rights, the denigration of their culture, and the questioning of their patriotism. Poets stand in the forefront of this effort to defend *la raza* against the Anglo-dominated government and economic system in the Southwest. The social poetry of this period falls into three categories: (1) poetry that addresses specific political issues or historical occurrences; (2) poetry that affirms the positive cultural aspects of Hispanics in general and Chicanas/os in particular; and (3) patriotic poetry that attempts to combat the negative stereotyping of Chicanas/os as cowardly or aliens who were more concerned about Mexico than the United States (Meyer 1996).

In response to accusations by Anglos that Chicanas/os, because of their Mexican ancestry, were aliens and cowards, poets wrote patriotic poetry affirming their loyalty to the United States. World War I precipitated an outpouring of patriotic sentiments by many Chicana/o poets. Virtually every newspaper that published literature carried love and religious poetry in its pages. Praise for a beloved person and unrequited love constituted the two most popular themes. Much of the love poetry was notable for its penchant to exaggerate the powers of love. Jesus Christ and the Virgin Mary constituted the most common subjects of religious poetry, but a few poets dealt with theological questions as well.

SPANISH-LANGUAGE NEWSPAPERS AND MÉXICO DE AFUERA (MEXICO ON THE OUTSIDE) Up until about the 1890s, there was little immigration from Mexico into the United States. The expansion of the Mexican and U.S. railroad systems brought increased immigration as a large number of Mexican workers, many of them from deep in Mexico, were afforded relatively inexpensive and readily accessible transportation to the border and within certain regions of the United States. By 1900, 127,000 Mexican-born immigrants added significantly to the approximately 200,000 Mexican Americans native to the Southwest (Rosales 1996, 20). Mexican immigrants or seasonal workers along with the Mexican American population became the main sources of labor for the growing commercial agricultural sector, especially in Texas and California. Industrial mining in California as well as in Arizona, Colorado, and New Mexico also attracted skilled Mexican miners and unskilled laborers. The violent revolution that erupted in Mexico in 1910 and lasted until 1917 dramatically increased the flow of Mexican immigration to the United States. Many civilians and military deserters sought refuge along the U.S.–Mexico border and eventually in the United States itself. Some returned to Mexico after the revolution ended but the majority stayed. The growth of the U.S. Mexican-origin population during this time was substantial. In 1910, 210,000 Mexican nationals lived in the United States whereas by 1930 there were approximately a million (Rosales 1996, 43).

Many of the Mexicans who fled to the United States during the Mexican Revolution were educated political refugees. Some of them played a key role in publishing in the Southwest, especially in the founding of new newspapers. As Nicolás Kanellos has pointed out, "From their upper class, expatriate perspectives, these intellectuals and entrepreneurs created and promoted—and here the newspaper was essential—the idea of a Mexican community in exile, or a 'México de afuera' in which the culture and politics of Mexico could be duplicated until Mexico's internal politics allowed for their return. The 'México de afuera' campaign was markedly nationalistic and militated to preserve Mexican identity in the United States" (Kanellos 1993, 110). Examples of Spanish-language newspapers founded by Mexican exiles are Clemente Idar's *La Crónica* (The Chronicle) in Laredo; *El Paso del Norte* (The Northern Pass) in El Paso; and Ignacio E. Lozano's *La Prensa* (The Press), which began publishing in San Antonio in 1913, and *La Opinión* (The Opinion), which began in Los Angeles in 1926. Lozano and his family also created a more extensive publishing enterprise that produced political tracts and creative literature. *La Opinión* is still published in Los Angeles today.

These and many other newspapers published *crónicas*, popular short weekly columns that humorously and satirically commented on current topics and social habits. Several of the Mexican satirists who contributed to crónicas assumed pseudonyms and commented as first-person witnesses on the customs, behaviors, morality, materialism, and religious and racial attitudes of both Anglos and the resident Chicana/o population; the latter often came in for a drubbing for not preserving Mexican customs, social practices, and especially a fluent and educated Spanish untainted by English.

The best known of these satirists was Julio G. Arce, who used the pseudonym Jorge Ulica. Under the title "Crónicas diabólicas" (Diabolical Chronicles), Arce published dozens of short satirical pieces in Spanish-language newspapers during the 1920s. As Clara Lomas (1978, 48) has pointed out in her study of a few of Ulica's works, he takes an ambivalent position on the cultural battle that was being waged between Chicanas/os and Anglos. While he is critical of the excesses of certain U.S. institutions and customs, he also tends to take an elitist stance toward Mexican-origin U.S. citizens, an attitude common among Mexican intellectuals who fled to the United States during the revolution.

◼ Narrative Fiction and Memoirs

Along with the impressive number of authors who published in Spanish-language newspapers in the late nineteenth and the first part of the twentieth centuries, there are several notable writers whose works were published in book form. Fortunately, several Chicana/o scholars have salvaged some of these works. For example, Rosaura Sánchez and Beatrice Pita have recovered two novels by María Amparo Ruiz de Burton: *Who Would Have Thought It?* (originally published in 1872 and republished in 1995 by the Recovering the U.S. Hispanic Literary Heritage project) and *The Squatter and the Don* (originally published in 1885 and republished in 1992 by the Recovering the U.S. Hispanic Literary Heritage project). Estevan Arellano discovered and has written about Manuel M. Salazar's short novel *La historia de un caminante, o sea Gervacio y Aurora* (A Traveler's History, or Gervacio and Aurora, originally published in 1881). Francisco Lomelí has brought to light and studied two short novels by Eusebio Chacón: *El hijo de la tempestad* (Son of the Tempest, originally published in 1892) and *Tras la tormenta la calma* (Calm after the Storm, also originally published in 1892). Doris Meyer has written about Felipe Maximiliano Chacón's short novella *Eustacio y Carlita* (the publication date is unknown but it was probably published early in the twentieth century). Nicolás Kanellos is responsible for recovering, translating, and publishing Daniel Venegas's *Las aventuras de don Chipote o, cuando los pericos mamen* (*The Adventures of Don Chipote or, When the Parrots Breastfed*, originally published in Los Angeles in 1928 and republished most recently by the Recovering the U.S. Hispanic Literary Heritage project in 1999).

María Amparo Ruiz was born of aristocratic lineage in the Mexican state of Baja California in 1832, only eleven years after Mexico's independence from Spain and sixteen years before Alta California was ceded to the United States. In 1849 when she was sixteen years old, Ruiz married Henry S. Burton, a U.S. Army officer, and moved to the newly created U.S. state of California. Ruiz de Burton moved east with her husband in 1859, then after he died in 1869 she returned to California with her two children. She was involved for the rest of her life in social and cultural causes and is best known for her literary accomplishments. Although English was not her native language, her published works are all in English. She died in 1895 (Ruiz de Burton 1995, 8–9). Her life thus spans a tumultuous time in the history of both Mexico and the United States, in particular because of the

U.S. occupation of California and the transition the californios were forced to undergo as they adapted to new circumstances as U.S. citizens after 1848.

As Sánchez and Pita have noted in their very informative introduction to Ruiz de Burton's first novel, *Who Would Have Thought It?* the novelist provides a historical perspective from the vantage point of an outsider during the Reconstruction period after the U.S. Civil War (Ruiz de Burton 1995, vii). Her extensive residence on the East Coast allowed her to observe firsthand the tumultuous process the U.S. government was going through shortly after the bitter war between the North and South had almost torn the nation apart. *Who Would Have Thought It?* is only superficially a romantic novel; in fact, it parodies both the mid-nineteenth-century sentimental novel and the novel of domesticity (Ruiz de Burton 1995, x). Ruiz de Burton takes on and strips bare the dominant myths of gendered women's roles as well as those pertaining to race that were prevalent not only in the South but also in the North among the country's elite wealthy class and government officials. In her second novel, *The Squatter and the Don*, Ruiz de Burton uses another literary genre popular in the nineteenth century, the historical romance, to take on another American myth dominant in the nineteenth century: Manifest Destiny, that is, the belief that the United States had a God-given right to expand its national territories to encompass the West and Southwest. At the same time, Ruiz de Burton links this popular myth not only with U.S. political and military actions, but also with corporate powers who aided and abetted federal interests to expand the United States to the Pacific Ocean and beyond in order to develop new markets. The fictional Almar family described in the novel is representative of the californio families who lost their land and their material wealth to Anglo interests in the mid-nineteenth century.

Manuel M. Salazar was a New Mexican known mainly for his poetry, but he also wrote what is perhaps the earliest published Chicano novel, *La historia de un caminante, o sea Gervacio y Aurora*, which follows the amorous adventures of Gervacio, who skips from affair to affair in the best Don Juan tradition. The work contains many romantic and bucolic elements that leave us with the impression that the New Mexico of Salazar's time was a utopia whose residents enjoyed an unequaled pastoral life.

Eusebio Chacón (1869–1948) was born in New Mexico but moved to Colorado, where he taught and was very active in civic and political affairs. He is best known for a pair of short novels in Spanish: *El hijo de la tempestad* and *Tras la tormenta la calma*. They are important for being among the first novels to be published (1892) by a Chicana/o author. The first novel revolves around a bandit chieftain whose men terrorize the populace. In both novels Chacón gives us a heavy dose of his erudition, especially his knowledge of prominent literary works and figures. In *El hijo de la tempestad* Chacón develops as his protagonist an amoral character who is more interested in satisfying his material and sexual needs than in championing the cause of his downtrodden people. In *Tras la tormenta la calma* Chacón creates a Don Juanesque character who is dedicated to pursuing young maidens. The theme of honor plays a prominent role in this short novel.

Born in Santa Fe in 1873, Felipe Maximiliano Chacón was a professional journalist who edited Spanish-language newspapers in various New Mexico cities. Among his prose publications is a thirty-page novella, *Eustacio y Carlita*, cut in the mold of nineteenth-century Romanticism. Just as they are about to consummate their marriage, the protagonists discover they are brother and sister.

Daniel Venegas was a Mexican immigrant who came to the United States in the 1920s like so many of his countrymen to escape political violence and to improve his economic status. *Don Chipote* draws on the Spanish-Mexican literary tradition of the sometimes comic picaresque novel in which a protagonist, a *pícaro*, reveals through his or her adventures some of the lesser-known and seamier aspects of society. Don Chipote and his sidekick leave their families and their humble existence in Mexico to come to the United States, eventually finding their way to Los Angeles, which in the 1920s is rapidly becoming a highly urbanized industrial center. Although laced with humor as Venegas pokes fun at U.S. culture as well as at his and his sidekick's own foibles, the novel has a very serious side. It recounts the difficulties that poor Mexican immigrants encounter in the United States, including racism and exploitation by ruthless Anglo and Mexican American labor contractors and bosses. *Don Chipote* is an early example of Chicana/o tales of immigration, which proliferate during the last quarter of the twentieth century.

Mexican Americanism

Beginning in the 1940s and increasingly in the 1950s, Mexican immigrants and U.S.–born Mexican Americans began to assimilate into U.S. society at greater rates. Together, these two groups created a powerful social and political force with which the dominant society would have to reckon. A new ideology, commonly referred to as *Mexican Americanism*, was actively promoted by new organizations such as the League of United Latin American Citizens (LULAC) and, after War World II, the GI Forum.

World War II (1939–1945) was the key event that gave Mexican Americanism its strong impetus and urgency. Hundreds of thousands of Mexican Americans from rural and urban areas throughout the Southwest and Midwest joined the military and served in both the European and Pacific theaters of the war. Meanwhile, at home in the United States, Mexican American women—most of them for the first time—assumed major financial responsibilities in the family and took jobs in war and other industries. At war's end, Mexican American veterans who returned to the United States, together with those at home who had proudly served the war effort through their jobs, had developed a very different set of expectations of U.S. society than had predominated before the war. Mexican Americans in great numbers now demanded their full due as citizens. The struggle against racism and discrimination in employment, housing, and education after World War II became a major rallying cry. Organizations, associations, and legal defense committees began systematically to challenge racist practices (Rosales 1996, 104–5). Mexican Americans also enjoyed some successes in electoral politics, as political leaders and strategists began registering larger numbers of Mexican-origin citizens and encouraging them to use their collective power at the ballot box in municipal, state, and federal elections.

Several writers stand out in this transitional phase in Chicana/o literature that bridges the 1920s or 1930s to the mid-1960s: Américo Paredes (discussed earlier in this chapter and in chapter 5), Jovita González, Nina Otero-Warren (discussed in chapter 4), Fabiola Cabeza de Vaca (discussed in chapter 4), Josephina Niggli, Fray Angélico Chávez, Mario Suárez, and José Antonio Villarreal.

Born in New Mexico in 1910, Fray Angélico Chávez, a Franciscan priest, was a prolific poet as well as writer of narrative fiction, historian, and scholar. The poet T. S. Eliot recognized one of his books of poetry, *The Virgin of Port Lligat*, as "a very commendable achievement" (Padilla 1987, 215). His short fiction is collected in two volumes: *New Mexico Triptych* (1940) and *From an Altar Screen: Tales from New Mexico* (1957). On a superficial level, his stories emphasize the folkloric, religious, and pastoral aspects of life in New Mexico from the eighteenth century up to World

War II, but as Genaro Padilla (1987, 219) has pointed out, "manifold social tensions come into sharp relief" beneath the surface. In Chávez's fiction there is a complex and subtle interplay between the author's religious and moral perspective and the troubling aspects of New Mexico's history, of which he was keenly aware as a scholar of history. Chávez teases out in several of his stories the class differences that existed among nuevomexicanas/os before the Anglo occupation of the region in the nineteenth century, as well as the tensions that soon developed between them and Anglos after the occupation. His stories also portray the prejudice and discrimination that nuevomexicanas/os and Anglos alike showed toward the indigenous Indian peoples of New Mexico. Chávez was equally critical of the Hispanic *patrones* (bosses) and what he considered to be the American "philistines" with their radically different values, mores, customs, and traditions. He is particularly harsh in his references to the collusion that took place between Anglos and wealthy nuevomexicanas/os to deprive the less privileged inhabitants of their land and other assets.

Mario Suárez was born in 1923 and raised in Tucson, Arizona. He received a BA degree from the University of Arizona (1952). Suárez is best known for his short story "El hoyo" (the hollow) and for one of the earliest uses of the term *Chicano* in a literary work. In this and several other short stories, he creates a barrio (roughly based on a 1940s Tucson barrio of the same name) that is richly textured with the sights, smells, and sounds of a vibrant community consisting of "social types and personalities defined by circumstances, character traits, psychological makeup, or language: pachucos, immigrants . . . perplexed or assertive women, rogues, womanizers, drunks, coyotes, dreamers, machos, priests, and outcasts" (Lomelí 2004, 148–49). His stories concentrate on the local customs and rich linguistic mixture of English and Spanish found in the barrio, while at the same time providing glimpses of a Mexican-origin population undergoing dramatic social change in the post–World War II era. Suárez's barrio is a place of refuge and regeneration. Beneath its sometimes rough and rundown exterior, he finds the enduring soul of a people whose values and language have survived hardship, conflict, and social strife.

Josefina Niggli was an accomplished novelist and short-story writer. All of her narrative fiction works are set in Mexico. Her novel *Step Down, Elder Brother* (1947), takes place in Monterrey in the years following the Mexican Revolution, and its romantic plot is linked to some of the conflict's important figures. Niggli's *Mexican Village* (1945) consists of ten stories centered around a fictitious town in the Mexican state of Nuevo León. The long cast of characters appears and reappears throughout the collection as the author weaves a tapestry of village life. A gifted writer, Niggli maintains a high level of suspense and tension throughout the collection and at the same time creates multidimensional and credible characters who fit within their local ambience without being stereotypical.

José Antonio Villarreal's novel *Pocho* (1959) is the last important work of the transitional phase of Chicana/o literature. It is structured around the lives of Juan Manuel Rubio, a Mexican immigrant, and Richard Rubio, his son, the *pocho* (Americanized Mexican) of the novel's title. The elder Rubio, a Mexican revolutionary officer in General Francisco Villa's army, abandons Mexico to start a new life in the United States. He crosses the border at El Paso and journeys west to California, where his wife Consuelo joins him. In the first part of the novel, Villarreal traces the changes in their relationship as Consuelo becomes progressively more restless being a subservient wife. Threatened by this challenge to his patriarchal authority, Juan leaves her for a young woman recently arrived from Mexico who has not yet been acculturated. The focus of the novel then shifts to Richard's personal development through his first eighteen years, which parallels and is integrally linked to broad cultural and social currents such as the Mexican immigrant family's disintegration, the unrest among American workers in the 1930s, the arrival in California of thousands of refugees from the Dust Bowl, the emergence of Chicana/o barrios in Los Angeles, and the relocation of Japanese Americans during World War II.

Pocho can best be described as a coming-of-age, or initiation, novel, in which we follow Richard's spiritual awakening in an often confusing world. His passage from boyhood to manhood is heightened by his perception of and sensitivity to his surroundings. Even as a boy he begins agonizing over such questions as the existence and immensity of a supreme being and the cosmos and suffers the guilt of nascent sexuality. He turns from these deep and conflicting emotions to take refuge in his innate inquisitiveness about the natural world of bugs and plants. At the same time, with the dissolution of his family, he is thrust between two cultures: Mexican-Chicana/o on one hand and Anglo on the other. He ultimately rejects the strictures of his father's cultural values as well as his mother's growing materialism, which he associates with Anglo culture. As he matures, he undergoes several waves of questioning and doubt while becoming more acutely aware of southern California's highly stratified society in which the

Chicana/o population occupies the lowest rung. He finally leaves his family and joins the U.S. Navy just as World War II erupts.

Beginning in the sixteenth century with the transplanting of important Spanish oral and written literary forms to the New World in general and to today's U.S. Southwest in particular, Chicana/o literary expression took root and flowered over the next several centuries. The Spanish-speaking communities of numerous towns (some isolated in the mountains of New Mexico and southern Colorado) and cities from Texas to California played an essential role in maintaining the oral traditions of their forbearers by passing on from generation to generation folk poetry, theater, and tales. And from as early as the 1820s, these communities founded newspapers that provided outlets for written expression, including poetry and short prose fiction. In addition, many writers found other outlets in which to publish their literary works. By the middle of the twentieth century, Chicana/o literature had a firm foundation on which to build a solid cultural edifice of literary creativity for the next several decades.

■ Discussion Questions

1. Discuss the persistence of the oral tradition and its various forms from the sixteenth century to well into the twentieth century.

2. Along with the oral tradition, the Spanish left many written documents. What different aspects of exploration, colonization, and settlement do these documents reflect?

3. What role did Spanish-language newspapers play in the lives of the Mexican-origin population during the nineteenth and early part of the twentieth centuries?

4. Discuss the contributions that scholars have made to the recovery and publication of literary texts.

5. Discuss the similarities and differences among the writers in the transitional period between the 1930s and the mid-1960s.

Suggested Readings

Acuña, Rodolfo. 2000. *Occupied America: A History of Chicanos.* New York: Longman.

Castañeda Shular, Antonia, Tomás Ybarra-Frausto, and Joseph Sommers, eds. 1972. *Literatura chicana: texto y contexto.* Englewood Cliffs, NJ: Prentice Hall.

Espinosa, Aurelio. 1985. *The Folklore of Spain in the American Southwest: Traditional Spanish Literature in Northern New Mexico and Southern Colorado.* Norman: University of Oklahoma Press.

Gonzales-Berry, Erlinda, ed. 1989. *Pasó por aquí: Critical Essays on the New Mexican Literary Tradition, 1542–1988.* Albuquerque: University of New Mexico Press.

Herrera-Sobek, María, ed. 1993. *Reconstructing a Chicano Literary Heritage.* Tucson: University of Arizona Press.

Kanellos, Nicolás. 1987. *Mexican American Theater: Legacy and Reality.* Pittsburgh: Latin American Literary Review Press.

——. 1990. *A History of Hispanic Theater in the United States: Origins to 1940.* Austin: University of Texas Press.

——. 1993. A Socio-Historic Study of Hispanic Newspapers in the United States. In *Recovering the U.S. Hispanic Literary Heritage,* eds. Ramón Gutiérrez and Genaro Padilla, 107–28. Houston: Arte Público Press.

Leal, Luis, and Pepe Barrón. 1982. Chicano Literature: An Overview. In *Three American Literatures: Essays in Chicano, Native American, and Asian American Literature for Teachers of American Literature,* ed. Houston A. Baker Jr., 9– 32. New York: Modern Language Association of America.

Limón, José. 1992. *Mexican Ballads, Chicano Poems: History and Influence in Mexican-American Social Poetry.* Berkeley: University of California Press.

Meléndez, A. Gabriel. 1997. *So All Is Not Lost: The Poetics of Print in Nuevomexicano Communities, 1834–1958.* Albuquerque: University of New Mexico Press.

Meyer, Doris. 1996. *Speaking for Themselves: Neomexicano Cultural Identity and the Spanish-Language Press, 1880–1920.* Albuquerque: University of New Mexico Press.

Paredes, Américo. 1958. *With a Pistol in His Hand: A Border Ballad and Its Hero.* Austin: University of Texas Press.

Paredes, Raymond A. 1982. The Evolution of Chicano Literature. In *Three American Literatures: Essays in Chicano, Native American, and Asian American Literature for Teachers of American Literature,* 33–79. New York: Modern Language Association of America.

Peña, Manuel. 1992–1996. Música fronteriza/Border Music. *Aztlán* 21 (1–2): 191–225. Available online at http://www.lib.utexas.edu/benson/border/pena/.

Rebolledo, Tey Diana. 1995. *Women Singing in the Snow: An Analysis of Chicana Literature.* Albuquerque: University of New Mexico Press.

Rosales, F. Arturo. 1996. *Chicano! The History of the Mexican American Civil Rights Movement.* Houston: Arte Público Press.

3

The Chicano Movement and the Flowering of Chicana/o Literature

Throughout the 1960s and early 1970s a general discontent existed among sizable segments of the U.S. population, much of it centering on a broad range of political and social institutions. The Civil Rights Movement and the rise of Black Power, the American Indian Movement, feminism, and other militant forms of political protest played key roles as well. During much of the latter part of the 1960s, social unrest, demonstrations, and riots in large urban areas heightened tensions between underserved minority groups and Anglo society. Finally, the profound discontent surrounding the war in Vietnam among millions of Americans of every race and sector of society led to a general sense of disillusionment and loss of faith in the presidency and Congress, which had repeatedly deceived its citizens about many different aspects of the war.

■ The Chicano Movement

The 1960s brought a dramatic shift in Mexican American politics with the rise of the Movimiento Chicano (the Chicano Movement), a highly complex social and political process that manifested itself in several different ways: (1) the unionization of farmworkers in the agricultural fields of California, Texas, and elsewhere in the Southwest led by César Chávez, Dolores Huerta, and others; (2) the Crusade for Justice founded by Denver activist Rodolfo "Corky" Gonzales; (3) the Alianza Federal de Mercedes (the Federal Alliance of Land Grants) inspired by Reies López Tijerina and based mainly in New Mexico; (4) La Raza Unida Party founded by José Angel Gutiérrez and others in Texas; (5) the walkouts and demands by high school and college students for curricular reform and the establishment of Chicano studies programs; and (6) the Chicano Moratorium against the War in Vietnam.

Rodolfo "Corky" Gonzales

Rodolfo "Corky" Gonzales, a Chicano activist from Denver and disaffected Democratic Party organizer, founded in 1966 the Crusade for Justice, a service-oriented cultural center that challenged the Denver city government and the Democratic Party to become more committed to eradicating poverty and to dealing effectively with racial injustice. The greatest contribution to the Chicano Movement of the Crusade for Justice was its sponsorship of the First Annual Chicano Youth Conference in 1969, which was attended by more than fifteen hundred Chicana/o community, high school, and college activists from throughout the Southwest. Through this organization and its sponsored events, Gonzales encouraged young Chicanas/os to join the struggle to claim their rights as American citizens.

Reies López Tijerina

Reies López Tijerina, a tejano, organized a New Mexico–based movement, the Alianza Federal de Mercedes, in the mid-1960s. Its purpose was to regain the lands that Spanish-speaking New Mexicans had lost in the nineteenth and early twentieth centuries due to legal, political, and economic manipulation and deceit. A charismatic orator and persuasive leader, Tijerina established a following mainly among northern New Mexico's rural Mexican Americans. Although he was not ultimately successful in restoring land to the original owners, he did galvanize a militant group of loyal followers who for a time seemed on the verge of creating an effective political force, particularly in the rural communities of northern New Mexico.

José Angel Gutiérrez

La Raza Unida Party (LRUP), founded by José Angel Gutiérrez and other tejana/o activists, was arguably the most successful example of the Chicano Movement's participation in electoral politics during the 1960s and early 1970s. The LRUP's underlying ideology relied heavily on cultural elements with which Texas Chicanos could identify: the role of the family, tejano music, Mexican history, and the Spanish language. It espoused a pragmatic nationalism that distanced itself from counterculture identification and Marxist rhetoric (Rosales 1996, 233). In 1970, Gutiérrez and other LRUP leaders targeted the Crystal City school board and city council for the party's first incursion into electoral politics; they succeeded in electing their candidates to both. The LRUP also enjoyed more modest gains in neighboring counties and municipalities. LRUP broadened its electoral participation in Texas by fielding a gubernatorial and other candidates in the 1972 statewide election.

César Chávez and Dolores Huerta

César Chávez and Dolores Huerta are generally recognized as two of the first and most important leaders of the Chicano Movement. Both were trained by the Chicago-based Community Service Organization (CSO) in the tactics of organizing. Their efforts and those of other organizers began in 1962, and over the next three decades the union they helped to found— the National Farm Workers Association (NFWA), which later became the United Farm Workers—enjoyed many successes in actions against large growers and other agriculture-related businesses in California's fertile central valleys as well as elsewhere. Through union-negotiated contracts, labor conditions and wages for thousands of farmworkers across the Southwest improved dramatically.

Chicano Moratorium against the War in Vietnam

By 1970, mass demonstrations against U.S. military involvement in Vietnam were occurring all across the country. Chicanas/os joined this wave of protests in August 1970 by holding the National Chicano Moratorium march in Los Angeles and simultaneously in other cities in the Southwest. On August 29, more than thirty thousand protesters marched through the streets of Los Angeles and later congregated in Laguna Park in East Los Angeles. The largely peaceful meeting ended tragically when police charged and dispersed the crowd. Three people were killed, many more were injured, and hundreds were arrested. Rubén Salazar, a prominent Chicano reporter for the *Los Angeles Times*, was killed in a separate but related police action. The Moratorium and the confrontation with police galvanized the Chicana/o community throughout the United States against the war in Vietnam.

Student Protests

High school and college students and their teachers and professors were at the forefront of the Chicano Movement, stamping it with a strong imprint of cultural nationalism, political radicalism, and militancy. For example, in March 1968, a loosely organized group of Chicano high school students staged a coordinated walkout in several Los Angeles high schools. Among their demands was a call for curricular reform. José Angel Gutiérrez and other activists had cut their political teeth in the mid-1960s in the Texas-based Mexican American Youth Association (MAYO). Student groups such as southern California's United Mexican American Students (UMAS) were formed on high school and college campuses in the late 1960s and early 1970s throughout the Southwest. By 1969, student and faculty activists began to plan and implement Chicana/o studies programs in some high schools, but mainly at colleges and universities in order to introduce more Chicana/o-oriented material into high school and college curricula in history, literature, political science, and other fields.

Chicana/o Publishing Efforts

The political aspect of the Chicano Movement was accompanied by various projects and initiatives to promote Mexican American culture. The best example is the founding in 1967 of a Chicana/o–oriented journal by a small group of Chicana/o faculty and students at the University of California, Berkeley. *El Grito: A Journal of Contemporary Mexican-American Thought* had a social sciences and literary focus, and its mission was to counteract false and distorted notions about Chicanas/os prevalent not only in society at large but also within academic circles. The same group quickly established Quinto Sol Publications and the Premio Quinto Sol (the Fifth Sun Award), also known as the Quinto Sol National Literary Award. The publishing company and the award were keys to the development of Chicana/o narrative fiction in the early 1970s. Later in this chapter, I will discuss the award-winning works: Tomás Rivera's . . . *Y no se lo tragó la tierra* (. . . And the Earth Did Not Part; 1970 award); Rudolfo A. Anaya's novel *Bless Me, Ultima* (1971 award); and Rolando Hinojosa's novel *Estampas del valle y otras obras* (Sketches of the Valley and Other Works) and Estela Portillo Trambley's collection of short stories *Rain of Scorpions and Other Stories* (cowinners in 1972).

El Grito ceased publication in 1974, but other journals were already in existence to take its place. The most notable was *Aztlán: Chicano Journal of the Social Sciences and the Arts* founded in the 1970s by a group of students and faculty members at UCLA. Still in publication today, it has become the most important scholarly journal for the dissemination of cutting-edge research on Chicana/o topics ranging from literature and women's issues to demography, politics, history, and sociology. Three other journals with a literary focus appeared in the early 1970s: *Revista Chicano-Riqueña* (later renamed *The Americas Review*), *Bilingual Review/Revista Bilingüe*, and *De Colores*. The first ceased publication in the late 1990s and the third lasted only a few years. *Bilingual Review/Revista Bilingüe* continues to be published. Other notable journals that lasted for only a few years included *La Palabra*, *Grito del Sol*, and *Caracol*.

As important as these cultural-literary journals were in providing an outlet for Chicana/o scholars and writers, in advancing the cultural and social ethos of the Chicano Movement, and in providing an alternative to the biased and often stereotypical literature that continued to appear in mainstream journals, the founding of two publishing houses was momentous. Arte Público Press came into existence in 1973 due mainly to the vision and social commitment of Nicolás Kanellos, then a young professor at the University of Indiana, Northwest, and presently at the University of Houston, where he holds an endowed faculty position. He has continued to create and guide many subsequent publishing, archival, and recovery projects. Gary Keller, who was largely responsible for creating *Bilingual Review/Revista Bilingüe*, founded Bilingual Review Press in 1974. Currently a Regents Professor at Arizona State University, he continues to oversee the journal, to provide leadership for the press, and to initiate numerous other highly meritorious projects. Kanellos and Keller together have been largely responsible for the publication of hundreds of young and established Latina/o writers, especially Chicanas/os, over the past three decades.

El Teatro Campesino and the Chicano Movement

An essential aspect of the activism of the Chicano Movement that galvanized thousands of Chicanas/os in the 1960s and early 1970s was the expression by dozens of writers and other artists of their combined frustration over and protest against racism and oppression through the written word (poetry, short stories, and novels) and theater. El Teatro Campesino (the Farmworkers' Theater) perhaps best embodies the essential linkage of creativity with commitment to social justice and change. It began in 1965 when Luis Valdez (see figure 9), with a fresh undergraduate degree in drama from San Jose State University and a stint with the politically progressive San Francisco Mime Troupe, founded El Teatro Campesino to support the César Chávez–led strike against the large and powerful grape-growing enterprises in California's San Joaquin Valley.

**9. Luis Valdez
(courtesy of Arte Público Press)**

Together with many others, including farmworkers, Valdez created the *acto* (act or skit), which became central to the repertory of El Teatro Campesino and other Chicana/o theater groups in the 1960s and 1970s. The acto is typically a ten- to fifteen-minute improvisational, bilingual dramatic work intended to educate and to rally the audience to take social action. The focus on collective creation was in keeping with the revolutionary ideology of the group and its commitment to social change.

Chicanas played important roles in all phases of El Teatro Campesino's evolution from 1965 until its dissolution in the early 1980s. Yolanda Broyles-González has carefully documented the ways in which women were an integral part of El Teatro Campesino, particularly as actors; unfortunately, however, they were marginalized in the key decision-making processes regarding production and roles. From the very beginning, men played all of the strong roles while women were relegated to playing roles such as the abject woman, the long-suffering and self-sacrificing mother or grandmother, the prostitute, the *vendida* (sellout), the abused wife, or the adoring girlfriend. In other words, El Teatro Campesino to some extent reinforced the secondary and inferior status of women in traditional Mexican and Chicano culture (Broyles-González 1994, 129–63).

An essential aspect of El Teatro Campesino's effective dramatizations of the farmworkers' plight and other social injustices is the simple device of using stereotypical characters very familiar to the audiences, including "Super Sam," the arrogant white cop; the Patrón, the Grower who exploits his workers while pretending to be their friend; the Vendidos, who have rejected their Mexican-Chicano cultural identity; the Coyote (Labor Contractor), who cynically exploits his fellow Chicanas/os for profit; the Esquirol (Scab), who is imported from Mexico to break the backs of the strikers by working for lower wages or crossing union picket lines; and the Huelguistas (Strikers), who form the picket lines and are committed to social change.

Like other alternative theater efforts, El Teatro Campesino used no sets, few props, and few devices except for signs hung around the actors' necks identifying their roles, masks, old pairs of pants, pairs of sunglasses, and other easily portable items. The advantage of the simple dramatizations was that the acto performances could be staged anywhere—in the streets, in union halls, in the fields—on improvised stages such as the back of a truck. Improvised stages gave the group high mobility, an intentional strategy to allow for flexibility and adaptability to local conditions, such as the avoidance of local law enforcement authorities who generally favored agribusinesses. Thus, the group could arrive at the edge of an agricultural field or on a city street, set up, do its performance, and leave a site before the authorities could arrive.

El Teatro Campesino's early actos were concerned exclusively with the farmworkers' and union's struggle against the growers. For example *Las dos caras del patroncito* (The Two-Faced Boss) focused on the hypocrisy of the grape grower and the innocence and vulnerability of the Mojado (Wetback) who was imported illegally from Mexico to help break the California grape strike. *La quinta temporada* (The Fifth Season), created by El Teatro Campesino in 1966, deals with the hated figure of the Coyote, the labor contractor who delivers undocumented Mexican workers to the growers in exchange for lucrative commissions. The Fifth Season refers to the improved working and living conditions offered by the United Farm Workers Union.

The focus of El Teatro Campesino broadened somewhat in 1967 when the theater ensemble left Delano for Del Rey, California, where it founded El Centro Campesino Cultural (The Workers' Cultural Center). The actos now began dealing with other problems that Chicanas/os faced. For example, *Los vendidos* (The Sellouts), one of El Teatro's most popular actos, reflects the shift from the fields to the urban centers where the majority of Chicanas/os lived and worked. The play deals humorously with the serious problem of Chicanas/os who abandon their language and culture as they climb the social ladder in a society dominated by alien Anglo values.

El Teatro Campesino moved again in 1969 as their reputation began to spread across the United States and abroad. In 1969, the troupe was invited to the Seventh World Theatre Festival in France, where they were well received by enthusiastic audiences. Later that year, the troupe performed in Los Angeles at the Inner City Cultural Center where, again, audiences received them enthusiastically.

El Teatro Campesino continued dealing with the larger Chicana/o perspective. *No saco nada de la escuela* (I'm Not Getting Anything out of School) is a three-part acto that follows Chicana/o students from elementary school through high school to college, presenting the problems they confront at every level, including insensitive, racist teachers and bewilderment in an English-speaking classroom. In *The Militants*, both the stereotyped bleeding-heart Anglo liberal and the young Chicana/o militant are satirized for their lack of effective action to bring about social change.

In 1970, El Teatro turned its attention to the Vietnam War with the production of *Vietnam campesino* (Vietnam Farmworker), a longer, five-scene acto more suitable for performance on a formal theater stage than in fields or union halls. The play focuses on the collusion between the growers and the Pentagon to exploit the Chicana/o farmworker both at home and in Vietnam. It calls for Chicanas/os to recognize that they have more in common with their Vietnamese brothers than with Anglos in their own country. The acto ends with a call for solidarity among Chicanas/os and a resolve to fight the real war in Aztlán, not Vietnam. Like *Vietnam campesino*, *Soldado razo* (The Chicano GI), first performed in 1971 at the Chicano Moratorium against the War in Vietnam in Fresno, makes an antiwar statement from a Chicana/o perspective. It centers on a father and son's false concept of machismo and the military.

The year 1971 signaled a major evolution in El Teatro Campesino. Luis Valdez and the troupe of actors moved to San Juan Bautista, California, and began experimenting with another form, the *mito* (myth), which differs significantly from the acto. The mito explores the content of Chicana/o culture, whereas the acto concentrates on political issues expressed in the cultural context of the audience. El Teatro thus began deemphasizing sociopolitical content to focus more clearly on legends, myths, and religion.

El Teatro Campesino's first public experimentation with the mito was its production of *La gran carpa de los rascuachis* (The Tent of the Underdogs), first performed in 1973 in Santa Cruz, California, and later in Mexico City. The work is divided into three parts: two mitos and an intervening acto that tells the story of Jesús Pelado Rascuachi, a Mexican national who with his family crosses the border to the United States in search of a better life. As a farmworker he is exploited and suffers discrimination. *Bernabé: A Drama of Modern Chicano Mythology* is a mito in which historical and mythological parallels are drawn between the sacred Aztec ritual of offering a gift of the human heart to Huitzilopochtli, the Sun God, and the campesinos of the Southwest who toil under the blazing sun. *The Dark Root of a Scream* once again draws a parallel between Aztecs and Chicanas/os. Just as the Indian priests created strife and promoted human sacrifice, the Catholic Church is portrayed in this mito as an instrument of destruction that sends young Chicanas/os to their death in wars.

The play *Zoot Suit*, first presented for fourteen performances in Los Angeles as part of the Mark Taper Forum's Theatre for Now Series in 1978, brought much critical acclaim to Valdez and El Teatro Campesino. It focuses on the famous Sleepy Lagoon murder of 1942. In the play, four young Chicanos represent the twelve pachucos who were indicted, convicted of murder, sentenced to long prison terms, and later pardoned. The play is the story of their release after the California Court of Appeals overturned their convictions for lack of evidence. In 1979, the troupe performed the play at the Winter Garden Theater on Broadway in New York City. While it received generally good reviews on the West Coast, East Coast critics treated it harshly.

Zoot Suit represented an important step forward for Chicana/o theater in the 1970s because for the first time a contemporary play by a Chicana/o successfully made the transition from the agricultural fields, urban barrios, and college campuses to commercial theater. With this dramatized social document, El Teatro Campesino carried its message to a wider audience without abandoning the simplicity and directness of its earlier actos or its commitment to social justice.

◼ TENAZ and Annual Theater Festivals

El Teatro Campesino was the major force in the late 1960s and the early 1970s that led to the formation of other Chicana/o theater groups and the founding of TENAZ (El Teatro Nacional de Aztlán [The National Theater of Aztlán]) and annual theater festivals. In 1970, El Teatro Campesino hosted the first national Festival de los Teatros Chicanos, attended by sixteen groups from all over the United States. Several festivals followed between 1971 and 1979, becoming larger and more sophisticated as they began including workshops on different aspects of theater management, acting, directing, production, and social content. In addition to theater groups from throughout the United States, groups from Mexico and other Latin American countries occasionally attended the festivals. One group, El Teatro de las Chicanas, a women's group, gave a series of performances challenging sexist stereotypes that had proved so harmful to the equality of men and women in the Chicano struggle.

El Teatro Campesino and TENAZ spawned more than forty regional Chicana/o theater groups, most of them affiliated with academic institutions or urban community organizations. No group other than El Teatro Campesino was able to generate enough income from performances and other activities (for example, workshops or television and movie rights) to be self-sufficient, nor were any as active as several members of El Teatro Campesino. Yet, following the creation of TENAZ in 1971, several teatros survived tenaciously and even prospered, at least for a few years. Some of the more successful groups include El Teatro de la Esperanza (Theater of Hope) at the University of California–Santa Barbara, San Jose State University, and San Jose City College; El Teatro de la Gente (People's Theater); El Teatro de Aztlán at California State University–Northridge; El Teatro Desengaño del Pueblo (The People's Theater of Disillusion) from Gary, Indiana; El Teatro Chicano de Austin; Carnales del Espíritu (Soul Brothers) from Austin; El Teatro de Ustedes (Your Theater) from Denver; El Teatro de la Revolución (The Theater of the Revolution) from Greeley, Colorado; El Teatro del Piojo (The Flea's Theater) from Seattle; El Teatro de los Barrios (The Theater of the Barrios) from San Antonio; El Teatro Mestizo of San Diego; El Teatro de los Niños (The Children's Theater) from Pasadena; and Teatro Causa de los Pobres (The Poor People's Cause Theater) from Denver.

Poetry and the Chicano Movement

Like Luis Valdez, some poets became participants in the Chicano Movement either directly through political action or indirectly by means of their artistic expression. Their poetry is socially committed, upholding the positive aspects of Chicana/o culture and its indigenous roots and denigrating the negative traits of the dominant society and its value system. While they use a variety of styles, language, imagery, modes, and tones, most of the prominent poets are committed to a combative poetics that parallels political activism in the service of the broad aims of the Chicano Movement. Several poets identify with contemporary Mexico and its indigenous Aztec and Mayan cultures. Language, which is of paramount importance to the poets whose works appear in Chicano Movement publications, tends to be direct and highly accessible rather than florid, resonant, or in any way affected. An embodiment of this directness is the use of a particular syntactic blend of English and Spanish characteristic of the speech of many Chicanas/os but elevated to the level of authentic poetic expression. In addition to this combined use of the two languages—variously known as the binary phenomenon, code-switching, and interlingualism—the unique slang of the pachuco and the *vato loco* (crazy dude), as well as prison jargon, become vehicles for authenticating the barrio experience and sources of cultural affirmation.

The most important poet-activists writing between the mid-1960s and the mid-1970s are Rodolfo "Corky" Gonzales, Abelardo "Lalo" Delgado, Ricardo Sánchez, Luis Omar Salinas, Tino Villanueva, and Angela de Hoyos. The poet Alurista could well be grouped with these poets, but I have decided it is more appropriate to discuss his works as representative of a later phase of Chicana/o poetry (see chapter 7).

Rodolfo "Corky" Gonzales

In addition to his crucial activities as a political activist, Rodolfo Gonzales also published *I am Joaquín* (1967), a long epic poem that conveys the spirit of the political agenda of the Chicano Movement, especially its call for cultural nationalism and its search for identity and cultural roots. Gonzales portrays Joaquín, the poem's central figure, as the collective voice of Chicanas/os who resist assimilation into Anglo society and subjugation to its oppressive forces and who search for strength in their cultural heritage in order to continue the struggle. In tracing the history of Chicanas/os from their Spanish and Indian past through Mexican history to the present era in U.S. history, Gonzales offers a frank appraisal of the "villains and heroes"; that is, both the positive and negative aspects of Chicanas/os' dual ancestry as mestizos, descendants of the Spanish and the indigenous peoples of Mexico. This dual heritage has produced both tyrants and slaves, exploiters and exploited, revolutionaries and anti-revolutionaries, and victors and vanquished.

The dominant theme running throughout the epic poem is endurance. Just as Joaquín has survived the many travails, conquests, wars, and other hardships in his past, he will continue to endure in the future. Gonzales ends the poem with a crescendo, calling on Chicanas/os to join in solidarity, to triumphantly seize their destiny as a liberated people.

Abelardo "Lalo" Delgado

Like Gonzales, Abelardo "Lalo" Delgado is a poet-activist whose actions and words have made him one of the most respected and influential figures among Chicanas/os who identified with the movement's goals. His four books of poetry, all published before 1975, have left their mark on many of his peers, who often speak of him as a model and inspiration. Although much of his poetry is characterized by a militant, critical view of the dominant society and its cultural values, he attempts to bring together alienated Chicanas/os and Anglos in a spirit of harmony and revindication.

Ricardo Sánchez

Ricardo Sánchez, like other Chicana/o poets writing during the same period, is harshly critical of the injustices perpetrated by Anglos on Chicanas/os, whom he urges to band together in unity to resist continued subjugation. But perhaps more than other poets, Sánchez is like a loud and rude trumpeter blasting strident notes as he calls our attention to the mostly grim social reality for Mexican Americans. His language and form are often jarring and jagged, his tone almost always irreverent, and his images shocking. Sánchez offers his opinions without restraint; he is extreme in his views and sometimes undisciplined in his form. In *Canto y grito mi liberación* (I Sing and Shout My Liberation, 1971) and *Hechizo-Spells* (*hechizo* is Spanish for *spells*, 1976), Sánchez expresses his personal struggle against an insensitive society more interested in profit than compassion. These autobiographical references are meant to represent the collective Chicana/o experience. Sánchez served time in prison, and many of the poems in *Canto y grito mi liberación* deal with the brutality and dehumanization of prison life and the poet's odyssey to find himself in a fragmented world where violence and inhumanity reign. He ultimately finds some solace in the nurturing love of the barrio and his family. *Hechizo-Spells*, a combination of prose and poetry, can best be described as a literary happening. In addition to his many antiestablishment diatribes, Sánchez takes on a number of sacred cows within Chicana/o youth culture of 1970s, such as the beliefs that drugs are a positive part of the Chicana/o tradition and that male superiority is a desirable aspect of Chicanismo. In this sense, he stands apart from most other Chicano poets writing during the same period.

Luis Omar Salinas

Luis Omar Salinas studied poetry at Fresno State University under Philip Levine, an outstanding U.S. poet and teacher who also influenced Gary Soto (see chapter 7) and other Chicana/o poets. Salinas is known for the surrealistic images seen throughout his early and later work. Best known for his first book of poetry *Crazy Gypsy: Poems* (1970), Salinas has gone on to publish several more collections of poetry: *I Go Dreaming Serenades* (1979), *Afternoon of the Unreal* (1980), *Prelude to Darkness* (1981), *Darkness under the Trees: Walking behind the Spanish* (1982), *The Sadness of Days: Selected and New Poems* (1987), *Follower of Dusk* (1991), and *Elegy for Desire* (2005). In *Crazy Gypsy*, Salinas shares with other Chicano Movement writers the intense anger and sense of alienation within dominant Anglo society. Like Luis Valdes and others he was highly critical of the Vietnam War, which he describes in poems like "Death in Vietnam" as a foreign engagement perpetrated by government officials who send the country's brown sons and daughters to die and be wounded in disproportionate numbers while at home in the United States their families continue to suffer from racism and discrimination, a certain fate that awaits Chicana/o soldiers when they return from abroad.

Tino Villanueva

Tino Villanueva has established a solid reputation as a fine and socially committed poet and perceptive scholar. His first book of poetry, *Hay otra voz: Poems* (There Is Another Voice: Poems, 1972), is a combination of two aesthetic approaches: poems that deal with historical realism—aspects of the Chicana/o experience—and those that are philosophical musings about time, death, love, beauty, and other themes. Time plays a key role in many of his poems, which are replete with images such as the hourglass and the wristwatch. The poet struggles to escape time's grip, which he does partially through his commitment to denounce injustice and racism. Several of the book's final poems focus on farmworkers as victims of their work, schools, and poverty.

Angela de Hoyos

Angela de Hoyos has led the life of a community activist and cultural worker in San Antonio from the 1960s forward. Two of her books of poetry, *Chicano Poems for the Barrio* and *Arise, Chicano! and Other Poems*, were written in the 1960s at the height of the Chicano Movement but not published until 1975. The movement's militancy is amply reflected in the books' titles and in most of the poems that comprise them. In the first book much more than in the second, Hoyos expresses her steadfast commitment to maintaining her people's cultural traditions and values, a distinctly anti-assimilationist stance that was consistent with the basic tenets of the movement and the views of many of its leaders and participants. Hoyos's use of code-switching between Spanish and English, which reflects the language usage of many barrio dwellers, is also a political statement that dignifies and underscores the legitimacy of Spanish and its admixture with English to express the uniqueness of a conquered but still proud ethnic minority. The fourteen poems in *Chicano Poems*, like many literary and nonliterary Chicano Movement publications, provide a type of informal record of the Chicana/o sociohistorical and political reality.

Narrative Fiction and the Chicano Movement

As I discussed earlier in this chapter, key to the development of contemporary Chicana/o narrative fiction in the early 1970s was the establishment of the Quinto Sol National Literary Award and the first Chicana/o publishing company, Quinto Sol. To reiterate, Tomás Rivera, Rudolfo Anaya, Rolando Hinojosa, and Estela Portillo Trambley received these prestigious awards in 1970, 1971, and 1972. I discuss these authors plus other notable authors in this section.

Tomás Rivera

Tomás Rivera (see figure 10) was born in Crystal City, Texas, in 1935 to Mexican immigrant parents. Much like other Chicano writers, musicians, artists, and filmmakers his education was frequently interrupted by the trips his family made every year in the so-called migrant stream to pick crops in the Midwest. Despite repeated interruptions, he finished high school and earned a BA degree from Southwest Texas State University and a PhD in Spanish literature from the University of Oklahoma in 1969. In his short career, Rivera served in several academic administrative positions, culminating in his appointment in 1979 as chancellor of the University of California, Riverside, a position he occupied until his tragic and untimely death in 1984.

Drawing on his own childhood and adolescence, Rivera uses the Texas-based migrant farmworker experience as the backdrop of . . . *Y no se lo tragó la tierra*. He draws heavily on the daily lives of the people he knows best while elevating their fears, struggles, and beliefs beyond the level of one-dimensional social-protest literature. While foregrounding the socioeconomic reality of his people, as a skilled novelist he gives this reality great force and credibility by creating characters, especially the novel's young, anonymous narrator, who are complex and multidimensional.

■ 10. Tomás Rivera
(courtesy of Arte Público Press)

The work consists of a series of short narrative units (that is, vignettes, anecdotes, or sketches) that are interrelated and in their entirety form a coherent and compelling work. The twelve thematically unified units are each framed by a brief fragment at the beginning. The fragments at the beginning of the units sometimes direct the reader backward by commenting indirectly on the thematic concerns of the preceding unit, or forward by prefacing the story that follows. In some instances, however, the anecdote does not relate directly to either what immediately precedes or follows it, but instead echoes themes and motifs found elsewhere in the novel. The effect is incremental; through the reinforcement, variation, and amplification provided by the twelve stories and the thirteen fragments, the picture of the community is gradually filled. At the end, the entire experience is synthesized and brought to a thematic conclusion through the consciousness of the central character (Grajeda 1979, 71–72).

The central character is the young, unnamed narrator of two of the framing pieces and of the longer narrative units. He is not explicitly identified with any of the other characters, but the experiences and landscapes of their lives all constitute part of his past and his memories of that past. Through him, we hear the voice of his people. The fact that he remains unnamed throughout the book indicates that Rivera chooses to focus on the migrants' collective experience rather than the experience of one particular character. At the same time, the frequent appearance of the young narrator does give structural unity to the work (Grajeda 1979, 72).

Rudolfo A. Anaya

Rudolfo Anaya's novel *Bless Me, Ultima* has probably been the best-selling contemporary Chicana/o novel since its publication more than thirty years ago. It has been translated into several foreign languages. Anaya (see figure 11) was born in 1937 in a small village in eastern New Mexico, and earned BA and MA degrees in English from the University of New Mexico where he was also a professor of creative writing until his retirement several years ago. He has published numerous novels (including detective novels that will be discussed in chapter 5), collections of short stories, and essays, and has received several important awards and honors.

Bless Me, Ultima revolves around a young boy growing up in rural New Mexico after World War II in a family whose roots go back to the original Spanish settlers. Antonio Márez, the young protagonist, is almost seven when he begins to have what can be described as a religious crisis. His first-person narration ends almost a year later after an intense period of spiritual growth during which the young boy has been influenced by Ultima, a local *curandera* (folk healer) of indeterminate age whom Antonio's family has brought to live in their home.

Anaya depicts Antonio's father, Gabriel Márez, as an intensely independent *llanero* (plainsman) who laments that he no longer lives on the *llano* (the plains) and has not fulfilled his lifelong dream of moving to California to seek a better way of life for his family. In contrast, Antonio's mother, María Luna Márez, comes from a long line of farmers who are firmly rooted in the land they have worked for generations. Critical of the wanderlust of her husband's side of the family, she hopes that Antonio will someday become a priest in order that she can vicariously live out a life of cultivation and learning that her marriage to Gabriel has not afforded her. Antonio's brothers, World War II veterans, are characterized as shiftless, unambitious young men who add to the keen disappointment their mother feels about her life. Antonio's sisters are barely mentioned.

Ultima's arrival in the family home saves Antonio from the torment and anguish he would probably have felt as he is torn between his mother's and father's attempts to influence his future. Ultima has a profound impact on Antonio as she invites him to see the possibilities of a magical world that is as much a part of him as his mother's faith in God and his father's sense of independence. She is his spiritual guide at a time when the death of people close to him leads Antonio to lose his faith in traditional Catholic beliefs.

Ultima awakens in him the memory of the timeless, mythological figures that inhabit his past, teaching him a profound respect for the mystical legends and folk wisdom that have survived through the centuries. She introduces him to the Golden Carp, a benevolent god who became a fish to be near his people.

Rolando Hinojosa

Rolando Hinojosa (see figure 12) intends each of his works, regardless of the genre, to form part of a lifelong novel that he has called his "Klail City Death Trip." He has created the fictional world of Klail City in Belken County, located somewhere in the

■ 11. Rudolfo Anaya

lower Rio Grande Valley of Texas (hereafter referred to as the "Valley") and filled it with memorable characters whose ordinary lives take on tragic-comic proportions as they go about their daily tasks, dealing with the conflicts arising out of generations of racial strife and cultural misunderstanding.

Born in the Valley in 1929, Hinojosa served in the U.S. Army during the Korean conflict, received a BA from the University of Texas, an MA from New Mexico Highlands University, and a PhD in Spanish from the University of Illinois. He held several academic and administrative positions during his long career and recently retired from the University of Texas at Austin, where he held an endowed faculty position for many years.

Hinojosa's *Estampas del valle y otras obras* (published in bilingual form in 1973 and in English as *The Valley* in 1983, not as a translation but as what Hinojosa calls a "rendering") does not have a novelistic plot or a climax, but is instead a series of sketches that form a tapestry of the Chicana/o community in and around Klail City. Each *estampa* forms an integral part of the complex mix of lives, joys, tragedies, and struggles of the community. The author tells us at the beginning of this work that his sketches are like individual strands of hair matted together with the sweat and dirt of generations of human toil. To separate them would be to interrupt the flow of vitality and spontaneity that surges through the work.

The work ranges in tone from a terse, direct presentation to a subtle folk

■ 12. Rolando Hinojosa
(courtesy of Arte Público Press)

humor. We follow dozens of characters through the novel's pages almost as though we were listening to the running commentary of a group of old friends who are reminiscing about a lifetime of relatives and acquaintances, marriages, romances, scandals, elections, deaths, burials, births, divorces, racial incidents, and other events. The interrelationships between characters are revealed slowly and almost coincidentally in order to create an overall impression of the collective nature of the community of Klail City. The few characters who do reappear throughout the pages of this novel serve as threads of unity among the seemingly disparate sketches.

Estela Portillo Trambley

Estela Portillo Trambley was born in El Paso, Texas, in 1936, received both BA and MA degrees in English from the University of Texas at El Paso, and for many years worked for the El Paso public schools. Her most important published work is the award-winning collection of short stories *Rain of Scorpions and Other Stories*. She is unusual for being one of very few Chicana writers with a strong feminist point of view to be recognized and published in an era when Chicanos were not only the principal spokesmen for the Chicano Movement, but also dominated publishing in Chicana/o venues such as newspapers, magazines, journals, and publishing houses. The recognition she received through winning the Premio Quinto Sol signaled the arrival of a wave of Chicana writers whose poetry, narrative, and drama burgeoned from the late 1970s forward.

Two stories in *Rain of Scorpions and Other Stories* are especially representative of Portillo Trambley's feminist perspective, a sentiment which was beginning to spread among Chicanas in the public sphere in the 1960s and 1970s. In the first, "If It Weren't for the Honeysuckle," two women of different generations living in the same house are trapped in an abusive situation perpetrated on them by the same man. In order to save a third, younger woman from the same destiny, the two women kill the man and bury his body in the garden. The title of the story refers metaphorically to the periodic need to prune parts of the honeysuckle plant in order to nurture and encourage its strength and survival. The family of women (and future males), now rid of its malignant part, is able to regain its vitality and prosper. In the second story, "The Paris Gown," Portillo Trambley creates a strong, liberated female character who rejects the expectations and strictures of her traditional, male-dominated culture to establish her own independent life path. Surprisingly, it is not a young 1960s woman but a grandmother who reminisces with her granddaughter about how she dramatically rejected Mexican society's constraints to express her true self. She foils her father's plans to marry her off to the suitor he has selected by announcing herself at a formal social event in the nude.

Portillo Trambley believed strongly in what she called "the female principle," which guides women who are listening closely to their hearts to seek roles that may appear by our standards to be traditional but which she believes are constantly thwarted by a male-dominated world. The strong female characters in both stories are illustrations of this principle.

Miguel M. Méndez

Miguel Méndez's first novel, *Peregrinos de Aztlán* (*Pilgrims of Aztlán,* 1971), captures some of the atmosphere of the Chicano Movement while at the same time exploring different aspects of life along the U.S.–Mexico border. His distinctly Mexican perspective of the border sets him apart from other Chicana/o writers of the 1960s and early 1970s. Miguel Méndez (see figure 13) followed a difficult path toward becoming a writer that seems more fictional than real. He was born in Bisbee, Arizona, in 1930 but scarcely five months after his birth his family was deported to Mexico as part of the U.S. government's general deportation campaign that included thousands of Americans of Mexican descent. He was raised on Mexican communal lands in the state of Sonora, where his mother taught him to read as a very young child, and he became a lifelong avid reader. His formal education ended in elementary school, and when he was fifteen he set out to look for work in the United States, finally settling in Tucson, Arizona, in 1946, where he became a bricklayer. Eventually, he became a community college instructor and a University of Arizona faculty member in 1984, a position from which he retired several years ago.

Peregrinos de Aztlán is a difficult and challenging work due mainly to the novelist's broad use of the Spanish language, which ranges from the slang then popular among young urban Chicanas/os to long baroque descriptions of landscapes. The rapid alternations among characters, times, and spaces make the novel all the more difficult to read. The author invites us

13. Miguel M. Méndez

into a complex and sometimes labyrinthine world of oppressed Yaqui Indians in Mexico and exploited Chicana/o barrio dwellers on both sides of the border. Although it is not easy to struggle through the novel's array of linguistic challenges, multiple points of view, and stream of consciousness narration, the reader is rewarded at the end by a penetrating view of various aspects of both Mexican Indian and Chicana/o experiences along the border. Méndez draws a parallel between the dominant Anglo society's oppression of Chicanas/os and the Mexican government's oppression of the Yaqui.

Alejandro Morales

Alejandro Morales was born in Montebello, California, and grew up in East Los Angeles. His parents were Mexican immigrants who settled in California before his birth. Morales received a BA from California State University, Los Angeles, and an MA and a PhD in Spanish from Rutgers University. He has been a faculty member at the University of California, Irvine, for most of his career.

In his 1975 novel *Caras viejas y vino nuevo* (published in translation as *Old Faces and New Wine* in 1981), Morales provides a more intimate view of life in the Chicana/o barrio than did any other novelist of the late 1960s and early 1970s. He presents two different but related perspectives of barrio life through the eyes of two Chicano adolescents, Julian and Mateo: weddings, dances, Christmas festivities, political confrontations, tragedies, and their passage into adulthood including their first sexual encounters and drug experiences. Morales is less interested in portraying a collective experience than in examining the individual choices the two young narrators make that ultimately decide their futures. Julian is characterized as an athletically gifted young man who has the greater potential of escaping the barrio to assimilate into Anglo society. Despite this, he becomes involved in drugs and alcohol and ends up in jail. Mateo, on the other hand, excels as a student and abandons the barrio, presumably to enroll in school in the East. His end is also tragic: He dies of leukemia.

Aristeo Brito

Like Paredes and Hinojosa, Aristeo Brito provides a broad historical perspective of the border in his award-winning novel *El Diablo en Texas* (1976 and translated as *The Devil in Texas* in 1990). The novel is divided into three sections: "Presidio 1883"; "Presidio 1942"; and "Presidio 1970." He traces the history of the border town of Presidio, Texas, and its long relationship to its border twin town, Ojinaga, Chihuahua. The first part focuses on the post-1848 period when Anglo landowners settled in what had been part of northern Mexico and began to take over Mexican American landholdings using various legal and quasi-legal means. Brito establishes the socioeconomic basis that would perpetuate the extreme stratification among Anglo Texans, wealthy Mexicans and Mexican Americans, and the majority population of poor Chicanas/os who would be disenfranchised politically and treated as social inferiors well into the twentieth century. The second part of the novel highlights the often disrespectful and even physically brutal treatment of the Mexican-origin population in the Presidio-Ojinaga region at the hands of largely Anglo Texas Rangers, U.S. Customs officials, local law enforcement authorities and, later, the Border Patrol. The devil referred to in the work's title plays a prominent role as the embodiment of evil clearly and closely associated with Anglo Texans.

■ Discussion Questions

1. Discuss the different manifestations of the Chicano Movement in terms of their similarities and differences.

2. Sometimes the production of art is related to the artist's political convictions. To what extent is this demonstrated by the founders of El Teatro Campesino?

3. How did El Teatro Campesino during its first few years differ from your understanding of traditional theater as performed in venues such as Broadway?

4. Discuss the role of publishers and journals in advancing the goals of the Chicano Movement.

5. How were the four literary works that received the Quinto Sol Literary Award similar and different from one another?

6. How is the poetry of the Chicano Movement similar to or different from the theater and narrative fiction of that period?

■ Suggested Readings

Acuña, Rodolfo. 2000. *Occupied America: A History of Chicanos.* New York: Longman.

Anaya, Rudolfo A., and Francisco Lomelí, eds. 1989. *Aztlán: Essays on the Chicano Homeland.* Albuquerque: Academia/El Norte Publications.

Camarillo, Albert. 1979. *Chicanos in a Changing Society.* Cambridge: Harvard University Press.

García, Ignacio M. 1997. *Chicanismo: The Forging of a Militant Ethos.* Tucson: University of Arizona Press.

Grajeda, Ralph F. 1979. Tomás Rivera's . . . *Y no se lo tragó la tierra:* Discovery and Appropriation of the Chicano Past. *Hispania* 62: 71–81.

Huerta, Jorge. 1982. *Chicano Theater: Themes and Form.* Ypsilanti, MI: Bilingual Press/Editorial Bilingüe.

——. 2000. *Chicano Drama: Performance, Society, and Myth.* Cambridge: Cambridge University Press.

Jiménez, Francisco, ed. 1979. *The Identification and Analysis of Chicano Literature.* Binghamton, NY: Bilingual Press/Editorial Bilingüe.

Lattin, Vernon E., ed. 1986. *Contemporary Chicano Fiction: A Critical Analysis.* Binghamton, NY: Bilingual Press/Editorial Bilingüe.

Melville, Margarita B. 1980. *Twice a Minority: Mexican American Women.* St. Louis: C. V. Mosby.

Rodríguez del Pino, Salvador. 1982. *La novela chicana escrita en español: cinco autores comprometidos.* Ypsilanti: Bilingual Press/Editorial Bilingüe.

Rosales, F. Arturo. 1996. *Chicano! The History of the Mexican American Civil Rights Movement.* Houston: Arte Público Press.

Ybarra-Frausto, Tomás. 1977. The Chicano Movement and the Emergence of a Chicano Poetic Consciousness. *New Scholar* 6: 81–109.

4

Chicana/o Autobiography

The term *autobiography* and its synonyms, such as *life writing*, *life narrative*, and *self-referential writing*, are difficult to define (Olney 1980, 15). In this chapter, I use *autobiography* to refer to narratives that are in my estimation intended to be predominantly nonfictional accounts of their authors' lives. Likewise, I have excluded works that contain autobiographical elements but seem to me to be largely fictional. Not all readers will agree with my selections. Some works (for example, Oscar "Zeta" Acosta's two works, *The Autobiography of a Brown Buffalo* and *The Revolt of the Cockroach People;* and *Canícula* by Norma Cantú), could well have been placed instead in chapter 5 on contemporary narrative fiction, where I discuss several largely fictional autobiographies.

The works included in this chapter are not all of similar length nor did they become known to readers in a uniform way. For example, some nineteenth- and early twentieth-century autobiographies are transcribed oral histories, and most of these transcriptions have been recovered from library archives. The majority, however, were published as books, and most were published in the past fifty years. I have organized the autobiographies into the following general categories: nineteenth- and twentieth-century oral histories, women's voices of nostalgia as resistance, the immigrant and migrant experience, life on the U.S.–Mexico border, the urban barrio experience, self-redemption, and self-identity. As complex narratives, several of the works could easily be included in two or more categories, but I have categorized them according to what I consider to be their primary focus.

■ Nineteenth- and Twentieth-Century Oral Histories

Chicana/o literary scholars have recovered and studied most surviving nineteenth- and early twentieth-century autobiographies. Genaro M. Padilla, in his groundbreaking book *My History, Not Yours: The Formation of Mexican American Autobiography* (1993), discusses the autobiographies of well-known nineteenth- and early twentieth-century figures (for example, the californio Manuel Guadalupe Vallejo, the nuevomexicano Rafael Sotero Chacón, and the nuevomexicana Cleofas Jaramillo), and also several women's oral histories he discovered in the Bancroft archives at the University of California, Berkeley.

In his book, Padilla situates the formative autobiographical works within a matrix of sociohistorical conditions that underlies the abrupt and often highly disruptive transition for the Southwest's Mexican population to life in the United States in the late 1840s and early 1850s. He lays out how those Mexicans who chose to stay in their newly adopted country whose borders had been redefined by the Treaty of Guadalupe Hidalgo and the Gadsden Purchase Treaty were forced in a few short years to adapt to new Anglo legal, financial, linguistic, and social traditions. By situating the formative period of Chicana/a autobiography within this very complex web of social, political, and cultural dynamics, Padilla provides a deep and nuanced understanding of the works he discusses. Of the fifteen narratives by women that Padilla discovered in the Bancroft archives, he focuses on three, those of María de las Angustias de la Guerra, Eulalia Pérez, and Apolinaria Lorenzana.

In 1878, an elderly Doña María de las Angustias, a member of an elite californio family, dictated her personal memoirs, "Ocurrencias en California" (California events), to one of Bancroft's assistants. Although the assistant tried to direct her to comment on the social manners and customs of her people, safe topics for women of the time, she chose instead to speak to him about political figures and events. The figure that emerges from her memoirs is that of a highly intelligent and politically savvy woman who although she conformed superficially to the social expectations of women at the time, led a very rich and active life among powerful political, social, and financial decision makers who were exclusively male. Her memoirs provide a detailed and precise account of political and social events from the time she was about three years old in 1818 through the American invasion of her native city of Monterey in the 1840s (Padilla 1993, 122).

Eulalia Pérez, another remarkable woman who lived more than a hundred years, dictated her memoirs to Bancroft's assistant in 1877. Despite her very advanced age, her mind was clear and her memory excellent. She had many different roles, including those of *partera* (midwife), *cocinera* (cook), *llavera* (keeper of the keys), and *mayordoma* (superintendent), during the fourteen years she worked at San Gabriel Mission prior to 1830 when the entire mission system in California began to fall apart. Her memoirs narrate the fascinating life of an early nineteenth-century woman of a humble background from childhood through adulthood, provide much ethnographic detail about how the mission system functioned, and document how a strong and persistent woman with an indomitable spirit was able to negotiate the male-dominated system to gain positions of increasing authority within it (Padilla 1993, 133).

The third transcribed narrative that Padilla discusses is Apolinaria Lorenzana's "Memorias de la beata" (A Saintly Woman's Memoirs). She, like Pérez, served the mission system as a mayordoma and as a nurse and teacher. Lorenzana had migrated to California from Mexico as a child with a group of orphans who were distributed among some of the most prominent californio families. Her memoirs reveal a precocious and focused young girl who had learned to read before emigrating from Mexico and who then taught herself to write. Even as an adolescent she began teaching others to read and write. Although she had ample opportunities to marry, she chose instead to minister to the young and the infirm. In addition to her multiple roles in the mission system, she also oversaw several *ranchos* (ranches). Padilla observes that Lorenzana's memoirs are "woman-centered," that is, they give a central place to women in a male-dominated culture with strict gender constraints and roles (Padilla 1993, 139–40).

Another rich source of women's autobiographical material was developed in the 1930s and early 1940s under the auspices of the Franklin D. Roosevelt administration's Works Projects Administration (WPA). The WPA established many public programs to give employment to the millions of unemployed and destitute U.S. citizens who had been devastated by the Great Depression of the 1930s. One such program was the Federal Writers' Project (FWP), which was designed to use the talents of unemployed writers to create a series of state guides containing a section on the culture and history of each state. FWP writers were directed to interview older residents and to create histories from which the cultural and historical material could be mined. The project was particularly vibrant in New Mexico, where work began as early as 1933 (Rebolledo and Márquez 2000, xix).

Like Padilla did in the Bancroft archives, Tey Diana Rebolledo and María Teresa Márquez conducted intensive research in archives containing hundreds of interviews of elderly nuevomexicanas that did not find their way into the state guide, *New Mexico: A Guide to the Colorful State* (most recently reprinted as *The WPA Guide to 1930s New Mexico*). Rebolledo and

Márquez selected from this extensive archival material dozens of women's tales that provide a rich source of New Mexico folklore as well as autobiographical material. Their 2000 book, *Women's Tales from the New Mexico WPA: La diabla a pie*, includes transcriptions of many of these short interviews. What emerges is a composite picture of the difficult lives of women from mainly rural areas of New Mexico during the early part of the twentieth century. The snippets of their personal histories as well as the folktales the women chose to share with their interviewers are indicative of behaviors, attitudes, values, and customs still very much alive in the villages and rural areas of Hispanic New Mexico in the 1930s and early 1940s. In drawing a contrast between the tales told by men and those told by women, Rebolledo and Márquez comment on the cultural complexities surrounding gender roles and expectations. For example, many of the tales have a cautionary moral message that seems designed to warn women not to stray from normative sexual behaviors. Other tales, as well as interviewees' comments, reveal a picture of a traditional society dominated by class differences as well as injustices perpetrated by the dominant Anglo society (Rebolledo and Márquez 2000, xlix).

Several Chicana/o scholars, including Rebolledo, have conducted oral history projects in order to collect and preserve the voices of the *ancianas/os* (the old ones). Nasario García and Patricia Preciado Martin in the past decade have also conducted fruitful oral history projects. These efforts are extremely valuable in capturing rich ethnographic detail of a way of life whose disappearance and loss rapidly accelerated after World War II when a general diaspora occurred from rural communities to urban areas as Chicanas/os sought social mobility through improved employment opportunities.

Drawing on his own childhood of summers spent with his maternal grandmother in New Mexico's Río Puerco Valley, Nasario García collected and edited the oral histories of dozens of nuevomexicanas. In his 1997 book, *Comadres: Hispanic Women of the Río Puerco Valley*, he organizes in a coherent, thematic way the many interviews he conducted among his grandparents' contemporaries and others between 1989 and 1992. Each of the nine chapters centers around a cluster of themes: the growing, harvesting, and preparation of food; household chores and responsibilities; parenting; women's roles as curanderas and parteras; maintaining and building homes; courtship and marriage rituals; and the nurturing social relationships maintained among the women.

Patricia Preciado Martin, a prolific creative writer who resides in Tucson, Arizona, has published several oral histories of Tucson and southern Arizona's Chicana/o men and women: *Del rancho al barrio* (From the Ranch to the Barrio, 1983), *Images and Conversations: Mexican Americans Recall a Southwestern Past* (1983), *Songs My Mother Sang to Me: An Oral History of Mexican American Women* (1992), and *Beloved Land: An Oral History of Mexican Americans in Southern Arizona* (2004). Six of the thirteen oral histories in *Images and Conversations* are conversations with some of the region's most prominent elderly women. The personal reminiscences, folktales, anecdotes, and traditions that emerge from all thirteen conversations are structured to reveal to the reader her or his cultural heritage in order to allow a better understanding of the present. In *Songs My Mother Sang to Me*, Preciado Martin records interviews with ten women who were of her mother and grandmother's eras. As in the case of other oral histories, her primary intent is to interview, transcribe, edit, and publish memories of the past before they disappear with the passing of generations. A secondary purpose is to counter the negative images of Mexican and Mexican American women perpetuated by Hollywood and the media. The results comprise a stunning collection of the reminiscences of immigrant and nonimmigrant ranching and farm women, urban working women, and stay-at-home wives and mothers.

Women's Voices of Nostalgia as Resistance

The majority of the women interviewed for the New Mexico FWP resided in small villages and rural areas. Most of them had not received formal education much beyond high school, nor were they completely comfortable speaking English. By contrast three nuevomexicana writers—Fabiola Cabeza de Baca Gilbert, Nina Otero-Warren (formerly Otero), and Cleofas Jaramillo—stand out as middle- or upper-class, educated women who were completely comfortable speaking and writing in English. They produced several books that, like the interviews conducted for the FWP, were intended to document the folklore and culture of Hispanic New Mexico while at the same time revealing "details of their lives and their families" (Rebolledo 1995, 29).

Chicana feminist critics have interpreted the three women's works very differently than male critics have. Rebolledo, for example, views their works as acts of subtle but strong resistance to the loss of Hispanic culture at a time when it was in very real danger of being forgotten or "erased" as Chicanas throughout the Southwest began to assimilate in greater numbers into the dominant culture after World War II. Rebolledo has also recognized that by highlighting their roles as vigorous and independent writers, the three nuevomexicanas were going against the grain of patriarchal expectations prevalent at a time when women were expected to seek fulfillment in their traditional roles as wives and mothers in the home (Rebolledo 1995, 29–47).

Rebolledo and Eliana Rivero (1993, 31) have documented what they identify as "the narrative strategies of resistance" embedded throughout the works of these three women writers. These strategies include a conscious struggle to retain their ethnic heritage in every way possible in the face of Anglo colonizing forces; a very sentimental attachment to the past as a means of implicitly questioning the viability of the imposed Anglo culture and society in contrast to the unified Spanish-speaking community it is trying to replace; an experimentation through the blending and blurring of borders between different narrative genres (for example, the mixing of the oral and the written, history and autobiography, recipes and narrative); the very act of writing down and transmitting traditions, values, and cultural practices as a challenge to the authority of the male voice; and the use of translation from English to Spanish and vice versa as subtle criticism of Anglo culture and its superficial understanding of Hispanic culture and history (Rebolledo and Rivero 1993, 17–18).

◼ The Autobiography of the Immigrant Experience

As I discussed in chapter 2, immigration from Mexico to the United States grew sharply during the Mexican Revolution and continued at a steady pace until the end of the last century, when it again burgeoned. Many individuals who have made the trek north to the United States in search of a safer environment and economic advancement have recorded their varied experiences either as oral histories or as authors of their own autobiographies. An example of the former is Manuel Gamio's *The Mexican Immigrant: His Life Story* (1931). Gamio, a Mexican anthropologist who dedicated his career as a scholar to studying different aspects of the Mexican immigrant experience, interviewed numerous legal and undocumented laborers in the 1920s and 1930s and published parts of these interviews in *The Mexican Immigrant.* His book of interviews is a mosaic of the hardships many of the immigrants encountered crossing into the United States and often suffering at the hands of ruthless and exploitative employers and even law enforcement personnel.

Ernesto Galarza

Ernesto Galarza describes his own immigrant experience in his autobiography, *Barrio Boy: The Story of a Boy's Acculturation* (1971). Galarza, a Columbia University–trained PhD sociologist and labor expert, recounts his family's abrupt departure for the United States from a small, mountainous village in the western Mexican state of Nayarit at the beginning of the Mexican Revolution. The family eventually settled in Sacramento, California. Galarza traces the slow, painful, but ultimately successful path of his acculturation to an alien Anglo culture. Genaro Padilla notes that Galarza tends to sentimentalize the Mexican village he and his family were forced to abandon and to treat the flight north as an adventure rather than what it was for millions of Mexicans: "the tragedy of death, starvation, and displacement" (Padilla 1993, 235).

Pablo Cruz

About the same time that Galarza's autobiography appeared and more than forty years after the publication of Gamio's work, Eugene Nelson published an extended oral history, *Pablo Cruz and the American Dream* (1975), based on his many interviews with Pablo Cruz, an undocumented Mexican worker, during the summer of 1964. Cruz's story is similar to those of many of the informants Gamio interviewed in several aspects: his upbringing in a large and poor Mexican family in rural Mexico; his having to help support his family as a ten-year-old; his desire to escape poverty by studying during high school to become a radio broadcaster; his illegal border crossing into California; troubles with a brutal and exploitative coyote; his constant fear of being deported by the authorities; his marriage under a false name; and finally his blending into the agricultural communities of central California. The transcribed autobiography is on one hand unremarkable, in that Pablo Cruz's life was like those of so many of the undocumented Mexican workers who preceded him, and inspirational on the other, in that he survived significant odds and adversity during his early life.

Ramón "Tianguis" Pérez

A more recent autobiography of immigration is Ramón "Tianguis" Pérez's *Diary of an Undocumented Immigrant* (1991). Pérez grew up in a mountainous and isolated village in the Mexican state of Oaxaca and became involved in revolutionary activities as a teenager during the Mexican Revolution. These activities are recorded in his *Diary of a Guerrilla* (1999). The account of his experiences as an undocumented Mexican worker is similar to those chronicled in Gamio's work, although sixty years separates the former from the latter. By the time Pérez and thousands like him came to the United States, a whole organized and smooth-running system for smuggling undocumented workers was firmly in place (that is, Mexican coyotes [smugglers] working closely with Chicana/o *contratistas* [labor contractors] to provide cheap labor to large U.S. businesses with the full complicity of corporate executives and their subordinates). Pérez provides graphic descriptions of negotiating the exploitative labor system while at the same time avoiding deportation by the Border Patrol and other authorities. Disillusioned by the constant alienation he feels in a culture not his own, he ultimately decides to return to Mexico rather than seek to qualify for residency in the United States.

Leonor Villegas de Magnón

Leonor Villegas de Magnón's memoir, *The Rebel* (1994), tells a different immigration story. She was born in Mexico in 1876 and fled to the United States in 1910 for political reasons. She had been a fierce critic of the Mexican dictator Porfirio Díaz and had allied herself with the revolutionaries who overthrew him. She settled in Laredo, where she continued her revolutionary activities from afar.

The Chicana scholar Clara Lomas is responsible for recovering, introducing, editing, and translating Villegas de Magnón's memoirs, which were originally written in Spanish. The memoirs provide a rare woman's point of view of some of the participants and events of the Mexican Revolution, especially along the U.S.–Mexico border. Villegas de Magnón looks at the revolution through the eyes of *fronterizas* (women border dwellers) on both sides of the border who used their privileged positions as members of wealthy and influential families to finance anti-Porfirian causes. Another valuable aspect of the book is the respect its author shows toward the poor and downtrodden, values that had been modeled by her parents.

■ The Autobiography of Life along the Border

The border between the United States and Mexico has different, interrelated political, cultural, and social dimensions. The 1848 Treaty of Guadalupe Hidalgo and the 1853 Gadsden Purchase Treaty established new boundaries between the two countries between the U.S. states of Texas, New Mexico, Arizona, and California and the Mexican states of Tamaulipas, Nuevo León, Coahuila, Sonora, and Baja California. These treaties and subsequent economic and political forces created a series of twin cities along the border: Brownsville/Matamoros, Eagle Pass/Piedras Negras, Laredo/Nuevo Laredo, El Paso/Ciudad Juárez, Nogales/Nogales, and San Diego/Tijuana. There are, of course, numerous other smaller twin towns and border crossings, but most of the U.S. and Mexican citizens who inhabit the border region live in the larger twin cities.

All of the writers discussed in this section spent at least some of their lives in these twin cities: Alberto Alvaro Ríos in Nogales/Nogales; Norma Cantú in Laredo/Nuevo Laredo; Luis Alberto Urrea in San Diego/Tijuana; and Ray Gonzalez and Gloria López-Stafford in El Paso/Juárez. Of the five writers considered in this section, Alberto Alvaro Ríos and Norma Cantú best capture in their respective autobiographical works the complexities of growing up Chicana/o on the U.S.–Mexico border. Yet all of them recount in their autobiographical works the experience of living in an area that is not entirely Anglo nor Chicana/o nor Mexican, but rather a complex combination of these cultures that contributes toward a dynamic and ever-changing border existence that some scholars have called a "liminal," or "in-between," space with its own characteristics. The writers included in this section portray through their memories a kind of fluid state of living on the border; there are at once vast and not-so-vast differences in cultural observances, values, expectations, and norms of behavior as well as different linguistic practices, foods, tastes, smells, sights, and sounds.

Alberto Alvaro Ríos

Alberto Alvaro Ríos's reflections on a young life spent in the twin cities of Nogales, Arizona, and Nogales, Sonora, evokes the complexities of life in the borderlands: "The trouble is, we talk about the border at Nogales as a place only, instead of an idea as well. But it is both *where* two countries meet as well as *how* two countries meet, and the handshake is rough" (Ríos 1999a, 12). Ríos was born in 1952 and grew up in Nogales, Arizona. His father was an immigrant to the United States who married an English-woman whom he had met during his military service in World War II.

What is immediately striking about Ríos's autobiographical work, *Capirotada: A Nogales Memoir* (1999), is the depiction of the twin cities as one: "Nogales in the earliest years I can remember had a smell of woodsmoke in the evenings. The town itself, which is where I grew up, was separated into two parts, the American and the Mexican, by a ten-foot-high hard wire fence" (Ríos 1999a, 2). He returns to this sense of unity numerous times throughout his narrative, yet without ignoring the obvious geopolitical boundary between the two cities. At the time Ríos wrote his work, it had become increasingly difficult to traverse the border—especially for undocumented Mexican workers. This was due in large measure to the construction of a long, solid fence between the two cities that Ríos describes as "a pathetic version of the Great Wall of China" (Ríos 1999, 12). Ríos expresses the tension between the unity and the separation of the two cities many times in his narrative.

Capirotada, the title of the autobiography, refers to a tasty Mexican bread pudding made during and just after Lent. Ríos uses it to typify the interdependence and the mutual respect and understanding between inhabitants of the two cities. The wonderful mélange of ingredients in capirotada, some of which—raw peanuts, *panocha* (unrefined brown sugar), *quesadilla* cheese—could only be purchased in Mexico, symbolizes how the individual cultural, linguistic, historical, culinary, and other parts from both sides of the border make up one entity.

Norma Cantú

Norma Cantú (see figure 14) was born in Nuevo Laredo, Tamaulipas in 1947, immigrated with her family to Laredo, Texas, in 1948, and became a naturalized U.S. citizen in 1968. She obtained her PhD in literature from the University of Nebraska and currently teaches at the University of Texas, San Antonio. Cantú describes *Canícula: Snapshots of a Girlhood en la Frontera* (1995) as a "fictional autobioethnography," indicating that her narrative is not always autobiographical. Nonetheless, I consider it sufficiently so to include in this section. In keeping with Cantú's intended blurring of the lines between fiction and nonfictional autobiography, she creates a fictional narrator, Nena, whose recounted memories of growing up in Laredo, Texas, are triggered when she discovers family photos in a cardboard box many years later. Cantú includes many of Nena's family photos—all apparently authentic photos of the author's family—at the beginning of many of the work's stories, scenes, and vignettes. In a further attempt to blur the lines between fiction and nonfiction, Cantú's individual narratives do not always correspond to the photos. The stories focus on Nena's growing out of childhood into womanhood as well as

■ 14. Norma Cantú
(photo by Macarena Hernández)

on her mother, father, grandmother, siblings, and friends, thus presenting a composite picture of a small community of individuals who negotiate sometimes harmonious and sometimes difficult lives within Laredo and between Laredo and its Mexican counterpart of Nuevo Laredo.

More so than Ríos, Cantú paints a picture of an economically, socially, and racially stratified U.S.–Mexico border society in which racial tensions between Anglo Texans, versus Chicanas/os and Mexican nationals play out in frequent clashes. She also describes the Spanish-speaking population on both sides of the borders as itself highly stratified along class lines. She alternates between profoundly disturbing and pleasant memories. That this area is often one of the hottest places in the United States in the summer is reflected in the title; *canícula* refers to the muggy and extremely uncomfortable climate during most of the summer. Canícula also refers metaphorically to social stratification, the multifaceted manifestations of racism, and Nena's increasing awareness as she matures of what is sometimes an oppressive existence within a traditional Chicano/Mexican family.

Ray Gonzalez

Ray Gonzalez, who was born in 1952, grew up in El Paso (see figure 15). He currently holds an endowed chair in English at the University of Minnesota. He has written extensively about the El Paso/Juárez area and the wider borderlands region in his poetry, fiction, and essays. His most explicitly autobiographical works are *Memory Fever: A Journey beyond El Paso del Norte* (1993) and to a lesser extent *The Underground Heart: A Return to a Hidden Landscape* (2002). He has returned frequently to El Paso

■ 15. Ray Gonzalez (courtesy of University of Arizona Press)

for family reunions, professional conferences, and "the need to immerse myself briefly in the power of the Southwest landscape" (Gonzalez 1993, vii). Landscape plays a much more important role in his autobiographical recollections than is true for other writers discussed in this section.

Gonzalez's evocation of his spiritual and emotional link to the Rio Grande and the stark Chihuahuan Desert landscape of far west Texas and southern New Mexico marks his two autobiographical works. At the same time that the river and landscape nurture him, they are a source of his lament for a past that cannot be relived. He reflects painfully on how both the river and the landscape have changed since he left El Paso. The once free-flowing river has given way to a slow-moving and increasingly polluted stream of water traversed daily by thousands of undocumented Mexican workers. The once-pristine landscape is now cluttered with housing developments built hastily to accommodate a rapidly increasing population. The Sunset Heights neighborhood where he was raised is now an unsightly barrio with a high crime rate. In his decidedly mournful words, *Memory Fever* "is about growing up in a place I will not see again" (viii).

Gloria López-Stafford

Like Gonzalez, Gloria López-Stafford situates her autobiographical narrative, *A Place in El Paso: A Mexican American Childhood* (1996), in El Paso during her childhood and early adolescence in the 1940s and 1950s. She was born in Juárez in 1938 and spent most of her early years in El Paso's Segundo Barrio (Second Ward), a well-known lower- and working-class district that abuts the Rio Grande. It was the source of the late-1930s pachuco culture that migrated to California in the 1940s. She recalls having a very difficult childhood. Her sickly mother died when she was a small child, and she was raised by her father and her stepmother, a Mexican woman from Juárez. Her Anglo godparents, who lived in a more affluent area of El Paso, eventually adopted her. Like many other Chicana/o autobiographies, *A Place in El Paso* focuses on the common, traumatic transition of a child raised in a Spanish-dominant home to a school where

English was dominant and where children caught speaking Spanish were humiliated and punished. Life in the Segundo Barrio was fraught with other difficult experiences for the small child, including the devastating poverty of the tenements, the menacing behavior of tough-talking pachucos, and the high incidence of petty and violent crimes. These experiences are the foreground for the rare instances of joy and security in the young girl's life, including the traditional religious celebrations of Advent, Christmas, and the Feast of the Three Kings, and the Christmas *tamaladas*, when families and friends gather to make traditional sweet and meat tamales.

Luis Alberto Urrea

Luis Alberto Urrea was born in 1955 in Tijuana, Baja California, and grew up in San Diego (see figure 16). The family first lived in a working-class community of Anglos, Chicanas/os, Mexicans, and African Americans, and then moved to a predominantly Anglo neighborhood. Urrea is currently a professor of creative writing at the University of Illinois, Chicago. Urrea's most autobiographical work is *Nobody's Son: Notes from an American Life* (1998), the third and final part of what the writer calls a border trilogy also consisting of *Across the Wire: Life and Hard Times on the Mexican Border* (1993) and *By the Lake of Sleeping Children: The Secret Life of the Mexican Border* (1996).

Urrea's autobiographical memories are distinct from those of the writers already discussed in this section in that a Mexican city plays a much more prominent role. His recollections of Tijuana, where he was born and where he would frequently return throughout his childhood to visit family and friends, are decidedly positive: "When I was a boy, Tijuana was a place of magic and wonder, a place of dusty gardens laden with fruit, of pretty women, dogs, food, music. Everywhere you looked, there were secrets and astonishments. And everyone was laughing" (Urrea 1998, 66).

As is common with most children as they grow older, Urrea's perspective changes dramatically over time, especially during the ten years he did relief work along the border after graduating from college. This change is amply reflected in the two first installments of his border trilogy and to a lesser extent in *Nobody's Son*, which focuses more on Urrea's anguished childhood. Urrea's view of the border through a different optic of adult experience is dominated by scenes of impoverished Mexicans struggling to eke out an existence while still retaining some sense of dignity. He also

16. Luis Alberto Urrea

reveals the tawdry underbelly of Tijuana which, like many border cities, has been for most of the twentieth century a sexual playground for tourists and military personnel stationed in U.S. border cities.

■ The Autobiography of the Urban Barrio Experience

Barrios first developed in the nineteenth century as whole sections of cities such as San Antonio, Houston, El Paso, San Diego, and Los Angeles became populated mainly by native-born Mexican Americans even as the Anglo population began to increase. Barrios then provided a welcoming home for successive waves of Mexican immigrants who crossed the U.S.–Mexico border; immigration accelerated with the outbreak of the Mexican Revolution in 1910. Later in the twentieth century, Chicanas/os and Mexicans who were part of the migrant stream to the Midwest and Northwest began new barrios in cities such as Minneapolis–St. Paul, Milwaukee, and Kansas City. At the same time, others resettled in and around cities like Chicago where there were employment opportunities in factories and the steel industry. Over the span of the twentieth century, barrios have sprung up in virtually every city in the Southwest as well as in Missouri, Florida, North Carolina, and elsewhere outside the Southwest.

Today, not all Chicana/o communities are barrios and not all barrios are poor, located in the inner city, or overcrowded. There are hundreds of communities throughout the Southwest and elsewhere that have none of these characteristics. Nonetheless, it is the poor, inner-city barrio where many contemporary Chicana/o writers situate works that highlight the cultural, socioeconomic, physical, psychological, spiritual, and other dimensions of this urban space. At the same time, they do not skirt the fact that barrios are increasingly socially and economically impoverished, with low-income residents; underfunded and low-performing schools; inadequate social and medical services; and high rates of drugs, gangs, and crime.

Included in this section are writers whose autobiographical narratives focus primarily on their childhood and adolescent years growing up in urban barrios in Pacoima, California (Mary Helen Ponce), Fresno, California (Gary Soto), and East Los Angeles (Luis J. Rodríguez). Like the writers in the previous section, Ponce, Soto, and Rodríguez recall living in border spaces, but along borders within cities as opposed to along the U.S.–Mexico border. One does not have to cross the international line to be in such spaces, for internal borders are common in cities with large ethnic populations living in ghettos and barrios that have unofficially prescribed boundaries that set them off from often more prosperous Anglo communities. The phrase "living on the other side of the tracks" metaphorically conveys this notion of internal borders. The writers in this section—who can therefore be thought of as growing up in internal urban border areas—range from Ponce's generally positive and benign view to Rodríguez's decidedly negative one; Gary Soto falls somewhere in between.

Mary Helen Ponce

Ponce was born in 1938 in Pacoima, California, a small city in the San Fernando Valley twenty miles northeast of downtown Los Angeles. Her parents were both Mexican immigrants. Ponce was one of eleven children, several of whom died before she was born or during the twelve years covered by her 1993 autobiographical narrative, *Hoyt Street: An Autobiography*.

Although Ponce focuses in her opening chapter on the economic deprivation of her barrio's largely lower- and middle-class Mexican-immigrant and first-generation Mexican American population, this description contrasts with the largely positive memories of living there that she evokes in the remainder of the book. She foregrounds the mutual generosity, kindness, and resourcefulness among neighbors and extended families despite their economic struggles. For example, many families, including her own, would accumulate piles of used building material and broken-down cars and trucks in their back yards to use themselves or give to needier families. Given the traditional values that governed their lives, the men, women, and even children were expected to make sacrifices for and be supportive of others, especially during times of great need such as a death in the family, an illness or accident, or a financial crisis.

A curious and bright young child, Ponce was eager to attend the barrio elementary school, where she excelled throughout the eight grades that she describes in the book. Although she was not exempt from the normal minor failures and small disappointments associated with childhood, her experiences were largely positive. There is no reference, for example, to the humiliation that Mexican-immigrant and first-generation Chicana/o children frequently experience when they leave the comfort of their homes in their familiar barrios for the first time to fend for themselves in a school atmosphere that can be hostile and unforgiving.

Gary Soto

Soto, who was born in Fresno, California, in 1952 overcame a difficult childhood of loneliness and alienation to become one of the finest and most acclaimed writers of his generation. In *Living up the Street: Narrative Recollections* (1985), he recounts the anguish he felt as a child when he lost his father, who died in an industrial accident, and had to adapt to a new life with a stepfather who treated him and his two siblings with a mixture of indifference and anger. Elsewhere, Soto also recounts that he was a poor student throughout his elementary and junior high school years in barrio schools; he barely graduated from high school in 1970. Fortunately, instead of going the route of most of his Chicana/o classmates, who either joined the military or took low-paying local jobs, he went to college, excelled, and earned an MFA in creative writing from the University of California, Irvine.

Memory and the ability to recall detail play important parts in Soto's creative process: "For me, streets have mattered. When I am ready to write, ready to sit down, usually at the kitchen table but also in bed, I conjure up inside my head an image of our old street in south Fresno, where, at the beginning of the 1960s, house after house was torn down in the name of 'urban renewal'" (Soto 2000, ix). He also comments that even in late childhood, he was conscious of his ability to notice and then recall details of growing up on Braly Street, in a rundown barrio of Fresno, and later on Van Ness and other streets in a somewhat more prosperous, working-class part of town.

In *Living up the Street* and other autobiographical works, Soto describes the bleak aspects of barrio poverty and the loneliness that dominated so much of his childhood and adolescence. He recounts how he and his two siblings developed "a streak of orneriness" in order to survive with some pride intact in a neighborhood in the shadows of factories that wore down and dehumanized the Chicana/o families on Braly Street. As he does throughout all of his creative works, Soto often unobtrusively inserts social commentary about the oppressive material conditions of the Fresno barrios where he grew up. His meanness and penchant for fighting became a self-protective shield to ward off the real violence that adults in the barrios perpetrated against children. Soto also comments on the larger societal forces that contribute heavily to the creation of these conditions. He recalls the disparities he perceived as a child between working-class poverty and the idealized middle-class Anglo existence portrayed in popular 1950s television shows such as "Father Knows Best" and "Leave It to Beaver." Soto's autobiographical depiction of life in the Fresno barrios is less positive than Ponce's characterization of the Pacoima barrio. Where Ponce emphasizes redeeming aspects of barrio life, Soto does not.

Luis J. Rodríguez

Luis Rodríguez (see figure 17), an award-winning poet, journalist, and essayist, was born in El Paso in 1954. His family moved to Los Angeles in 1956. Rodríguez attended the public schools in East Los Angeles, the home of many other Chicana/o writers and the site of very intensive political activity during the Chicano Movement of the late 1960s and early 1970s. As he describes in vivid detail in his autobiographical work, *Always Running: La vida loca, Gang Days in L.A.* (1993), Rodríguez spent much of his adolescence in the streets of East Los Angeles as a member of different gangs that engaged regularly in violence and other antisocial behaviors. He was also active in political activities such as the Chicana/o school walkouts in 1967, which were organized to protest prejudice and discrimination in the schools.

Rodríguez presents a much more graphic and raw vision of barrio life than does either Ponce or Soto. He recounts how he joined gangs in a

■ 17. Luis J. Rodríguez

misguided effort to escape the harassment he suffered from Anglo students as a first-generation Chicano with poor English language skills. The gangs also afforded him a network of friends and the protection that such friendships offered. He neither glorifies nor demonizes gangs, but instead provides an overview of the socioeconomic conditions that create gang life. Rodríguez describes in stark detail some incidents of violence, crime, and cruelty in which he participated—robberies and petty theft; abusive experimentation with drugs, alcohol, and sex; severe physical beatings; drive-by shootings; and murder—as well as how he became calloused to the pain that he was inflicting on others. He was eventually jailed for attempted murder and then released.

Rodríguez finally came to terms with the brutal behavior that almost earned him a life prison sentence. He recalls rejecting the gangs and turning to education and public activism as much more positive and promising life paths. His intent in writing his autobiography was to give his teenaged son a frank and honest perspective on gang life within a violent urban barrio before he, too, was sucked into its vortex. Unfortunately, in 1998, five years after the publication of *Always Running*, his son was sentenced to prison for attempted murder.

■ The Autobiography of Self-Redemption

Several Chicana/o writers discussed in this chapter trace their trajectories from growing up in extremely difficult conditions to eventually leading productive lives as adults. We know from sociological studies that many Chicana/o contemporaries of these writers have not been so successful. And although the writers do not highlight in their autobiographical accounts the combination of will and sense of purpose that perhaps inspired them to continue the struggle to succeed, it is definitely present. There is, then, a redemptive aspect running through many of the works already discussed, but the 2001 autobiography of Jimmy Santiago Baca, *A Place to Stand*, is one of the most dramatic stories of self-redemption.

Baca was born in Santa Fe in 1952, the son of poor Mexican mestizo parents. After his parents divorced, his mother abandoned him and his two siblings, and his father was largely absent during most of his childhood and adolescence. The children lived for a time with their grandparents, but then Baca, who was barely six years old, and his younger brother were sent to an orphanage in Albuquerque. He escaped repeatedly from the orphanage, was later sent to a juvenile home, and then served several short jail sentences for theft and other crimes in New Mexico, Arizona, and California. Baca grew up in decidedly bleak conditions, constantly engulfed in extreme poverty, criminality, chronic unemployment, hard drug and alcohol addiction, homelessness, and broken, despairing, and dysfunctional families.

Baca recounts in his autobiographical narrative that when he was twenty-one he was convicted in Arizona for drug possession and served five years in the Florence, Arizona, maximum security correctional facility, where he struggled to survive among hardened criminals including many violent offenders. At this juncture, Baca had fallen to a new low in his life and seemed destined to spend the rest of his days in and out of jails and penitentiaries or worse.

One of the most moving sections of *A Place to Stand* is the slow and painful process that Baca, drawing on sheer willpower, went through to learn to write by phonetically sounding out words from a textbook he had stolen from a prison official. Over the course of several years in prison, he overcame the inferior education that had left him a functional illiterate and began to write rudimentary phrases; whole sentences and paragraphs; and then simple, naïve, and sentimental poems. Aided by a prison workshop on writing, he eventually began to produce more sophisticated poems, some of which were published in magazines and literary journals. By the time he left prison, he had come to the attention of some prominent U.S. poets such as Denise Levertov and the Native American critic Joseph Bruchac. Baca's prison experience in general and the brutality of prison life in particular play a central role in much of his subsequent award-winning poetry, essays, and most explicitly, his autobiography. Today, he is considered to be one of a handful of Chicana/o poets who are recognized across the United States.

■ The Autobiography of Self-Identity

In general, autobiographers implicitly or explicitly express a desire to better understand themselves and to reveal at least an aspect of who they are. In some cases, their autobiographical narratives reveal their process of self-discovery and self-identity. Chicana/o autobiographers are no exception; the writers discussed in this chapter all engage in this process at some level. But two writers stand out for doing so: Oscar "Zeta" Acosta and Richard Rodríguez.

Oscar "Zeta" Acosta

Acosta was an irreverent and energetic social rebel and political activist who wrote brilliantly but lived self-destructively, all the while serving as a defense lawyer. Acosta was born in El Paso, Texas, in 1935 and raised in California's San Joaquín Valley. He received his law degree in 1966 and immediately dedicated himself to defending poor clients and activists in East Los Angeles. He went to Mexico in 1974, where he mysteriously disappeared and was never heard of again.

In his autobiographical narratives, *The Autobiography of a Brown Buffalo* (1972) and *The Revolt of the Cockroach People* (1973), Acosta captures a sense of the tumultuous times of civil unrest and social and political turmoil associated with the Chicano Movement and with the militant civil rights struggles and confrontations in general that occurred throughout California in the 1960s and early 1970s. Acosta's two autobiographical works together describe his personal odyssey to discover himself and his relationship to his cultural past. In the first work, Acosta becomes progressively more disenchanted with his life as an urban lawyer, feelings he attributes to an acute sense of feeling culturally rootless. His experiences with drugs, alcohol, and sex provide him with little relief from this anguish, and it is only through the quest for and attainment of his true identity as a Chicano that Acosta reckons with his internal struggle. In the second work, after he decided to dedicate himself to defending his people, his life takes on direction and meaning.

Acosta begins his six-month quest to find his identity in *The Autobiography of a Brown Buffalo*. In an attempt to come to terms with his frequent bouts of depression and self-doubt, he journeys to Juárez, where he discovers his true mestizo roots. It is at this point that he begins to take pride in himself as a "beautiful brown buffalo." He sets out for Los Angeles, determined to put his newfound identity to good use.

In *The Revolt of the Cockroach People*, a sequel to the first work, Acosta recounts passing through an intense period in the Chicano Movement as a fearless attorney who participates in demonstrations, marches, and dramatic courtroom defenses of militants falsely accused of crimes. Acosta adopts his middle name, "Zeta," which comes from General Zeta, the revolutionary hero of a Mexican movie classic. The novel contains many thinly veiled references to both Anglo and Chicana/o figures of the late 1960s and early 1970s. They include Rubén Salazar, the Chicano journalist who was killed during the August 1970 National Chicano Moratorium against the Vietnam War; Sam Yorty, the mayor of Los Angeles; "Corky" Gonzales, the Denver political activist; César Chávez; and California Governor Ronald Reagan.

Acosta's "shoot from the hip" style in both novels is energetic, direct, and seemingly undisciplined, reflecting the chaos in his own life as well as the swirl of unrest and experimentation of the times. He seems most interested in plumbing the depths of a time when people of all ethnic backgrounds, especially young people, were questioning an older generation's values and priorities while living out their own and collectively producing a sea of social change that made its mark on American society.

Richard Rodríguez

Richard Rodríguez was born in San Francisco in 1944 to Mexican parents. Soon after his birth, the family moved to an Anglo neighborhood in Sacramento, where he grew up and attended parochial schools. He received a BA degree and went on to do advanced graduate work in literature. Rodríguez's primary autobiographical work is *Hunger of Memory: The Education of Richard Rodríguez: An Autobiography* (1982). Two other books, *Days of Obligation: An Argument with My Mexican Father* (1992) and *Brown:*

The Last Discovery of America (2002), are also autobiographical, but much less so.

In the first part of *Hunger of Memory*, Rodríguez describes his early years of struggle in school. As was true for several generations of Chicanas/os and Mexican immigrant families, the dominant language in his home was Spanish. Rodríguez recalls his extreme discomfort in first grade attending a school in which most of his classmates were from middle- and upper-class Anglo families. The linguistic and class disparities were a source of embarrassment and shame, heightened by his growing perception that his parents, who barely spoke English, had somehow failed him.

One of the aspects of *Hunger of Memory* that has made Rodríguez a pariah for many Chicana/o scholars is his attack on bilingual education, which he connects throughout his work to his "journey from social disadvantage to social acceptance, from public alienation to public integration" (R. Saldívar 1990, 157). Rodríguez differentiates between Spanish as a private family language among U.S. Latinas/os and English, especially written English, as a "public" language that he believes all U.S. citizens must learn to be socially accepted and economically successful. One of the reasons that Rodríguez has been so controversial is his insistence that Spanish speakers must not let their native language become an impediment to their becoming successfully assimilated into U.S. society. Adding to the controversy is his failure to acknowledge what millions of bilingual speakers of Spanish and other heritage languages know from experience: that an individual can retain and further develop her or his ability to communicate orally and in writing in a native language while at the same time becoming fully articulate in spoken and written English.

Rodríguez's dichotomy between private Spanish and public English and his attack on bilingual programs have made him popular among conservative Anglo politicians and educators, who generally praise *Hunger of Memory*. On the other hand, Chicanas/os have been critical, describing the work as portraying at best a naïve and uninformed point of view and at worst an expression of self-hate and a self-serving act in Rodríguez's journey to find self-acceptance. One of the most critical responses to *Hunger of Memory* is by Ramón Saldívar, who states, "His writings against bilingual education (because it is a hindrance to the access to a 'public' language) and against affirmative action (because it denigrates the achievements of those who have made it on their own merits) involves him, whether he admits it or not, in a political service to the Right" (R. Saldívar 1990, 157). Soon after the publication of *Hunger of Memory*, Rodríguez became a spokesman for ideologues with specific political agendas like the "English only" movement.

■ Discussion Questions

1. Discuss the importance of oral histories in the development of Chicana/o autobiography.

2. How does nostalgia function as a strategy of resistance in Chicana/o autobiography?

3. What do the autobiographies of immigration have in common?

4. Discuss the similarities and differences between the autobiographies situated in U.S.–Mexico border cities and those situated in urban barrios far from the border.

5. Discuss your understanding of an autobiography that has aspects of self-redemption.

6. In what sense do many autobiographies explore issues of identity? Give examples from the works discussed in this chapter.

■ Suggested Readings

Folkenflik, Robert, ed. 1993. *The Culture of Autobiography: Constructions of Self-Representation*. Stanford: Stanford University Press.

Gamio, Manuel. 1931. *The Mexican Immigrant: His Life Story*. Chicago: University of Chicago Press.

Olney, James, ed. 1980. *Autobiography: Essays Theoretical and Critical*. Princeton: Princeton University Press.

——. 1998. *Memory and Narrative: The Weave of Life-Writing*. Chicago: University of Chicago Press.

Padilla, Genaro M. 1993. *My History, Not Yours: The Formation of Mexican American Autobiography*. Madison: University of Wisconsin Press.

Rebolledo, Tey Diana. 1995. *Women Singing in the Snow: An Analysis of Chicana Literature*. Albuquerque: University of New Mexico Press.

Rebolledo, Tey Diana, and María Teresa Márquez, eds. 2000. *Women's Tales from the New Mexico WPA: La diabla a pie.* Houston: Arte Público Press.

Rebolledo, Tey Diana, and Eliana Rivero. 1993. *Infinite Divisions: An Anthology of Chicana Literature.* Tucson: University of Arizona Press.

Smith, Sidonie, and Julia Watson. 2001. *Reading Autobiography: A Guide for Interpreting Life Narratives.* Minneapolis: University of Minnesota Press.

5

Trends and Themes in Contemporary Chicana/o Narrative Fiction

T he Chicano Movement of the 1960s and early 1970s generated a flurry of cultural activity, including the publication of anthologies and newspapers, the establishment of literary prizes, and the founding of scholarly journals and literary presses. Poetry, drama, nonfiction autobiography, and narrative fiction flourished. Chicana/o writers performed and read their works at literary festivals, on high school and college campuses, and in venues in the urban barrios of the Southwest. Colleges and universities as well as high schools began offering courses in Chicana/o literature as part of Chicana/o studies or ethnic studies programs and in departments of English and Spanish.

The firm foundation established during the Chicano Movement served to encourage and support writers in their creative endeavors. During the 1980s and especially the 1990s, an explosion of literary publication took place. Established writers such as Rolando Hinojosa, Miguel Méndez, and Alejandro Morales continued to publish and at the same time a large group of new writers emerged. Arte Público Press and Bilingual Review Press published most of the literary works during these two decades, but Chicana/o writers increasingly began to be published by university presses and by mainstream commercial presses located on the east and west coasts.

In this chapter, I discuss some works of narrative fiction by a few of the established as well as many other less well recognized writers. I have organized the chapter according to what I believe are some important themes and trends in contemporary Chicana/o narrative fiction. As is the case throughout this book, my choice of writers is selective, not comprehensive; I have excluded many writers because they did not seem to be representative of these themes and trends. If you would like to study specific themes and trends of Chicana/o narrative fiction in greater depth, you may want to consult the "Suggested Readings" section at the end of the chapter.

Keep in mind that works of narrative fiction, particularly novels, suggest not just one but multiple themes. This is especially true of works that are artfully done, nuanced, and complex. For example, a novel on the Chicana/o experience in the Vietnam War can also deal with a theme such as the corrosive and suffocating effects of patriarchy. As I did with the nonfiction autobiographical works presented in chapter 4, I have attempted to identify a work's primary thematic focus and to place it within one specific thematic or trend category in this chapter: living on the U.S.–Mexico border, the migrant experience, the barrio, the family, growing up Chicana, other forms of feminist expression, war, the mystery novel, and recent trends.

▪ Living on the U.S.–Mexico Border

In chapter 4, I discussed several nonfiction autobiographical works in which the U.S.–Mexico border was a primary focus. In terms of narrative fiction, the border has long been a popular theme for both U.S. and Mexican writers stretching back to 1848 when the geopolitical border was established between the two countries. Some examples are Helen Hunt Jackson's *Ramona: A Story* (1884), María Amparo Ruiz de Burton's *The Squatter and the Don* (1885), Jovita González's *Caballero: A Historical Novel* (1930), Carlos Fuentes's *Frontera de crystal* (1995), Cormac McCarthy's *All the Pretty Horses* (1992), and Rosina Conde's *Arrieras somos* (*Women on the Road*, 1994).

The multidimensional and highly complex theme of the U.S.–Mexico border is also very well represented in contemporary Chicana/o narrative fiction by established writers including Américo Paredes, Rolando Hinojosa, Alicia Gaspar de Alba, and Helena María Viramontes. Among less well-known Chicana/o writers who have dealt with this theme are David Rice, Lucrecia Guerrero, Oscar Casares, Alicia Alarcón, and Richard Yáñez. Several Chicana/o authors have created fictional towns and even whole regions that are rooted in the history of border peoples. Américo Paredes and Rolando Hinojosa are two writers representative of this important current in contemporary Chicana/o narrative fiction.

Américo Paredes

Paredes wrote his novel *George Washington Gómez* in the 1930s but did not publish a revised version of it until 1990. The novel is set in the period during and immediately after a 1915 uprising by Mexican anarchists and Mexican American seditionists in south Texas and northern Mexico. They were resisting the Texas Rangers, the U.S. Army, and other law enforcement agencies that had carried out more than fifty years of sometimes brutal repression of the Spanish-speaking population on both sides of the international line.

Paredes creates the fictional town of Jonesville on the Rio Grande, where Gumersindo and María Gómez give birth to a son, George Washington Gómez, who is soon nicknamed Gualinto. Paredes uses both this character's English first name and his Spanish nickname throughout the novel as a way of highlighting the dilemma George Washington/Gualinto faces living in two cultures in a border community. He graduates high school, attends the University of Texas in Austin, marries an Anglo, and adjusts—sometimes with difficulty—to survive and prosper in two very different cultural milieus and in both English and Spanish. By the end of the novel, he decides to embrace his mestiza/o roots, which have always sustained him.

Rolando Hinojosa

As I discussed in chapter 3, Hinojosa has deep roots in the border region of south Texas. His award-winning novel *Estampas del valle y otras obras* and his subsequent works are all set in the fictional town of Klail City in fictional Belken County located somewhere in the lower Rio Grande Valley of Texas, where Hinojosa was born and raised. Hinojosa published *Klail City y sus alrededores*, winner of the prestigious Casa de las Américas international literary prize in 1976 (published in English in 1987 as *Klail City: A Novel*). His long poem *Korean Love Songs from Klail City Death Trip* appeared in 1980. *Mi querido Rafa* was published in 1981 and its English translation, *Dear Rafe*, in 1985. *Rites and Witnesses* was published in 1982, followed by *Partners in Crime: A Rafe Buenrostro Mystery* (his first detective novel) in 1985; *Claros varones de Belken/Fair Gentlemen of Belken County* appeared in bilingual form in 1986; *Becky and Her Friends* was published in 1990 and the Spanish version, *Los amigos de Becky*, in 1991; *The Useless Servants* appeared in 1993, and *Ask a Policeman* (his second detective novel) in 1998.

Although the Klail City Death Trip series focuses on twentieth-century events on both sides of the U.S.–Mexico border, Hinojosa draws on the social and economic displacement of Mexicans that occurred in the nineteenth century as Anglos began to arrive in increasing numbers and their military, economic, and political forces slowly pushed Mexicans and later

Mexican Americans to the margins of society (Sánchez 2004, 300). Much of this historical perspective is provided by Esteban Echevarría, the narrator in *Rites and Witnesses* and other works, who functions as the voice of memory. He carries forward to later generations the dark history of Anglo domination as well as accounts of Valley Mexican Americans going south during the Mexican Revolution to fight with the revolutionary forces. The cumulative construction of a historical context reinforces that the mexicano communities north of the border are inextricably and continuously linked to those on the Mexican side. These linkages form the underpinning of transborder relations between whole communities and individuals that are present throughout the Klail City Death Trip series.

Richard Yáñez

Richard Yáñez also deals with the U.S.–Mexico border in his short story collection *El Paso del Norte: Stories on the Border* (2003). Unlike Paredes and Hinojosa, Yáñez does not create a fictional setting for his stories, but rather situates them in El Paso. In several of his stories, he deals with the phenomenon of internal borders existing in the very heart of border cities. For example, in his short story "Desert Vista," a teenaged narrator relates the transition of his Chicano family from the working-class barrio of La Loma (the hill) to a new home in Desert Vista, a housing development for upwardly mobile El Pasoans. Shortly after the move, the narrator encounters a barrier of wooden posts and metal rails with a "No Passing" sign designed to deny access to the development by illegal border crossers from Juárez and less fortunate Chicana/o families. The barrier functions as an internal border on the U.S. side just as the Rio Grande functions as a barrier to hinder undocumented Mexicans from crossing over to El Paso. In stories like "Good Time" and "Rio Grande," Yáñez also brings into focus the common practice among U.S. law enforcement authorities—both Anglo and Chicana/o—along the border, particularly the Border Patrol, of treating Chicanas/os as they do illegal Mexicans.

Alicia Gaspar de Alba

Like other Chicana/o narrative fiction writers whose works are situated on the U.S.–Mexico border, Alicia Gaspar de Alba (see figure 18) publishes some of her narrative short fiction in Spanish, but unique to her work is the clear delineation she draws between English and Spanish in her short story collection *The Mystery of Survival and Other Stories*. Two of the eleven stories are written entirely in Spanish, whereas the other nine are largely in English with occasional use of a Spanish word or phrase. The use of the two languages in this way offers a different perspective on the concept of the U.S.–Mexico border. To write stories entirely in Spanish sends a potent message to the reader that the border should be considered as a clear delineator between two distinct languages and cultures.

Other Writers

18. Alicia Gaspar de Alba (photo by Deena J. González; courtesy of Bilingual Review Press)

Several Chicana/o writers, including Helena María Viramontes and Demetria Martínez, have written about the plight of Central American political refugees who flee their countries, make the difficult trek across Mexico, and land in U.S. border cities, where they blend in and are welcomed into Chicana/o barrios. Helena María Viramontes's short story "Cariboo Café," from her collection *The Moths and Other Stories* (1985), captures the fear and confusion of a Central American family that has successfully negotiated the terrifying journey north and must now avoid being detected by *la migra* (the Border Patrol); local authorities; and the ever-present drug dealers, pimps, and drunks in the Chicana/o barrio on the U.S.–Mexico border where the family has landed. The Cariboo Café is described as a common meeting place, a refuge, for many undocumented workers who are trying desperately to establish new lives but must avoid deportation, which could result in death. The café is a microcosm of social ills: a drug addict overdoses and dies in the bathroom, several illegals who work across the street in a garment factory hide in the bathroom to avoid la migra, the café's Anglo cook betrays the workers, and the same cook betrays the Central American woman, who dies in a police shootout.

The Migrant Experience

Less than thirty years after the signing of the Treaty of Guadalupe Hidalgo, Anglo Texans had taken over vast tracts of fertile land owned originally by mexicanos and tejanos. Poor, landless tejanos provided much of the labor for these commercial enterprises. Human labor was desperately needed, as labor contractors negotiated seasonal contracts between tejano communities and agricultural interests in Texas, in the Midwest, and to a lesser extent in the Northwest. Thousands of tejano families would make the annual trek from their homes in Texas to the Midwest and then return for the winter months after the end of the harvest season, a cycle they would repeat year after year. While some tejano families did settle permanently in towns and cities in the Midwest and Northwest, the seasonal pattern of migrant labor was solidly in place by the beginning of World War II. This seasonal pattern is popularly referred to as the "migrant stream," referring to the established routes that workers would follow each year in search of crops to be picked.

In California, large-scale farming, which had begun at the end of the nineteenth century, escalated in the 1920s with rapid expansion in labor-intensive crops like cotton, fruit, nuts, and vegetables (Acuña 2000, 225). As large agricultural enterprises became more industrialized, a labor pattern much like that in Texas was established and would persist throughout much of the rest of the century: labor contractors, usually Mexican or Mexican American, would enter into profitable contracts with owners/growers to provide a steady, reliable, and cheap source of workers during harvest season. In this way, a second migrant stream was established involving many thousands of Mexican, Mexican American, and other workers from Mexico, Texas, and California itself.

A number of serious problems were associated with the system of agricultural contract labor: contractors and growers/owners were often unscrupulous in their labor practices and treatment of workers, who were often not provided with adequate housing; wages were extremely low; conditions in the agricultural fields were harsh and workdays long, especially in the brutally hot summers in California's central valleys; there was inadequate sanitation and drinking water in the fields; and increasingly after the 1950s the use of toxic pesticides and herbicides on the crops threatened workers' health.

Many contemporary Chicana/o writers were members of families who seasonally joined the migrant stream, leaving their homes and schools to make the annual trek to the Midwest, California, or the Northwest, and these personal experiences are amply reflected in their narrative fiction. I have already discussed in chapter 3, Tomás Rivera's 1971 award-winning work, . . . *Y no se lo tragó la tierra*, in which he draws on the many years his family was a part of the migrant stream. There are many other writers like

Rivera; I have selected several to discuss in this section. A few writers, like Elva Treviño Hart, deal with the Texas migrant labor experience, but the majority of writers—including Helena María Viramontes, Francisco Jiménez, and Rigoberto González—draw on the California experience.

Elva Treviño Hart

Elva Treviño Hart was born in Pearsall in south Texas to Mexican immigrant parents. As a young girl, her life was disrupted annually when her family would leave their community to join the migrant stream to Minnesota and Wisconsin. Her novel *Barefoot Heart: Stories of a Migrant Child* (1999) is a retrospective narration of a young adult who looks back on a childhood of hardship buffered by a caring and nurturing family. She recalls the difficulties that resulted from her immigrant parents' inability to support their rapidly growing family in rural Texas, material conditions that forced them to enter the migrant stream. She reenacts their first trip in the spring months from south Texas to Minnesota in a covered truck filled with families like her own under the watchful eye of a labor contractor who would deliver them directly to the migrant camps close to the beet fields in fulfillment of his agreement with Anglo owners and growers.

Francisco Jiménez

The title of Francisco Jiménez's collection of tightly interrelated short stories, *The Circuit: Stories from the Life of a Migrant Child* (1997), refers to the circuit, or cycle, of the migrant stream. Some of the experiences are told from the point of view of a young narrator whose parents leave the poverty of rural Mexico to bring their young family to California in the 1940s. Early in the work, the narrator recalls his family's being sent to a labor camp somewhere in central California to join a large group of strawberry pickers.

Jiménez includes many of the same details about the very negative aspects of the migrant labor experience that other Chicana/o writers have emphasized in their works (for example, unscrupulous contractors and farm owners, subsistence-level wages, inadequate temporary housing, disrupted schooling, long working days in the fields, health crises, and the constant menace of the Border Patrol). He focuses, however, on his young narrator's intellectual curiosity and strong desire to educate himself.

Helena María Viramontes

Helena María Viramontes (see figure 19) and her nine siblings would often supplement the family's barely adequate income by working summers in the California agricultural fields. She dedicates her novel *Under the Feet of Jesus* (1995) to the Chicano labor leader César Chávez and to her parents. The work focuses on Estrella, a young Chicana on the verge of womanhood, and her family, who are a part of the migrant stream in California. Viramontes reenacts the conditions under which these migrant workers eke out a subsistence wage, the largest part of which goes to pay for their transportation, food, and primitive housing.

■ 19. Helena María Viramontes (courtesy of Arte Público Press)

Viramontes portrays the family as a source of physical and psychological nurturing, but also suggests that a traditional family can constrain women by insisting on rigid adherence to traditional practices and values. In the pursuit of her own sense of worth, independence, and identity, Estrella often clashes with her mother, Petra. Like Jiménez's narrator, Estrella is buoyed by her innate curiosity about the world beyond the migrant labor camps despite the woefully inadequate teachers she encounters in the schools where migrant children are sent. Viramontes's young Chicana narrator embodies the hope that she and others like her can break away from the endless and burdensome cycle of the migrant labor stream to seek more promising futures as fully capable women.

Rigoberto González

Rigoberto González, in his novel *Crossing Vines* (2003), emphasizes the complexity and multidimensionality of the various characters who are involved with different aspects of California's vast grape-growing agribusinesses. The novel contains three parts—"Fuego" (fire), "Viña" (vine), and "Cruz" (cross)—and is structured around a single day, beginning in the early morning and ending in late evening. The day, in fact, is the day in 1993 when César Chávez died. Each chapter focuses on a different character at a different time of day. As the title implies, as the day progresses, the web of interrelationships and interactions—the "crossing vines"—among the characters begins to take shape and take on different grades of importance. By the end of the novel, the reader has formed a collective impression of individual lives all related directly or indirectly to the mundane tasks of growing, picking, sorting, washing, and packing table grapes.

The Barrio

The mix of positive and negative aspects of the barrio is reflected in the works of several Chicana/o writers discussed in earlier chapters. In contemporary Chicana/o narrative fiction, writers such as Miguel Durán, Luis J. Rodríguez, and Yxta Maya Murray amply represent some positive but mainly negative images, recollections, connotations, and associations with the barrio.

Miguel Durán

In his novel *Don't Spit on My Corner* (1991), Durán draws on his own experience as a member of a barrio gang. He narrates different aspects of a Los Angeles barrio of the 1940s through the eyes of Miguelito (Little Mike), a teenage pachuco whose loyalties are divided among his family, his girlfriend, and his gang. Durán uses the so-called Zoot Suit Riots as both a backdrop to and a major cause of Little Mike's changing attitude toward the military and his country's involvement in the war against Nazi Germany and fascist Japan. His generally patriotic feelings turn to bitterness and resentment when he and other pachucos are regularly assaulted and beaten by off-duty soldiers and sailors who come into his barrio to pursue them. Durán highlights the role of newspapers and radio in fomenting hostility among Los Angeles–area Anglos toward barrio residents in general and pachucos in particular. Local police authorities turn their backs on the violence visited upon Chicana/o youth, turning against the victims rather than the perpetrators of the violence.

Luis J. Rodríguez

Luis Rodríguez who presents in his 1993 autobiography, *Always Running: La vida loca, Gang Days in L.A.* (discussed in chapter 4), a graphic and detailed account of gang life in a Los Angeles barrio, returns to the topic in his collection of short stories, *The Republic of East L.A.* (2002) and his recently published novel, *Music of the Mill* (2005). Both works evoke the familiar sights and sounds of many East and South Los Angeles barrio sites.

Much of the short story collection and at least part of the novel deal with the lives of troubled Chicana/o and Central American youth, who suffer from the pernicious effects of deep poverty, abandonment, child abuse, neglect, drug addiction, and alcoholism in a barrio setting. Many of his characters fall prey to gangs, as in the story "Las chicas chuecas" (the crooked girls), in which Noemí, a young Chicana, is coerced into joining a violent all-female gang, from which the story takes its title. Rodríguez describes the barrio housing projects as spawning grounds for gangs, but at the same time he highlights the projects' positive attributes, such as their role in identity formation, which grows out of cultural and political activities.

Yxta Maya Murray

Murray has published several works of narrative fiction including two novels, *Locas* (1997) and *What It Takes to Get to Vegas* (1999), that deal with some of the corrosive effects of barrio life, especially the role of male and all-female gangs in the lives of young Chicanas. *Locas* is structured around the lives of two first-person narrators, Cecilia and Lucía, who are young, impressionable, and vulnerable Chicanas. During much of the first part of the novel, they struggle for the attention of Manny, Cecilia's brother and Lucía's lover, who has founded the Echo Park Lobos gang. Cecilia and Lucía come from dysfunctional families in which their mothers are abused by husbands and boyfriends. Lucía searches for a way out of the limited gender roles assigned to her by her family and young Chicanos. Unfortunately, her search for an alternative public and community identity ends when she founds her own gang, the Fire Girls, but she never fully abandons her dependence on men—boyfriends, fathers, and father figures. Cecilia's path after becoming pregnant at fifteen and leaving her brother's gang is different from Lucía's; she decides to leave behind "la vida loca" to work at "the good life." Despite their different choices, both unwittingly remain within the dominant Chicano patriarchal order that is prevalent in the barrio (Brown 2002, 94).

What It Takes to Get to Vegas is also set in East Los Angeles during the 1980s where the first-person narrator, Rita Zapata, and her younger sister, Dolores, live with their divorced mother, a sexually alluring woman who entertains male guests in her home. Unlike *Locas*, in which gangs are foregrounded, in this novel the East Los Angeles boxing scene is prominent. Instead of joining a gang, Rita attaches herself to a group of young men and women who hang around the boxing gyms. She quickly becomes romantically involved with Billy, a promising young Mexican boxer who is attempting to break into the more lucrative life of boxing away from the barrio. Most of the novel develops around Billy's rise through the boxing ranks in Los Angeles and then Las Vegas. He abruptly ends his relationship with Rita, who fatally wounds him with a gunshot. Dolores chooses a more traditional path, marrying José, her longtime boyfriend. Her relationship ends as tragically as Rita's when her husband is killed in a police shootout in the barrio.

The young lives of Murray's two women protagonists play out against the backdrop of the 1990s, when the Border Patrol conducted frequent raids in the barrios to round up and deport illegal Mexican and Central American workers and families and at the same time harassed Mexican-origin U.S. citizens. In the novel, many of the locally owned businesses experience financial difficulties due to the raids and either close or move out of the barrio, leaving behind block after block of bleak, boarded-up buildings. The novel ends with a riot in the barrio, a conflagration that leaves buildings gutted by fire and hundreds of rioters bloodied and arrested by the riot police. This apocalyptic fate mirrors the social reality of many urban barrios during the last years of the twentieth century.

Other Writers

Other Chicana/o writers of narrative fiction who deal with different aspects of the barrio include Stephen Gutiérrez, Dagoberto Gilb, Laura del Fuego, Max Martínez, Daniel Cano, Ricardo Pimental, and Genaro González. Writers such as Michele Serros, Jack López, and Guy García touch on the transition from the barrio to a more assimilated lifestyle in mainstream Anglo society.

The Chicana/o Family

The Chicana/o family is a complex institution that is difficult to define when considerations of class, gender, race, ethnicity, sexual orientation, education, and location are taken into account. It does not conform to a homogeneous and static ideal, but rather is highly heterogeneous, multifaceted, and always evolving. The family is amply represented across all genres of contemporary Chicana/o literature in works such as *Pocho* (see chapter 2), in the four Quinto Sol award-winning novels (see chapter 3), and in nonfiction autobiographical works (see chapter 4). In this section, I discuss several representative works of narrative fiction in which the family is a central thematic concern: four of Nash Candelaria's novels—*Memories of the Alhambra* (1977), *Not by the Sword* (1982), *Inheritance of Strangers* (1985), and *Leonor Park* (1991)—Arturo Islas's *The Rain God: A Desert Tale* (1984); Alfredo Véa's *La Maravilla* (1994); and Sandra Cisneros's *The House on Mango Street* (1984) and *Caramelo* (2002).

The historian Richard Griswold del Castillo has studied the dissolution of the nuclear Chicana/o family, a theme several of these authors address. This process has accelerated in the past few decades as a consequence of economic, social, and cultural pressures. The desire to move up the economic ladder toward greater assimilation into the Anglo mainstream, the changing nature of life in the barrio, and other factors have slowly eroded traditional values and norms largely in place among Chicanas/os up to the 1940s. Diversity in the family lives of Chicanas/os has also resulted from many historical forces: Mexican immigration, economic class, intermarriage, urbanization, industrialization, regional differences and discrimination (Griswold del Castillo 1984, 128).

Nash Candelaria

Nash Candelaria (see figure 20) has written a fictional but loosely biographical account of the Rafa clan from their origins in Spain through their settlement in New Mexico and the changes in the family they have experienced since the mid-1850s. *Memories of the Alhambra*, the first of the four novels, lays the foundation for the rest of the family saga. It begins with the controversial topic of heritage that nuevomexicanas/os, especially those from the northern part of the state, have debated for centuries: Are nuevomexicanas/os primarily Europeans of relatively pure Spanish blood, or are they mestizos of mixed Spanish, Mexican, and (later) Pueblo and other American Indian extraction? Candelaria's protagonist, José, the patriarch of the Rafa family, sets out to trace what he believes to be his pure Spanish lineage. His quest ends tragically and unanswered when he dies in Spain. The second novel, *Not by the Sword*, focuses on the two-year Mexican War (1846–1848), when José Antonio Rafa III (also called "Tercero") and his twin brother, Carlos, are suddenly forced to grapple with the Rafa family's loss of land and civil rights under the new Anglo military and political regime. Following the introduction of alien customs, traditions, and values, the Rafa family begins to change from the traditional patriarchal model to a somewhat different one in which, for example, Carlos's daughter refuses to marry the man selected for her. The third novel, *Inheritance of Strangers*, covers the period of heightened Anglo–nuevo-mexicana/o antagonism in the fifty-year period after the Treaty of Guadalupe Hidalgo. Tercero tries to hold together a traditional nuclear family on his inherited lands. The narrative loosely reflects some of the historical events and sociopolitical changes that took place during this period, as well as the tremendous strains on the traditional family unit. In the first three novels and in the final novel, *Leonor Park*, Candelaria underscores the great changes that have taken place in Chicana/o culture, including the family, over the past 150 years. At the same

20. Nash Candelaria (photo by Doranne Godwin; courtesy of Bilingual Review Press)

time, however, the Rafa family remains staunchly patriarchal as it clings to the vestiges of traditional values.

Arturo Islas

Arturo Islas's novels *The Rain God: A Desert Tale* and *Migrant Souls* are, like Candelaria's four novels, a family saga, but they tell a different story; as the literary critic Wilson Neate (1998, 225) explains, "Rather than chronicle the construction and development of the traditional familial community, it traces [its] demise." *The Rain God* consists of six interrelated narrative threads that focus on the Angels, a family whose ancestors had fled the violence of the Mexican Revolution to settle in a U.S. border town. The family matriarch, Mama Chona, bridges several generations of the Angel clan and functions as the guardian of the family's Mexican traditions. Although she and the rest of the family are of mixed Spanish and Mexican Indian lineage, Mama Chona insists that the Spanish side of their heritage is worth honoring and protecting, whereas the Indian side is not and must be suppressed at all times. Mama Chona is a strong and authoritarian figure who keeps the family together under trying circumstances. Islas portrays her as a repressive force whose sentiments are shared by her son,

21. Alfredo Véa

Miguel Grande, a male guardian of traditional values, including the prevailing belief that women are inferior.

Miguel Chico, a writer who is Mama Chona's grandson and Miguel Grande's son, rejects both the racist and sexist attitudes in traditional Mexican family values. In doing so, he comes into conflict with his grandmother, his father, and other family members, including his own siblings. Miguel Chico liberates himself from this oppressive family circle as he begins to recognize his homosexuality and to practice the lifestyle of a gay man. The death of Mama Chona symbolically signals the end of the traditional Chicana/o family and the acceptance and celebration of the changing mores and values of the late twentieth century.

Alfredo Véa

In his novel, *La Maravilla* (The Marvel), Alfredo Véa (see figure 21) creates a family unlike those in Candelaria's or Islas's novels. An omniscient narrator gives continuity to the work's sometimes disparate and seemingly unconnected sixteen chapters, and links many of its characters—who are briefly introduced, disappear for pages, then reappear. Beto, a young Chicano boy, is the novel's central protagonist. Abandoned by his mother, Lola, who gave birth to him out of wedlock, he lives during the 1950s with her parents in their simple adobe dwelling in Buckeye, Arizona, a small desert community on the western edge of the rapidly growing metropolis of Phoenix. Beto's grandmother, Josephina, was born in Spain and raised in Mexico before coming to the United States. His grandfather, Manuel, is a Yaqui Indian from the northwestern Mexican state of Sonora.

Beto's grandparents love and nurture him, but he is also cared for by an unusual extended family circle of poor and socially shunned Native American, African American, Asian, homosexual, and transvestite neighbors. Together with his grandparents, they introduce him into a highly multiracial, multicultural, and multi-gendered world unlike anything found in any other Chicana/o work of narrative fiction. Manuel describes himself,

Josephina, and this mélange of diverse individuals as "people of the gaps." He teaches his grandson to respect and honor their ethnic, sexual, racial, cultural, and religious differences because "only we know that the gaps are where life really is" (Véa 1993, 221). Although baptized a Catholic, Beto is exposed as a child to a wide range

22. Sandra Cisneros (photo by Ray Santisteban; courtesy of Susan Bergholz Literary Services)

of other religious traditions practiced by his grandparents and others in his small community. By the time Beto's mother finds her way back to Buckeye to take him away, Beto has been formed as a young child by a highly diverse immediate and extended family who, despite setbacks and marginalization of all kinds, maintain their personal dignity and pride—valuable lessons for a maturing young Chicano.

Sandra Cisneros

Two novels by Sandra Cisneros, *The House on Mango Street* (1984) and *Caramelo* (2002), are discussed elsewhere in this chapter under different thematic categories. But I briefly introduce both novels here as representative examples of the complexities of growing up female in a traditional but evolving Chicana/o family. In the first novel, Cisneros (see figure 22) draws extensively on her own background of being reared in a Chicago barrio as the only daughter in a family of six brothers. Esperanza, the adolescent female narrator, expresses her growing frustration over feeling marginalized within the family circle and in school as well. She depicts the family house in which she grows up as a constraining physical space that amply reflects this frustration. A counterbalance to this space is the house that she imagines as being her own in her future. Like the first novel, *Caramelo* is based on Cisneros's own childhood and adolescence, but now she focuses on the annual pilgrimages the entire family would make from Chicago to Mexico City to spend the summers in the house of her paternal grandparents. Celaya, the young narrator, recalls both the happy and sad aspects of these summer sojourns, but the focus is on her dawning awareness of some the family's dark secrets.

■ Growing Up Chicana: The Bildungsroman Novel

Growing up has for centuries been a theme in literature. In terms of Chicana/o literature, it is found in some of the nonfiction autobiographical works discussed in chapter 4 (for example, Alberto Alvaro Ríos's *Capirotada* and Norma Cantú's *Canícula*), in some of the fiction summarized in chapter 2 (for example, José Antonio Villarreal's novel *Pocho*), and in some of the works associated with the Chicano Movement (for example, Rudolfo Anaya's novel *Bless Me, Ultima* and Tomás Rivera's . . . *Y no se lo tragó la tierra*).

In dozens of novels and short stories published since the 1970s, growing up Chicana/o is either a major or minor theme. In her book *Daughters of Self-Creation: The Contemporary Chicana Novel* (1996) Annie Esturoy identifies a strong trend in contemporary fictional autobiography; namely, Chicana novelists' use of the *bildungsroman* genre (a literary form traditionally used to portray the process of male self-development) to explore the theme of the quest for authentic female self-development through self-discovery and self-definition (Esturoy 1996, 3). I have selected four works by Chicanas that I believe best represent this important trend in contemporary Chicana narrative fiction: Isabella Ríos's (Diana López) *Victuum* (1976), Sandra Cisneros's *The House on Mango Street* (1984), Denise Chávez's *The Last of the Menu Girls* (1986), and Lucha Corpi's *Delia's Song* 1989).

Isabella Ríos

Isabella Ríos situates her novel *Victuum* (1976) in Oxnard, California. Relying almost exclusively on a series of dialogues and stream of consciousness, the author reveals the lives of several characters, particularly that of her narrator-protagonist, Valentina Ballesternos, from birth through marriage, from roughly 1925 to 1971. Along with other Chicana/o Oxnard residents, Valentina weathers the Depression, World War II, and the tumultuous 1960s. Adolfo, Valentina's father, exercises the traditional role of a controlling and disciplining patriarch who attempts to control his daughter's sexuality so that she can marry a Chicano as an "unspoiled" virgin. Valentina's husband then takes on the patriarchal mantle, which she largely accepts until she discovers she has psychic powers that give her a sense of self-worth and meaning largely outside the realm of male control. In a revelatory moment, she realizes that that she is master of her own destiny (Ríos 1976, 338) and that as a mother she must pass on a new set of values to her children.

Sandra Cisneros

The House on Mango Street, a work composed of forty-four closely inter-related stories, is set in a large urban area where Esperanza, her parents, and several brothers live in a house that reflects the family's always precarious economic situation. Esperanza questions not only the socioeconomic conditions of their existence but also the confining atmosphere within the home for her, a sole female child subjected to the traditional gender-role expectations of both her parents and her siblings. She tells her own coming-of-age story in the house on Mango Street, where the larger Latina/o community reinforces the confining values that have historically limited the expectations and self-development of Chicanas from childhood through womanhood. As Esperanza comes to realize that the relative safety of the house and her family are suffocating her budding aspirations to forge her own identity and right to self-definition, she concludes that she must search for a new house of her own in which she alone will live as an independent and self-sufficient young woman.

Denise Chávez

Denise Chávez's *The Last of the Menu Girls* (1986), a work consisting of seven interrelated sections, is set in a Chicana/o barrio in a southern New Mexico city. Rocío Esquibel, the female protagonist/narrator, recounts her adolescent experiences growing up as an only child in a bicultural/bilingual milieu during the 1960s. As in *The House on Mango Street*, the family home plays a crucial role; it is central to her memories, and like Esperanza, she searches futilely for female role models in her own family and in the wider Chicana/o community. The pervasive, stultifying atmosphere in which Rocío lives ultimately triggers in her a strong desire to escape and determine her own destiny (Esturoy 1996, 119). Like Esperanza, Rocío's self-expression through language allows her to define her own identity.

Lucha Corpi

Lucha Corpi's *Delia's Song* (1989) is also a coming-of-age-as-a-writer story of self-discovery through the written word. It is set in Berkeley, California, in the late 1960s where the narrator-protagonist, Delia Treviño, is a student at the University of California, Berkeley. Reflecting the author's own student days at the same university during roughly the same period, Delia joins the Chicana/o component of the Third World Student Movement. The narrative alternates between scenes of Delia's academic progress and her participation in student meetings, campus protests, and confrontations with police. In graduate school, Delia suffers long periods of loneliness and despondency, knowing that she cannot return to her very traditional family home for solace. She visits her Aunt Marta, who shares with her a rich family history of remarkable women including her great-grandmother, Asunción, who becomes a model worthy of emulation. Marta describes her as " 'The Storyteller.' The weaver of words. The weaver of silver threads. The writer. The silversmith" (Corpi 1989, 181). In a revelatory moment, Delia decides to weave her own words, to write a novel about herself and share it with her lover, Jeff Morones, a fellow activist during their undergraduate days with whom she has reestablished a relationship. The act of writing about herself and sharing her words is not only therapeutic but a necessary step toward self-awareness, self-definition, and fulfillment as a young woman. Like Cisneros and Chávez, Corpi has her Chicana protagonist symbolically take control of "writing" her own life.

Other Forms of Feminist Expression

In chapter 3, I discussed some of the issues that Chicana activists confronted during the years of the Chicano Movement and long after as they often found themselves in a double bind. On one hand, they struggled against traditional and misogynistic values and behaviors exhibited by many of the male leaders, who expected that the women would play subservient roles. On the other hand, as members of an ethnic minority in a dominant Anglo society, Chicana activists suffered from racism and discrimination. Chicana activists who rejected this double bind began to coalesce into their own separate groups and to hold meetings apart from the men. Chicana academics organized in a similar fashion by forming, for example, a Chicana caucus within the National Association of Chicano Studies (NACS) and their own organization, Mujeres Activas en Letras y Cambio Social (Women Active in Arts and Letters and Social Change, or MALCS). Chicana lesbians had to confront a triple bind; in addition to racism, they were often the brunt of overt wrath and ridicule from not only the men but also many of their heterosexual Chicana sisters who would not tolerate their different lifestyles.

In chapter 1, I discussed the multiple and varied expressions of Chicana feminist criticism that address some of the issues Chicana writers and critics confront and grapple with. In this section, I discuss various strategies and thematic approaches outside the bildungsroman that Chicana feminist writers use in their narrative fiction to counter negative stereotypes of women in a highly regimented, patriarchal culture.

The Reappropriation and Reinterpretation of Myths, Legends, and Cultural Figures

Tey Diana Rebolledo has identified several mythical and archetypal figures and cultural heroines whom Chicana writers have used to combat the existing and dominant mythology that defines Chicanas as passive; subservient to men; and incapable of active, energetic, and vital lives (Rebolledo 1995, 49). These figures include the Virgin of Guadalupe; La Llorona (the legendary weeping woman who is said to have drowned her own young children in an act of desperation); women warriors in the form of *guerrilleras* (guerrilla fighters) and *soldaderas* (women soldiers); Sor Juana Inez de la Cruz; Doña Marina/La Malinche; and the Aztec/Nahuatl goddesses Coatlicue and Tonantzín.

Both Mexican and Chicana/o Catholics have historically revered the Virgin of Guadalupe (also known as the mestiza virgin), the mother of Jesus Christ, who is said to have appeared in the sixteenth century in a location that the pre-Columbian Nahuatl goddess Tonantzín already occupied. As a virginal figure free of sin, the Virgin of Guadalupe embodies for many Mexicans and Chicanas/os traits considered positive among women and thus worthy of being emulated: purity, nurturing, unselfish giving, intercession between earth and spirit, and the ideal qualities of motherhood (Rebolledo 1995, 53). Despite the overwhelmingly positive role she plays in Chicana/o culture, she is a controversial figure whom some writers and scholars depict as a negative symbol of compliance and passivity; others have simply reinterpreted her role. An example of the latter is seen in Sandra Cisneros's short story "Little Miracles, Kept Promises" (Cisneros 1991, 116–29). Chayo, the female protagonist, who has inherited from her mother and grandmother a passive notion of the Virgin, begins to associate this religious figure with her own gradual escape from patriarchal strictures. Cisneros has given to the Mexican Virgin some of the attributes of the Aztec/Nahuatl goddesses the Spaniards tried desperately to squelch as part of their attempt to subdue the conquered indigenous tribes in Central Mexico (Rebolledo 1993, 50–51).

La Malinche/Malintzín/Doña Marina is the Mexican cultural-historical figure that Chicana narrative writers use most frequently to represent the passive traits associated with the Virgin of Guadalupe. This sixteenth-century indigenous Mexican woman served Hernán Cortés as a translator and as one of his lovers. Some historians believe she played an important role in Cortés's campaign to conquer the Aztecs and other indigenous peoples. Today, many Mexicans view La Malinche as a traitorous figure and use the term *malinchista*, derived from her name, to condemn compatriots whom they believe have sold out to foreign interests or who ape and copy foreign styles, music, and other fashions; U.S. Chicanas who were perceived not to be supportive of the Chicano Movement's agenda were also labeled malinchistas.

Contemporary Mexican feminist writers have resurrected the figure of Marina, endowing her with the positive qualities of female assertiveness, defiance, and resistance to patriarchal values and behaviors. For example, Erlinda Gonzales-Berry in her novel *Paletitas de guayaba* (Little Flavored Guava Suckers), uses a linguistic device (Mari/Doña Marina) to blur the temporal and spatial separation between a young Chicana who journeys to Mexico City and the sixteenth-century historical figure. As Rebolledo observes, "In her feminist revision of history, Marina, as the voice, expresses her understanding of how women, as oppressed in her time as in the present, overcome their silence to speak" (Rebolledo 1995, 75). In her short story "Los derechos de La Malinche" (Malinche's Rights), from her short story collection *The Mystery of Survival*, Alicia Gaspar de Alba depicts La Malinche as a co-conspirator with the Aztec/Nahuatl goddesses Tonantzín and Coalitcue, who avenge the brutal acts of a bearded white man, presumably Hernán Cortés. La Malinche lines her vagina with spiny cactus, which destroys the man's penis when he attempts to have sex with her.

In her short story "Woman Hollering Creek" Sandra Cisneros uses the figure of La Llorona in a positive way. She depicts Cleófilas, the protagonist, as a desperate young Mexican woman who has married a macho Mexican man and moved to the United States. She soon learns that he is an adulterous and abusive husband from whom she knows she must flee. Felice, a kind of contemporary La Llorona, drives her back to Mexico in her pickup so that she can rejoin her family. Crossing the creek that separates the two countries, Felice celebrates noisily by letting out a yell "as loud as any mariachi" (Cisneros 1991, 55). The yell of triumph replaces the lament of the traditional La Llorona figure, and in this way Cisneros reinterprets the mythological figure, giving her assertiveness and other positive traits.

■ 23. Alma Luz Villanueva (photo by Alma Luz Villanueva; courtesy of Bilingual Review Press)

Alma Luz Villanueva (see figure 23) also endows the figure of La Llorona with positive traits as an empowering feminine force in her collection of short stories, *Weeping Woman: La Llorona and Other Stories* (1994). Villanueva portrays the many ways in which children are lost and endangered through abduction, murder, rape, incestuous abuse, and poverty (Madsen 2000, 189). The women in these short stories do not enact the traditional role of La Llorona as a wailing or weeping woman who has drowned or injured her children, but rather are caring and nurturing mothers who labor endlessly to lessen their children's pain and nurture them as suffering victims.

Along with the Aztec/Nahuatl goddesses, La Malinche, and La Llorona, Sor Juana Inez de la Cruz has emerged as another important cultural heroine who has come to symbolize for Chicanas the autonomous intellectual woman (Rebolledo 1995, 58). Sor Juana was a young, beautiful, and aristocratic Spanish-Mexican woman from the seventeenth century who purportedly rejected both matrimony and a frivolous and pampered role in the viceroy's court to become a nun and follow her intellectual pursuits. She left behind a considerable body of challenging poetry, drama, and essays that continues to be intensively studied. She also openly challenged Catholic Church authorities on several occasions.

Alicia Gaspar de Alba has in her narrative fiction depicted Sor Juana not only as an intellectually free spirit but also as a lesbian who violated rigid social codes in an era when overt love between women met with catastrophic consequences. In her lengthy novel *Sor Juana's Second Dream* (1999) Gaspar de Alba creates a fictionalized biography of Sor Juana, drawing on her poems and essays as well as on the considerable body of critical and biographical material on this extraordinary woman. Lesbian relationships with not only the viceroy's wife but also one of Sor Juana's assistants, both before and after entering the convent, are central to the novel. Gaspar de Alba informs us about Sor Juana's scientific experiments, the scientific instruments she was allowed to have in the convent, and her extensive library, thought to be one of the finest in seventeenth-century Mexico. The writer interprets some of Sor Juana's love poetry as expressing lesbian love rather than love of God; legions of literary critics have heavily favored the latter interpretation. This reinterpretation of Sor Juana provides a very apt example of how Chicana writers have reappropriated cultural heroines.

The Control and Exercise of Chicana Sexuality

In rejecting the patriarchal definition of women as passive, subservient mothers, daughters, and ultimately inferior companions to men, Chicana writers often posit in its place women's control of their sexuality as an act of resistance, independence, and self-definition. Rebolledo comments that for Chicana writers "sexual politics in all its forms, hetero- and homosexual, has been an important step towards healing the wounds of racism, homophobia and marginalization" (Rebolledo 1995, 183).

Ana Castillo is representative of how a Chicana writer has redefined traditional notions of female sexuality. In *The Mixquiahuala Letters* (1986), an epistolary novel, the reader follows the exchange of letters between Teresa, a Chicana, and Alicia, a Puerto Rican friend. The letters recount and reflect upon their chance meeting in Mexico and their encounters with males, especially Mexican ones. We learn that Teresa has gone to Mexico to escape the pain of not being accepted as a fully independent and self-reliant Chicana in the United States. She embodies the double racist and sexist bind that Chicana feminists experienced during and after the Chicano Movement. In addition, she is aware that her working-class background defines her as inferior in a class-conscious society. Her journey to Mexico is a search for a social milieu that is more accepting of the ways in which she is different in her own country. Unfortunately, she discovers the reality that Mexico is a highly racialized, sexist, and class-conscious country where clear distinctions are made among Indians, mestizos, and so-called white Mexicans. Above all, Teresa discovers that Mexican machismo is deep rooted and unyielding. She comes to realize her choice to exercise control over her own sexuality in Mexico as well as in the United States is at once self-empowering and painful, as any break from cultural norms and expectations always is.

In *Sapogonia: An Anti-Romance in 3/8 Meter* (1990), Castillo examines the relationship between the culturally formed male who has a propensity toward violence against women and the feminine process of self-development and the ethic of sharing (Madsen 2000, 88). The former is represented by Máximo Madrigal, a prototypical Chicano macho who attempts to control the life of Pastora Velásquez Aké, the novel's female protagonist, who represents the latter. Unable to relate to Pastora in any way that is not controlling and sexual, Máximo murders her when she rejects his advances. Unlike Teresa, Pastora is ambiguously portrayed as both an independent woman and a manipulative temptress who seduces and sexually teases men. She, like most of Castillo's Chicana protagonists, deliberately and consciously transgresses established norms of behavior, especially sexual behavior. Castillo clearly equates transgression with a strategy of liberation.

■ Lesbian Expression

Among the several Chicana narrative fiction writers who through their writing combat homophobia and oppression are lesbian writers, including Alicia Gaspar de Alba—her novel *Sor Juana's Second Dream* is discussed earlier in this section—Sheila Ortiz Taylor, and Terri de la Peña. The publication of the works of most of these writers was preceded by the groundbreaking anthology *This Bridge Called My Back: Writings by Radical Women of Color* (1981) edited by Cherríe Moraga and Gloria Anzaldúa. As the title indicates, the anthology contains works by Chicana as well as other women of color who boldly and forthrightly express their various takes on feminism. In part, the work is a rejection of white Anglo feminism as a model for women of color. Rebolledo has identified *This Bridge Called My Back* as a landmark for giving Chicana lesbian writers a forum to define their voices in an uncompromised way. The 1991 anthology *Chicana Lesbians: The Girls Our Mothers Warned Us About* (edited by Carla Trujillo) was also instrumental in advancing awareness of Chicana lesbian expression.

Sheila Ortiz Taylor

Sheila Ortiz Taylor's novel *Faultline* (1982) is one of the earliest examples of Chicana narrative fiction in which a lesbian lifestyle is embraced and treated openly. The novel's protagonist is Arden Benbow, a woman of mixed Mexican Indian and Anglo ancestry who is a single parent of six children. In a sardonic tone, Ortiz Taylor confronts directly society's discomfort and outright opposition to homosexuality in general and lesbians as parents in particular. The writer sets out to disprove the popular assumption that lesbians cannot be good parents.

Terri de la Peña

Terri de la Peña's novel *Margins* (1992) deals with the struggles that a Chicana lesbian undergoes to break free from a loving but traditional family that has difficulty coming to grips with their daughter's decision to live a lifestyle that is contrary to their expectations. The novel's protagonist, Verónica Meléndez (Roni), a graduate student in literature at UCLA, loses her longtime friend and lover, Joanna, who is killed in an automobile accident in which Verónica suffers severe physical injuries. During her recovery, she gravitates between two women who in different ways help her to heal: Siena and Renée Talamantes, a Chicana film student. Her mainly sexual relationship with the former ends abruptly but her relationship with the latter is more profound and ultimately more complete. Renée, who is portrayed as politically savvy and culturally knowledgeable, helps Roni come to terms with not only her Mexican Indian heritage but also her family and the Catholic Church, which repudiate her sexuality as both sinful and a betrayal of traditional values. Roni's open embrace of her own lesbianism parallels her newfound cultural pride. De la Peña affirms that Chicanismo has many definitions and is manifested in a variety of different ways.

 War

From 1848 on, Americans of Mexican descent have participated in military actions ranging from resistance and rebellion on U.S. soil against both Anglo military forces and in the Civil War, to U.S. foreign wars including the Spanish-American War, World War I, World War II, the Korean conflict, the Vietnam War, and most recently the military actions in Kuwait, Afghanistan, and Iraq. Chicanas/os have served proudly, patriotically, and often in numbers disproportionate to their percentage of the total U.S. population. Many Chicanas/os have felt a sense of betrayal upon returning to the United States after serving honorably to face racism and discrimination, particularly after World War II, the Korean conflict, and the Vietnam War.

A few contemporary Chicana/o authors have written about World War II and the Korean conflict. For example, Américo Paredes refers to World War II in his short story "The Hammon and the Beans." Sabine Ulibarrí, in his 1997 semiautobiographical work, *Mayhem Was Our Business: Memorias de un veterano* (A Veteran's Memories), recounts how he and thousands of nuevomexicanos "came out of the mountains, out of the valleys, from all the surrounding villages to volunteer for combat duty for their country . . . we heard the roll of distant drums, and we answered the call" (Ulibarrí 1997, 2). Ulibarrí volunteered for service in the U.S. Air Force, served for three years, and was decorated for his bravery with the Distinguished Flying Cross and Air Medal. His memories of returning home after several grueling years abroad are tinged with a sense of patriotism mixed with some bitterness and defiance: "When we came back from the war, we were not the same. We had left homes without running water, without electricity, with outside toilets. We had seen London, Paris, Berlin, Rome, Manila, Singapore, Tokyo. There was no way we were going back to the following: the sheep, the plow, or the political *patrón*" (Ulibarrí 1997, 29). Rolando Hinojosa's Klail City Death Trip series, discussed earlier in this chapter, contains numerous references to the Korean conflict. His long narrative poem *Korean Love Songs* (1980) is, as the title indicates, about serving in Korea. As the scholar Rosaura Sánchez has observed, this work documents "the pain, the male bonding, the friendships made and lost with death all around, and the psychological scars that will last beyond the war" (Sánchez 2004, 312).

Chicanas/os have written most extensively about the Vietnam War in their creative works, and it has emerged as a major theme for narrative fiction writers, both veterans who have shared their experiences in Vietnam and activists who protested the war at home. The Chicano scholar Jorge Mariscal lists some of the important aspects and questions about the war raised by these and other Chicana/o writers in his very important anthology, *Aztlán and Vietnam: Chicano and Chicana Experiences of the War* (1999): the sights, sounds and emotions of technological warfare; structures of interethnic relations in Vietnam, both within the U.S. military and between the U.S. soldiers and the Vietnamese people; the debates within U.S. Chicana/o communities about the conduct of the war; the racist practices associated with the military draft of that era; the meanings of patriotism and of manhood; the complex relations between ethnic identity and class identity; the solidarity or lack of solidarity among peoples of color, including those at home and those in Vietnam; and the struggle to live with personal tragedies and the scars of war (Mariscal 1999, 2).

Joe Rodríguez

Joe Rodríguez, a Vietnam-era veteran, reflects in his novel *Oddsplayer* (1989) on the racial and class stratification in U.S. society that greatly determined who would serve in Vietnam. Thousands of middle- and upper-class Americans were able to avoid service by invoking educational deferments and using other legal loopholes, while members of underrepresented minority groups, as well as poor urban and rural Anglos, were not able to do so. Consequently, they made up the bulk of the infantrymen, the "grunts," who repeatedly were called on to assume the greatest risks in confronting enemy troops during much of the Vietnam War.

Daniel Cano

In his novel *Shifting Loyalties* (1995), Daniel Cano reveals the horrors of Vietnam through the eyes of five young Chicano soldiers who have banded together in mutual support and protection. An important part of the novel is focused on Jesse Peña, a tejano who is thought to have crossed over to the enemy. He expresses doubts about what he is doing in Vietnam attacking and maiming not only enemy combatants but also Vietnamese civilians and farmers who cultivated their rice paddies and lived peacefully among each other much like tejano small farmers back home in Texas. Cano questions the morality of the war and the vexing role that Chicanas/os play in carrying out the questionable U.S. policy.

Ricardo Pimentel

Pimentel's collection of short stories *House with Two Doors* (1997) alternates between Vietnam and life at home in San Bernardino, California, between 1967 and 1971. The story "July 1969" poignantly captures the connection that Bert, a young Chicano soldier, makes between life with his wife and baby, and a young Vietnamese mother and her baby and small daughter whom he comes across during a lull in the fighting in Vietnam. He persuades the woman to allow him to cradle her baby just he would cradle his own child back home. Bert observes of the Vietnamese children who cluster around him, " 'They're not so different from us. . . . If this were back home, they'd all be hanging out at Gus's, scamming for soda and candy'" (Pimentel 1997, 131).

Leroy Quintana

In the short story "And All Your Children" (in *La Promesa and Other Stories*) Leroy Quintana, himself a Vietnam veteran, has his Chicano protagonist returning to the United States haunted by scenes of frequent and senseless violence against defenseless Vietnamese children. In contrast, he remembers a Vietcong soldier who spares his life: "for an instant, one long indefinable instant, we stand face to face, no more (and no less) than two feet away from one another. We are brothers, enemies, sons, soldiers, yin and yang, East and West" (Quintana 2002, 134).

Alfredo Véa

The novel *Gods Go Begging* (1999) by Alfredo Véa, another Vietnam veteran, is perhaps the best and most moving work of narrative fiction to deal with the complex theme of solidarity among underrepresented minority soldiers in Vietnam and their relationship to their declared enemies. Jesse Pasadoble, the novel's protagonist, is a defense attorney who served in Vietnam. Véa weaves into the novel's plot the many threads that interconnect the social issues of racism and discrimination at home in the United States and how they play out in Vietnam through the experiences of minority soldiers. Sergeant Pasadoble finds common bonds with Latino, African American, and Native American soldiers, most of whom have been drafted into military service. He observes that the U.S. military did not generally draft college kids and that it was always the sons of the poor—including Anglos—who ended up in the infantry and consequently took the heaviest casualties in Vietnam.

One of the most moving moments in the novel occurs when Sergeant Pasadoble befriends a North Vietnamese Army prisoner, Hong, who attracts his attention: "'You same-same me,' he said in pidgin. His voice was high-pitched and musical. War had not altered his civilian timbre. . . . 'You same-same me,' he repeated." (Véa 1999, 79). They soon discover that they can communicate in French, their lingua franca. Hong has learned French at the end of the French colonial occupation of Vietnam and has spent time in Marseilles as a younger man. Pasadoble has studied French in high school and dated a French-speaking woman. During their several meetings through the wire fence that separates the prisoner from the sergeant, they find they have a great deal in common as they draw a parallel between the French occupation and the internal colony within the United States that consists of Latinas/os, African Americans, and Native Americans dominated by a more powerful white power structure. Days later, Pasa-doble recognizes the prisoner in a long line of dead and mutilated North Vietnamese soldiers, and he secretly mourns him.

Several Chicana/o narrative fiction writers have addressed the short- and long-term physical and psychological effects of the Vietnam experi-ence on veterans once they returned home. For example, Leroy Quintana frequently draws on his own life-altering experience in Vietnam. In his short story "La Matanza" ("The Killing," 2002) Popeye, one his characters, remembers his reconnaissance unit coming upon a Vietcong officer and riddling him with M-16 bullets to send a message to his troops. Two months later, his buddy, who is boarding a helicopter for his final trip before leaving Vietnam, has his head blown off by a Vietcong sniper. Popeye tersely comments, "When I got home I started drinking, and I haven't stopped since. I go to the VA [Veterans Administration] hospital once a month for some pills. A few pills, a lost year, and a bucketful of nightmares—that's all I got to show for serving in Vietnam" (Quintana 2002, 122). Another character, J. K. Singh from the Navajo Reservation, shares his own personal horrors in Vietnam and, like Popeye, he returns home to receive medications from the local VA hospital "drinking them down with alcohol—beer, whiskey, whatever." Popeye and J. K. Singh are only two of Quintana's characters who are destroyed by the war.

Patricia Santana

Patricia Santana, in her novel *Motorcycle Ride on the Sea of Tranquility* (2002), deals with, among other aspects of her protagonist's coming of age in southern California in the late 1960s and early 1970s, the disastrous ripple effects a returning damaged Vietnam veteran has on an entire fam-ily. Fourteen-year-old Yolanda Sahagún eagerly awaits the return of her brother, Chuy, from Vietnam in April 1969. She remembers him as a loving and caring older brother who paid special attention to her, but at the welcoming party at the family home she begins to realize that he has changed dramatically and has become a surly and aloof young man who barely greets his family and friends. He suffers from posttraumatic stress syndrome, which manifests itself in his distancing behaviors, rage, abuse of alcohol and drugs, demonstrable lack of responsibility, and ultimate inability to take care of himself.

The Mystery Novel

The Chicana/o mystery novel is a new genre that has emerged during the past two decades. Among the established writers who have cultivated this genre with success are Rudolfo Anaya, Lucha Corpi, Rolando Hinojosa, and very recently, Alicia Gaspar de Alba. Michael Nava and Manuel Ramos are known exclusively for their mystery fiction. In this section, I briefly discuss the works of all six authors.

Rudolfo A. Anaya

Rudolfo Anaya has produced four mystery novels since 1995: *Zia Summer* (1995), *Rio Grande Fall* (1996), *Shaman Winter* (1999), and *Jemez Spring* (2005). In each, Sonny Baca, an Albuquerque-based Chicano private investigator becomes involved in a fascinating labyrinth of intrigue, myth, magic, and good old-fashioned crime investigation. Anaya sets these mysteries against a backdrop of urban Chicana/o culture in which he raises social issues related to the deep divisions that still exist in the Southwest between Anglos and Americans of Mexican descent. He also draws on the spiritual dimensions of connectedness with the land that characterize his classic novel *Bless Me, Ultima*. His knowledge of and respect for the cultural traditions of both indigenous and Hispanic peoples is evident in all four mystery novels.

In *Zia Summer*, Sonny Baca becomes enmeshed in a web of mysterious and baffling circumstances that affect him personally: the murder of his cousin Gloria Dominic. His investigation takes him into a world of dreams and myth. He discovers that Gloria had been in contact with a cult led by a man named Raven that worships the sun and is planning to blow up a truck transporting nuclear waste to a waste site in southern New Mexico. Sonny foils the plot to blow up the truck, solves the mystery of his cousin's gruesome death, and at the same time reveals a power struggle for control of Albuquerque's financial and commercial future. *Rio Grande Fall* begins with a woman's fatal fall from a hot-air balloon. Sonny discovers that she has been murdered and that Raven, who has now become Sonny's nemesis, is implicated in the murder. Anaya has endowed Raven with superhuman qualities and has Sonny availing himself of the assistance of his guardian spirit, the animal Coyote, as he engages Raven in a second epic struggle of good against evil. As in the first mystery novel, Anaya effectively foregrounds elements of New Mexico's old nuevomexicana/o culture and indigenous Indian shamanistic practices even as the plot plays out in the context of a contemporary urban environment of political intrigue. In *Shaman Winter*, more than in the first two novels, Anaya draws on Native American and Hispanic spiritualism, myth, and magic. An epic battle takes place between Sonny and Raven in a world of dreams, as the private investigator's enemy repeatedly tries to enter his dreams in order to attack and carry off his soul. They also confront each other in the real world as Sonny discovers that Raven is perpetrator of yet another heinous crime that is part of a much larger plot to seize control of municipal, state, and national political and financial institutions. Sonny momentarily triumphs over Raven at the end of this novel, but the reader is prepared for the battle to continue in the next novel, *Jemez Spring*. In this novel, the governor of New Mexico is murdered and in a related act, a bomb is planted close to the Los Alamos National Laboratories. Sonny once again takes on his archenemy Raven to solve the crime and prevent the detonation of the bomb. Anaya weaves into this plot a classic battle over the control of water rights, a resource that will determine the shape of future growth throughout the West.

Rolando Hinojosa

Partners in Crime: A Rafe Buenrostro Mystery (1985), Rolando Hinojosa's first mystery novel, follows the pattern of many modern detective stories. Hinojosa's thorough research of police procedures and crime along the border and his use of a clipped, hardboiled style give this novel much credibility as detective fiction. Rafa (Rafe) Buenrostro, the central character of this and his second mystery novel (*Ask a Policeman*), is a detective lieutenant on the Belken County homicide squad. Buenrostro and his fellow detectives go about the often tedious work of solving homicides, answering phone calls, and filling out endless reports. They also cooperate with Mexican police officials across the border in Barrones to solve a horrible crime, the brutal slaying of an American and two Mexican nationals. They eventually link the crime to a cocaine smuggling ring. Hinojosa's second mystery novel, *Ask a Policeman* (1998), like his first one, reflects the escalation of deadly violence associated with drug trafficking along the U.S.–Mexican border. Rafa, who has now been promoted to chief inspector of the Belken County Homicide Squad, is forced to deal with the tragic consequences of this violence when a former Mexican government official and convicted murderer is freed from jail by his henchmen. Once again, Mexican and U.S. police officials cooperate closely to track down and incarcerate the perpetrators of crime who threaten civic order on both sides of the border.

Lucha Corpi

Lucha Corpi (see figure 24) has published several detective novels. In the earliest of them, *Eulogy for a Brown Angel* (1992), her central charac-

■ 24. Lucha Corpi (courtesy of Arte Público Press)

ter is Gloria Damasco, a civil-rights activist who lives and works in the Bay Area. Gloria becomes involved in the murder of a young child on a Los Angeles street during a demonstration in 1970. She collects information about the victim and the circumstances of her death for several years until unexpected revelations lead her to the killer. Corpi's second Gloria Damasco mystery novel, *Cactus Blood* (1995), involves the horrifying and bloody murders of three social activists as well as the rape of a young Chicana who was exposed to pesticide contamination many years before. Damasco and a fellow Chicano detective follow several false leads until finally Damasco links the three murders to the incident involving the young woman. In Corpi's most recent mystery novel, *Black Widow's Wardrobe* (1999), Gloria Damasco witnesses an assassination attempt on a woman who has just been released from prison. She sets out to investigate the identity of the woman and the motive for the violent act against her, only to discover that the solution is to be found in the world of high-level Mexican politics and intrigue.

Alicia Gaspar de Alba

Alicia Gaspar de Alba's *Desert Blood: The Juárez Murders* (2005) is a mystery novel only in a general sense. It is based on the series of horrific and unsolved sex crime murders of mainly young Mexican women that have taken place in and around Juárez since the early 1990s. More than two hundred bodies, many of them mangled and dismembered beyond identification, have been found buried in shallow graves or garbage dumps. The murders have come to the attention of the Mexican national government and the international press, but as of 2005 authorities still have not found the perpetrators of these heinous crimes. Gaspar de Alba's interest is not to create a gripping mystery novel but to give concrete form to the travesty of the murders, which are thought to involve prominent drug lords and corrupt officials at the highest levels of government. The novel is thus a vehicle for protesting femicide within a highly patriarchal culture.

Unlike the other Chicana/o mystery novels, *Desert Blood*'s protagonist is not a police officer, a lawyer, or a private investigator, but a college literature professor who accidentally becomes involved in the murders. Ivon Villa and her partner, Brigit, have decided to adopt a child, and Ivon's cousin, an El Paso social worker, has arranged for them to adopt the unborn child of a young, unwed Juárez woman. Ivon returns to El Paso from California for the birth of the child, but the night she is to meet the woman, she and her unborn child disappear and both are soon discovered murdered. Ivon's sister Irene is kidnapped days later in Juárez, a victim of the ring that is suspected of committing all the murders. Through dogged persistence born of desperation to find her sister before she is murdered, Ivon pursues some possible leads that eventually lead her to her sister's kidnappers, one of whom is a corrupt Immigration and Naturalization officer.

Michael Nava

Michael Nava, a practicing attorney in Los Angeles, has published several mystery novels whose protagonist is a San Francisco Bay Area gay criminal lawyer named Henry Ríos: *The Little Death* (1986), *How Town* (1990), *The Hidden Law* (1992), *The Death of Friends* (1996), *Goldenboy: A Mystery* (1996), *The Burning Plain* (1999), and *Rag and Bone* (2001). Nava handles Rios's homosexuality in a sensitive and natural way in all of his novels while raising issues such as homophobia and AIDS.

When we first meet Henry Ríos in *The Little Death*, he is ten years out of law school and has chosen criminal defense law over more comfortable and higher-paying jobs in corporate law. Nava depicts Ríos as a principled individual dedicated to defending the downtrodden even when they seem to resent him. We follow his sputtering career over the next fifteen years through several excellent and compelling mystery novels. Ríos soon leaves the public defenders office to set up his own private criminal defense law practice, but the material conditions of his life as a lawyer never improve; he grows older but not more prosperous. Most of his clients are losers, down-

and-outers, and desperate petty criminals who cannot pay Ríos to represent them and rarely express their appreciation for keeping them out of jail.

Manuel Ramos

Manuel Ramos is, like Michael Nava, a practicing lawyer, but in Denver. He has written a series of mystery novels whose protagonist is the lawyer Luis Montez: *The Ballad of Rocky Ruiz* (1993), *The Ballad of Gato Guerrero* (1994), *The Last Client of Luis Montez* (1996), *Blues for the Buffalo* (1997), and *Brown-on-Brown* (2003). A sixth novel, *Moony's Road to Hell* (2002), features Danny Mora, a private investigator.

Montez is a middle-aged lawyer who was an idealistic student activist in the early 1970s but by the 1990s has become somewhat disillusioned. Ramos immerses us in the ambience of the last stages of the Chicano Movement in Colorado when Montez was a member of a militant group called Los Guerrilleros (The Warriors) battling for social justice. His life after law school has been mostly aimless on both personal and professional levels. In *The Ballad of Gato Guerrero* Montez regains some of his idealism, optimism, and self-confidence. Always the loyal friend, he comes to the aid of Felix "Gato" Guerrero, a Vietnam veteran who has been falsely accused of murder. He finally exonerates his friend. In *The Last Client of Luis Montez*, Montez is falsely accused of murdering a wealthy young client whom he has successfully defended against drug charges. He eventually solves the case, but at the end of the novel he is described as psychologically drained and physically exhausted by both his professional and family responsibilities. *Blues for the Buffalo* finds Montez recovering from his weakened state on a beach in Mexico. He meets Raquel Espinoza, a beautiful young Chicana writer who disappears in Mexico. Montez joins with Conrad Valdez, a private investigator hired by her father, to solve the mystery of her disappearance. In *Moony's Road to Hell*, Danny Mora (known to his friends as "Moony"), becomes involved in investigating the murder of a Chicano Immigration and Naturalization Service (INS) agent and his links to a Mexican drug lord. He solves the crime but not before he comes close to losing his own life several times.

Recent Trends in Chicana/o Fiction

Literary critics have carefully studied the evolution of trends that began to appear in Chicana/o narrative fiction in the 1970s and have become more

25. Ron Arias (photo by David Martínez; courtesy of Bilingual Review Press)

prominent over the past decade. One of the earliest contemporary works that illustrates innovative narrative features is Ron Arias's novel, *The Road to Tamazunchale* (originally published in 1975; see figure 25). The novel's central character, Fausto Tejada, is a retired bookseller and collector who is dying. After he loses his wife, Evangelina, his niece, Carmela, cares for him in her house in an unidentified Los Angeles Chicana/o barrio. Fausto's dead wife and Mauricio Hunca, a Peruvian shepherd who plays a flute and herds alpacas, make several appearances in the novel, much of which takes place in Fausto's dreams and imagination.

The novel alternates between a world grounded in the realism of a large, ugly metropolis and the realm of magic and fantasy. Arias frequently blurs the boundary between the two. Fausto, who has been dying slowly for six years, is beginning to try to exert some control over the process during his last days. There are numerous signals in the novel that alert the reader to be watchful for other indicators of the novel's altered reality (for example, the sound of the shepherd's distant flute, which throughout the novel comes to symbolize Fausto's approaching death; a journey to Cuzco, Peru, home of the ancient Incan civilization; Fausto's encounters with Mauricio and his alpacas on a busy Los Angeles freeway; the discovery of a dead *mojado* [wetback] who has mysteriously drowned in a completely dry concrete flood control channel; and the mysterious appearance of a cloud that dumps snow on different parts of the barrio).

The seamless and rapid interspersing of fragments of dreams, imagination, and fantasy, as well as other elements such as spatial and temporal fragmentation and displacement have led scholars to celebrate this novel as truly innovative, at least within the context of contemporary Chicana/o narrative fiction. Eliud Martínez (1977) identifies the novel's emphasis on play and make-believe as emblematic of the modern novel. An excellent example of this emphasis, which serves to blur further the border between illusion and reality is a dramatic performance that is incorporated into the text of the novel.

Magical Realism

Another trend seen in contemporary Chicana/o narrative fiction is magical realism. Magical realism is commonly associated with the 1967 novel *Cien años de soledad* (*One Hundred Years of Solitude*), by the Colombian novelist and Nobel Prize winner Gabriel García Márquez. At least two other twentieth-century Latin American authors, the Cuban Alejo Carpentier and the Guatemalan Miguel Angel Asturias, are frequently cited as precursors of magical realism. Briefly defined, magical realism is the borderless combination of and alternation between so-called magical elements and settings, characters, and events in the real world. Examples in *Cien años de soledad* are the raining of butterflies (magical) versus the exploitation of plantation workers (reality). Other examples of magical and realistic elements, respectively, are the pope's flight on a magic carpet from Italy to Colombia in "Los funerales de la mamá grande" (Big Mama's Funerals), a García Márquez short story, and the unspeakable cruelty toward political enemies in Asturias's novels. This melding is quite different from what Arias achieves in his novel through drawing on Fausto's imagination and fantasy and combining this inner consciousness with elements of external reality.

Many, many works of contemporary Chicana/o narrative fiction are imbued with a sense of magical realism through the omnipresence of such elements as La Llorona, curanderas, shamans, and *brujos* and *brujas* (male and female witches). At the same time, contemporary Chicana/o narrative fiction offers several complete works of magical realism. Representative of these works are Cecile Piñeda's novel, *The Love Queen of the Amazon* (1992); Kathleen Alcalá's short stories, including "Mrs. Vargas and the Dead Naturalist" (collected in a 1992 work by the same name); and Ana Castillo's novel *So Far from God* (1993).

Piñeda's female protagonist, Ana Magdalena, becomes immersed in a world of real and fantastic events in rural Peru. The writer presents her main male character, Don Federico Orgaz y Orgaz, as a caricature whose name, similar to the Spanish word for orgasm, *orgasmo*, suggests his masculinist, macho attitude toward women in general and Ana Magdalena in particular. Like the real-unreal world that surrounds Ana, Piñeda's stories are gems of magical-realist ambiguity.

Alcalá's short story takes place in an unidentified setting, presumably a rural and isolated village somewhere in Mexico. Mrs. Vargas, a mother of several children, awaits the arrival of a guest, Dr. Ellis, the naturalist referred to in the story's title, whom she has never seen before. She assumes that the "greenish-white" Anglo who arrives at her door one day, collapses, and dies of a heart attack, is the expected guest. The village dwellers cannot explain how this stranger arrived in their midst. Three days after his burial, another Anglo who identifies himself as Dr. Ellis, an ornithologist, arrives in the village in search of an extremely rare bird. Finding no trace of the bird, he returns to the United States. Mrs. Vargas is awakened from her sleep a few days later. She goes to the door of her hut and confronts the first Dr. Ellis, whose complexion looks unhealthy and whose coat is dusty and torn. She flings his portfolio far from her hut, and he picks it up, "a wistful look on his face," having found what he had left behind. Alcalá manipulates two related underlying concepts of magical realism with a Mexican and Chicana/o twist: that there exists a very porous border between life and death and that souls in pain wander the earth until they find peace.

Ana Castillo's novel *So Far from God* is set in the real village of Tomé, in north central New Mexico. It is where Sofía, a Chicana matriarch, lives with her four daughters: Esperanza (hope), Caridad (charity), Fe (faith)—also known as La Gritona (the loud one)—and the youngest known only as La Loca (the crazy one). The magical-realist nature of the novel is set from the very beginning with the death of La Loca and her resurrection when as a three-year-old, she sits up in her casket, talks, and floats to the ceiling. She keeps these magical powers throughout her life and practices them in sometimes beneficent ways, as when she restores Caridad's health and beauty. La Loca also has the ability to see the future and continues performing a variety of miracles until she dies of AIDS. Caridad becomes a successful curandera who communes with La Llorona and other spirits. Several of Castillo's characters are similar to those in García Márquez's works, and like the Colombian writer and other Latin American magical realists, Castillo comments on social injustices, including the patriarchal misogamy prevalent in Chicana/o culture and the racist violence and widespread discriminatory practices perpetrated by Anglos against nuevomexicanos.

Concepts of Aztlán and Mestizaje

As I point out throughout this book, Chicana/o narrative fiction and non-fiction writers, poets, and dramatists have in the past twenty years expanded their focus beyond the major concepts that drove the cultural-nationalist agenda of the 1960s and 1970s. This is not to say that they have totally abandoned or rejected this agenda, but rather they have attempted to integrate it into their works in less explicit and more nuanced ways. For example, the concept of Aztlán, which was central to many works of 1960s and 1970s narrative fiction, began to lose its geographic specificity as a mythical region encompassing the American Southwest in the 1980s and 1990s. The relocation of Aztlán is evident in the works I have discussed by Ana Castillo and Erlinda Gonzales-Berry, and in other works by Kathleen Alcalá, Montserrat Fontes, Graciela Limón, and Sylvia López-Medina. Recently published novels by Alejandro Morales (*The Rag Doll Plagues*, 1992), and Sandra Cisneros (*Caramelo*, 2002) are two excellent examples of the repositioning of Aztlán.

As the Chicano scholar Javier Durán has pointed out, Alejandro Morales (see figure 26) conceptualizes Aztlán in much broader terms than earlier writers to include the borderlands (Durán 2004, 394). At the same time, the writer greatly expands the notion of borderlands beyond the contiguous areas along the U.S.–Mexico border. In his novel, the border-lands/Aztlán stretches from Los Angeles in the north to Mexico City in the south, and in the latter part of the novel the border between the United States and Mexico all but disappears, returning the geopolitical boundaries to where they were prior to 1848.

Morales describes Mexico City as a cultural hub for Mexicans with some of the same characteristics as the Los Angeles–to–San Diego corridor. The three sections of the novel take place in and around these two hubs during different historical periods: the era of Spanish colonial rule; the 1980s, when Mexico City and Los Angeles were two very distinct metropolitan areas; and the end of the twenty-first century, when the entire two-thousand-mile expanse between these cities is known as the LAMEX corridor. In the first section, Gregorio, a representative of the Spanish crown, arrives from Spain in late eighteenth-century Mexico City to cure a plague that has

26. Alejandro Morales (photo by John Michael Margotta; courtesy of Bilingual Review Press)

already devastated the populace. In the novel's second section, which takes place in 1980s Los Angeles, Morales deals with another devastating disease, AIDS, which is on the verge of becoming an epidemic among certain sectors of the barrio's population. A Chicano physician, Gregory (the English equivalent of Gregorio) Revueltas, and his HIV-infected lover search for a cure, first in the barrio and then in Mexico City. The novel's third section, which takes place mainly in Mexico City at the end of the twenty-first century, focuses on the search for cures to new epidemics caused in part by environmental pollution, which threaten the LAMEX corridor. Gregory discovers that Mexico City's population has developed genetic mutations that are resistant to the new diseases and allow them to adapt and survive in plague-infected environments.

The salvation of the entire LAMEX corridor is found not in the north but in the south; a cure derived from the blood of brown people in the south rescues the largely white Anglo population in the north. This constitutes Morales's ironic commentary on the fear of miscegenation, or the mixing of races, that seems to be an undercurrent among contemporary rabid anti-immigrationists.

Sandra Cisneros's most recent novel, *Caramelo* (2002), also represents an extension of the 1960s–1970s concept of Aztlán, as it ranges freely among Chicago, Texas, Mexico City, and Acapulco in an interesting and innovative way that is not seen in any other contemporary Chicana/o novel other than Morales's *The Rag Doll Plagues*. The novel's spatial alternation between the United States and Mexico is reflected in the complexity the narrator repeatedly encounters in negotiating gender and generational obstacles in three different sets of cultural dynamics: Anglo, Mexican, and Chicana/o. *Caramelo* consists of eighty-eight vignette-like chapters in which the reader weaves in and out of the lives of four generations of Mexican–Chicana/o families as individual members, especially the narrator, Celaya (called Lala), seek to find their own destinies.

The color of caramel (*caramelo*) has two primary functions in the novel: first, to reinforce the generational and matrilineal aspect through the continuous presence of a caramel-colored *rebozo* (shawl) that is passed down from mother to daughter. The shawl's intricate weaving serves as a metaphor for storytelling, which is very important to Lala's maturation process. The shawl also functions as a metaphor for the role of race in Mexican as well as Chicana/o society; historically, men and particularly women with light skin have been favored over those with dark skin, light skin signifying European Spanish roots, and dark, signifying Mexican Indian, or mestizo, roots.

Graciela Limón also explores the complex question of Chicana/o mixed Spanish–Mexican Indian heritage. Born in 1938 in Los Angeles to Mexican-immigrant parents, Limón published prolifically in a ten-year span, with five novels to her credit: *María de Belén: The Autobiography of an Indian Woman* (1990), *In Search of Bernabé* (1993), *The Memories of Ana Calderón* (1994), *Song of the Hummingbird* (1996), and *The Day of the Moon* (1999). She earned a PhD in Latin American literature from UCLA (1975), and has taught at Loyola Marymount University in Los Angeles.

Limón's exploration of the interplay of ethnicity and race in Mexico and the United States began with *María de Belén* and appears again in *Song of the Hummingbird* and *The Day of the Moon*. In the first novel, narrator Natalia Roldán, a professor of literature, reflects on this interplay as she translates a recently discovered manuscript, the autobiography of a sixteenth-century Mexican Indian woman who witnessed the Spanish military conquest of Mexico's powerful Aztec civilization, which culminated in 1521. Early into her translation, Roldán becomes aware that this version of the conquest provides a marked contrast to several accounts written by Spaniards. Limón once again situates the reader in the Latin American colonial world in *Song of the Hummingbird*. Almost the entire novel is a dialogue between Huitzitzilín, a very elderly Mexican Indian woman, and Benito Lara, a Spanish Franciscan friar. The context of the dialogue is the former character's confession to the latter, in which the indigenous woman ostensibly seeks the priest's absolution; however, the dialogue reveals to the reader that the indigenous woman is morally superior to the friar. Again, Limón presents an alternative version of the conquest in which the Spanish conquerors' justification for the terrible acts of violence they carried out against Mexican Indian peoples is called into question. Limón not only questions the morality of the conquest but contrasts moral truths found in Spanish Catholicism versus indigenous religions.

In *The Day of the Moon*, Limón explores the mestizo ancestry of Chicanas/os in Mexico and the United States during the early part of the twentieth century and shortly before and during the Chicano Movement of the 1960s and 1970s. In contrast to the cultural-nationalist exaltation of indigenous roots and mestizaje apparent during the Chicano Movement, Limón explores both the positive and negative aspects of Chicana/o ancestry.

Elements of Popular Culture

Another relatively recent phenomenon in contemporary narrative fiction over the past several decades has been the use of images, icons, and content from popular culture. Perhaps the best example of the use of popular culture is Denise Chávez's 2001 novel *Loving Pedro Infante*. Pedro Infante, a singer and actor who was killed in an airplane crash in 1957, is an icon of Mexican popular culture. As is the case with Elvis Presley in the United States, there are regular sightings of Pedro Infante, and millions of his fans continue to come together to view his films, listen to his music, and collect and exchange memorabilia.

In her novel, Chávez (see figure 27) brings together several women, including Teresina "Tere" Avila, her narrator, who form the Pedro Infante Club #256 in the fictional New Mexico community of Cabritoville somewhere close to El Paso and Juárez where Infante's films on video and his recorded music are readily available. Tere, the club organizer, convener, and secretary, knows more than any other club member about the minutiae of Infante's life and works. Her idealization of him as a model of Mexican manhood contrasts with her own love life, which consists of a longstanding affair with Lucio, a married man with children, who strings her along. This affair and the unrequited love lives of the other fan club members constitute a kind of ongoing soap opera or—more appropriately—a movie script. The women look to Pedro Infante and his legions of lovers as a kind of substitute for their mundane and bittersweet lives. The fan club also serves to bring them together in solidarity to express their feelings and

■ 27. Denise Chávez (photo by Daniel Zolinsky)

commiserate about men, their inadequate economic circumstances, disappointments, tragedies, and occasionally their joys.

Children's and Young Adult Literature

The proliferation of children's and young adult literature is another recent trend in contemporary Chicana/o narrative fiction. Well-known writers such as Rodolfo Anaya, Pat Mora, and Gary Soto have branched out over the past ten years, producing an impressive array of this literature. Other Chicana/o writers who have published children's and young adult narrative fiction are Tito Campos, Ofelia Dumas Lachtman, Mary Sue Galindo, and Víctor Villaseñor.

Anaya has published several illustrated children's books, including *Maya's Children: The Story of La Llorona* (1996), *Farolitos for Abuelo* (1998), *My Land Sings: Stories from the Rio Grande* (1999), and *Roadrunner's Dance* (2000). As the titles reflect, Anaya emphasizes Hispanic cultural themes and customs and traditional family values. For example, *Maya's Children* is about the legend of La Llorona, the so-called weeping woman who mourns the tragic and early loss of her children. *Farolitos for Abuelo* deals with respect for one's elders and the importance of continuing to remember and celebrate their lives when they are gone.

Pat Mora has been a prolific author of children's literature since about 1992; she has published almost twenty narrative fiction picture books and readers and several poetry books, some of them bilingual. She draws on some of the same themes found in her adult books of poetry and nonfiction narrative: various positive aspects of Mexican and Chicana/o culture such as customs and traditions, the loving relationship that we should have with nature (especially the desert), and the importance of family. Several of her books, which are celebrations of traditional festive days such as Christmas and birthdays, are filled with rich images of food, sound, and music that are reinforced by fine illustrations. A few of her representative children's literature books are *Listen to the Desert/Oye al desierto* (1994), *Delicious Hullabaloo/Pachanga deliciosa* (1998), *The Bakery Lady/La señora de la panadería* (2001), and *Doña Flor: A Tall Tale about a Giant with a Great Big Heart* (2005).

Like Pat Mora, Gary Soto is also a prolific author of narrative fiction for younger readers. The majority of his more than twenty-five books are written for ages four to eight, eight to twelve, or for teenaged readers. Soto draws generously on his hardscrabble boyhood and adolescence spent in the working-class neighborhoods of Fresno, California. Like his adult poetry, narrative fiction, and narrative nonfiction, his books for younger readers are replete with bittersweet memories of these years. He touches lightly on the loneliness of growing up without his biological father, who was killed in an industrial accident when Soto was a boy. But at the same time, Soto inspires his young readers with scenes of magic, joy, wonder, and curiosity that were also a part of his childhood and adolescence. His young adult books portray young Chicanas/os making their way in a sometimes hostile mainstream culture as they mature toward adulthood. Some representative titles of Soto's books are *Living up the Street* (1985); *Baseball in April* (1990); *Taking Sides* (1991); *The Pool Party* (1993); *Boys at Work* (1995); and *If the Shoe Fits* (2002).

■ Discussion Questions

1. The border is a theme found in both Chicana/o autobiography and narrative fiction. Discuss the range of different ways writers treat this theme in their works.

2. Many contemporary Chicana/o writers were at one time part of the so-called migrant stream. How is this experience manifested in their works?

3. Discuss the different perspectives that Chicana/o writers have on growing up in an urban barrio.

4. Chicanas often found themselves in a double or even a triple bind during and after the Chicano Movement. What were the causes of these binds and how are they reflected in contemporary narrative fiction by Chicanas?

5. Discuss the different narratives strategies that Chicana writers use to break with traditional stereotypes of women as passive and subservient to men.

6. Discuss the theme of war in contemporary Chicana/o works of autobiography and narrative fiction.

7. What are some emerging trends in recent Chicana/o narrative fiction?

■ Suggested Readings

Aldama, Frederick Luis. 2003. *Postethnic Narrative Criticism: Magicorealism in Oscar "Zeta" Acosta, Ana Castillo, Julie Dash, Hanif Kureishi, and Salman Rushdie.* Austin: University of Texas Press.

Brady, Mary Pat. 2002. *Extinct Lands, Temporal Geographies: Chicana Literature and the Urgency of Space.* Durham: Duke University Press.

Brown, Monica. 2002. *Gang Nation: Delinquent Citizens in Puerto Rican, Chicano, and Chicana Narratives.* Minneapolis: University of Minnesota Press.

Day, Frances Ann. 1999. *Multicultural Voices in Contemporary Literature: A Resource for Teachers.* Portsmouth, NH: Heinemann.

Esturoy, Annie O. 1996. *Daughters of Self-Creation: The Contemporary Chicana Novel.* Albuquerque: University of New Mexico Press.

Ikas, Karin Rosa. 2002. *Chicana Ways: Conversations with Ten Chicana Writers.* Reno: University of Nevada Press.

King, Rosemary A. 2004. *Border Confluences: Borderland Narratives from the Mexican War to the Present.* Tucson: University of Arizona Press.

Kutzer, M. Daphne. 1996. *Writers of Multicultural Fiction for Young Adults: A Bio-Critical Sourcebook.* Westport, CT: Greenwood Press.

Madsen, Deborah L. 2000. *Understanding Contemporary Chicana Literature.* Columbia: University of South Carolina Press.

Mariscal, Jorge, ed. 1999. *Aztlán and Vietnam: Chicano and Chicana Experiences of the War.* Berkeley and Los Angeles: University of California Press.

McCracken, Ellen. 1999. *New Latina Narrative: The Feminine Space of Postmodern Ethnicity.* Tucson: University of Arizona Press.

McKenna, Teresa. 1997. *Migrant Song: Politics and Process in Contemporary Chicano Literature.* Austin: University of Texas Press.

Neate, Wilson. 1998. *Tolerating Ambiguity: Ethnicity and Community in Chicano/a Writing.* New York: Peter Lang.

Quintana, Alvina. 1996. *Home Girls: Chicana Literary Voices*. Philadelphia: Temple University Press.

Rebolledo, Tey Diana. 1995. *Women Singing in the Snow: A Cultural Analysis of Chicana Literature*. Tucson: University of Arizona Press.

Rivas-Rodríguez, Maggie, ed. 2005. *Mexican Americans and World War II*. Austin: University of Texas Press.

Rodríguez, Ralph. 2005. *Brown Gumshoes: Detective Fiction and the Search for Chicana/o Identity*. Austin: University of Texas Press.

Walter, Roland. 1993. *Magical Realism in Contemporary Chicano Fiction*. Frankfurt: Vervuert Verlag.

6

Contemporary Chicana/o Theater

From the mid-1960s to the early 1970s, Chicana/o theater constituted an important manifestation and expression of the social and political agenda of the Chicano Movement (see chapter 3). El Teatro Campesino played a crucial artistic and cultural role in taking socially committed theater to the fields and small towns of California's agricultural valleys as part of the successful campaign to unionize farmworkers. From its very beginning in 1965, Luis Valdez and others viewed their theater as working outside of commercial, mainstream, elite, or "legitimate," theater, which was limited to performances in established theaters in urban settings. TENAZ (Teatro Nacional de Aztlán), the organization of Chicana/o regional theaters that El Teatro Campesino helped to birth, also subscribed to this alternative mission of serving as the voice of the Chicano community.

1970s Chicana/o Playwrights

Fausto Avendaño

A university professor and scholar of Chicana/o literature, Fausto Avendaño wrote an important three-act play, *El corrido de California* (The Ballad of California, 1979), in which he uses a historical setting to dramatize the facts surrounding the Anglo military invasion of California in 1846. Don Gerónimo, a well-to-do Mexican rancher and official who professes great faith in the ideals of American democracy, slowly comes to realize that Anglo military forces intend to occupy his beloved California; his disappointment soon turns to resistance. His son Rafael, an official in the Mexican army who has repeatedly tried to warn his father of the dangers of Manifest Destiny, returns to his native California with a small military force to defend his compatriots against the advancing U.S. army. The dominant American spirit of the period is most dramatically represented by the allegorical figure of America, whose appearance early in the third act augurs the defeat of the Mexicans and the triumph of U.S. expansionism.

Rubén Sierra

Rubén Sierra's plays, *La Raza Pura, or Racial, Racial* (1976) and *Manolo* (1976), are hard-hitting works that address two different aspects of the Chicana/o social condition. *La Raza Pura*, a technically complex and humorous work, makes a powerful statement about the myth of being able to maintain racial purity in a rapidly changing society. Sierra's intent is to provide his Chicana/o audience with a mirror of its foibles in a humorous way. *Manolo* deals with an internal social problem: drug addiction among Chicano Vietnam veterans. Unlike Sierra's first play, this work is written in a realistic style, presenting what is tantamount to a case history of a returning veteran whose life has been significantly altered by his war experiences and his subsequent addiction. Much of the play focuses on the veteran's struggle against tremendous odds, including the oppressive atmosphere of the barrio. He triumphs in the end but dies tragically, shot down by a drug pusher who has also killed his brother.

Nephtalí de León, Francisco Burruel, and Ysidro Macías

Other Chicana/o playwrights who present similar social themes in their works are Nephtalí de León, Francisco Burruel, and Ysidro Macías. The plays in León's book *Five Plays* (1972) focus exclusively on the bitter history and present-day socioeconomic conditions of Chicanas/os, encompassing police brutality, protests against injustice and their similarity to revolutionary movements in Latin America, the educational abuses Chicanas/os suffer in Anglo-dominated public education systems, the difficulty of surviving injustice, and the constant struggle against overwhelming odds. Francisco Burruel's play, *The Dialogue of Cuco Rocha* (1970), is more hopeful. It consists of a lengthy dialogue between an imprisoned Chicano activist and an Anglo prison official. Their relationship changes during the play from antagonism to mutual respect. In *Mártir Montezuma* (1976), Ysidro Macías compares the Spaniards' mistreatment of the Aztecs to the Anglo growers' exploitation of Chicana/o farmworkers. Macías implicitly criticizes César Chávez's nonviolent philosophy as ineffectual. Macias's *The Ultimate Pendejada* (1976) focuses on a couple who have rejected their Mexican ancestry to embrace fanatic Anglo patriotism only to realize their mistake and seek authentic Chicana/o values in the barrio.

Carlos Morton

Carlos Morton (see figure 28) has been writing plays since he was a student in the early 1970s. He received his MFA in 1978 at the University of California, San Diego, and his PhD in theater at the University of Texas, Austin, in 1987. He has taught at several universities and is currently a professor of theater at the University of California, Santa Barbara. Morton is both a published scholar and a prolific playwright. He has published three anthologies of his plays—*The Many Deaths of Danny Rosales and Other Plays* (1983), *Johnny Tenorio and Other Plays* (1992), and *Rancho Hollywood y otras obras del teatro chicano* (2000)—as well as several individual plays. He has also translated and published an anthology of Mexican playwrights.

Many of Morton's plays are highly symbolic in that the characters represent and play out age-old struggles between good and evil, redemption and condemnation, and other dichotomies. An exception is *The Many Deaths of Danny Rosales*, in which Morton experiments with social realism. Perhaps his best-known and most produced play, it has been translated into Spanish and produced in Mexico. The play is a docudrama based on the murder of a young Chicano, Richard Morales, by a Texas police chief in Castroville in 1974. Morton indicts the legal, judicial, and police systems that in Texas and elsewhere all too frequently have applied a double standard to people of color.

More characteristic of Morton's theater are *El jardín* (The Garden) and *El cuento de Pancho Diablo* (The Tale of Pancho Devil). *El jardín* is a full-length play in which Morton uses stock biblical figures (Adam, Eve, God, and the Serpent) and barrio characters (Matón [killer], Ladrón [Thief], and Cabrón [Bastard]), who are readily familiar to a Chicana/o audience. Morton also uses barrio youth slang to enhance his connection with this audience. For example, Eve is identified as a *ruca* (chick) who is *media coquetona* (flirtatious), and the Serpent is a dissipated barrio type *lleno de mota y vino* (full of marijuana and wine). The play is a parody on the human fall from grace, as Morton uses the biblical tale to suggest that the real tragedy of the fall is that humans have lost touch with their spirit, the basis of ethnic and cultural pride. *El cuento de Pancho Diablo* is also a farcical Chicana/o version of biblical stories and Milton's *Paradise Lost*. The Devil quits his job in hell and returns to the earth, only to discover that conditions in the barrio are as bad as where he came from. Morton indicts the police, the Texas Rangers, the Immigration and Naturalization Ser-

28. Carlos Morton

vice, the Teamsters Union, the Catholic Church, and vendidas/os (sellouts) who forsake their cultural heritage and communities to get rich.

These three plays and some of Morton's other plays demonstrate his technical versatility and thematic range. An additional example is *Rancho Hollywood* in which he uses farce to indict the Hollywood film industry for its distortion of history and creation of racial stereotypes. Employing the device of rapidly changing stage scenes that parallel historic events, he highlights the disparities between official historical records and Hollywood's false version of them. *The Savior* is an examination of the assassination of Archbishop Oscar Romero in El Salvador in 1980.

Theater Projects

Luis Valdez majored in drama at San Jose State University and landed an apprenticeship with the San Francisco Mime Troupe after graduation. Carlos Morton also formally studied drama and theater in graduate school. The members of El Teatro Campesino's ensemble worked intensively together to perfect their acting and to help shape the theater's aesthetics. They were fortunate in being afforded such opportunities, which undoubtedly shaped their craft as playwrights. It was not until the late 1970s and early 1980s, however, that other Chicana/o playwrights, actors, and directors were able to take advantage of these kinds of intensive educational and workshop opportunities. Two of the most important theater projects, unfortunately both no longer in existence, were the South Coast Repertory Theatre's Hispanic Playwright Project (HPP) and INTAR (International Arts Relations, Inc.) located in New York City. The first, the HPP, was responsible for the development of many Latina/o plays (including Chicana/o plays) from across the United States from the mid-1980s to the mid-1990s. Playwright María Irene Fornés taught and directed INTAR's laboratory from 1981 to 1992 (Huerta 2000, 8–10).

A third project, the Latino Theatre Lab, was created under the auspices of the Los Angeles Theatre Center, a mainstream theater company located in an impressive 80,000-square-foot former bank building in downtown Los Angeles. The lab, which was directed from 1985 to 1991 by José Luis Valenzuela, a Mexican director, producer, and teacher, was unique in that it brought together an ensemble of Chicana/o theater, television, and film artists working in a mainstream theater company. Valenzuela and his staff were responsible for more professional Latina/o theater productions, readings, and workshops than any other mainstream or Latina/o theater company in the country. Valenzuela later founded his own company, the Latino Theatre Company, in East Los Angeles.

Many Chicana/o playwrights and directors who came into prominence in the 1980s and 1990s were associated at one time or another with at least one of these theater projects, where they participated in intensive workshops on different aspects of writing for the theater or had their plays produced. This was especially the case for Chicana playwrights and producers.

 ## The Prominence of Chicana Theater in the 1980s and the 1990s

If Luis Valdez and El Teatro Campesino, and to a lesser extent Carlos Morton, dominated Chicana/o theater from the mid-1960s to the early 1980s, most of the 1980s and the 1990s saw the rise and success of an unprecedented number of Chicana playwrights. Many of these playwrights had participated in some capacity in El Teatro Campesino or in one of the regional theaters it spawned. They had learned their craft well, and by the 1980s they had begun to emerge from the shadow of their male counterparts and to reject their machista attitudes and behaviors. This evolution was part of the general rejection of both Anglo and Chicano misogyny and patriarchy that was fundamental to the rise of Chicana feminism in the 1970s and 1980s.

The emergence of Chicana playwrights, producers, directors, and actors was also a key aspect of the dramatic increase in successful Chicana writers in all genres in the 1980s and 1990s (see chapters 4, 5, and 7). They began to organize and to found their own theater groups, allowing them for the first time to foster and promote their specific political concerns and feminist agendas unfettered by the obstacles that many Chicano male directors, producers, and actors had created for them in the past. Chicanas began bringing to the stage strong leading roles for women and debunking stereotypes of women as weak, subservient, and inferior wives, daughters, and sisters dependent on strong and assertive males for their identities. Their experiences as women served as the basis for many of the works they wrote and produced. Many of their plays focus on relationships between women, especially those between mothers and daughters as well as lesbian relationships (Sandoval-Sánchez and Saporta Sternbach 2001, 57–73).

Chicana playwrights began in the early 1980s to create new dramatic forms that foregrounded and gave value and meaning to the daily work of women both inside and outside the home. One of these forms was *teatropoesía*, "a creative fusion of drama and poetic texts" (Yarbro-Bejarano 1983, 79). Due to the paucity of Chicana-written plays, novice playwrights turned to the abundance of poetry written by Chicanas throughout the 1970s (see chapter 7) as a source from which to build dramatic presentations that reflected a strong female perspective and sense of self-identity. These staged montages of poetry written by their sisters provided very powerful models and motivators to would-be Chicana playwrights to tap their own potential and create their own plays.

Factors that contributed to the advancement of Chicana theater in the 1980s and 1990s include the informal networks that sprung up around arts events, the publication of anthologies that included Chicana playwrights, and the academic positions that playwrights occupied. In terms of informal networks, the Border Book Festival held annually in Las Cruces, New Mexico, since 1994 under the artistic direction of the Chicana writer Denise Chávez has attracted established and novice Latina/o writers including Chicana/o playwrights. The Chicana writer Cherríe Moraga's work with the San Francisco—based Brava! For Women in the Arts Theatre has highlighted interesting and innovative work in Latina dramatic arts. Moraga has also brought together both heterosexual and lesbian young women in the Bay Area to encourage their development as writers and playwrights. In Texas, the Cara Mía Theatre Company continues to produce quality plays by women, including works by Chicanas such as Moraga.

The inclusion of Chicana dramatic works in anthologies has gone far in contributing to the visibility of Chicana playwrights. The publication of *Shattering the Myth* (Feyder and Chávez 1992) represented an important breakthrough for Moraga, Edit Villarreal, and Josefina López, whose plays were included. The 2000 publication *Puro Teatro: A Latina Anthology*, edited by Alberto Sandoval-Sánchez and Nancy Saporta Sternbach, includes works of the following Chicana playwrights: Moraga, Yarelí Arizamendi, Amparo García Crow, Alicia Mena, Mónica Palacios, Diane Rodríguez, Edit Villarreal, Elaine Romero, and Silviana Wood.

Beginning in the 1990s, the following Chicana playwrights opened up another venue—college and universities—that allowed them to develop as artists and produce their own plays: Edit Villarreal and Mónica Palacios at UCLA; Cherríe Moraga at Stanford; Amparo García Crow at the University of Texas, Austin; Laura Esparza at the University of Washington; Yarelí Arizamendi at California State University, San Marcos; and Elaine Romero at the University of Arizona (Sandoval-Sánchez and Saporta Sternbach 2001, 63–65). In the remainder of this section, I highlight key works by these and other Chicana playwrights.

Estela Portillo-Trambley

Estela Portillo-Trambley (1936–1999) was not only an award-winning narrative fiction writer (see chapter 3), but also an excellent playwright. As the Chicano theater scholar Jorge Huerta (2000, 20; see figure 29) has commented, she "is regarded by most Chicana/o critics and scholars as the woman who inspired and opened the doors for all the Chicana writers that followed her." Portillo-Trambley was the first Chicana to publish a play, her best-known and most important dramatic work, *Day of the Swallows*, which originally appeared in 1972. In 1983, she published *Sor Juana and Other Plays*, which included the play by the same name as well as *Autumn Gold*, *Puente Negro*, and *Blacklight*.

Day of the Swallows is a three-act play set in a small Mexican village that is described in the stage directions as a "stepchild" of the local hacienda, whose owners along with the Catholic Church have dominated the rural and village poor around them for many decades. The play's main character is Josefa, a middle-aged woman and a powerful figure embittered by the

29. Jorge Huerta

humiliation and denial the women have had to endure at the hands of males. She symbolizes life's vitality and hope on one hand, but on the other she lives in fear that the secret that she and another woman are lovers will be revealed. Her life ends tragically; after cutting out the tongue of a boy who has witnessed her and her lover making love, she commits suicide. She is thus denied her full human potential as a woman by a repressive and rigid set of traditional mores. The theater scholars Alberto Sandoval-Sánchez and Nancy Saporta Sternbach (2001, 79) consider this play to be "nothing short of the inaugural moment of Latina playwriting," a work that profoundly influenced contemporary Chicana playwrights such as Cherríe Moraga.

Cherríe Moraga

Born in Los Angeles in 1952, Moraga is not only a superb playwright but has also authored or edited very important works of narrative fiction and nonfiction and poetry. She and Gloria Anzaldúa coedited the groundbreaking anthology *This Bridge Called My Back: Writings by Radical Women of Color* (1981) as their response to the exclusionary practices of Anglo feminists vis-à-vis feminists of color. In 1983, Moraga published *Loving in the War Years: lo que nunca pasó por sus labios* (What Never Passed through Her Lips), a semi-autobiographical collection of her essays and poems and an eloquent expression of Moraga's sentiments about being a Chicana lesbian.

Moraga began to develop as a serious playwright in 1984 when her first play, *Giving Up the Ghost* (1986), was selected for its first reading at INTAR, where she spent an entire year in an intense workshop atmosphere perfecting the play. The play premiered and was produced in 1989 by San Francisco's gay/lesbian theater company, Theatre Rhinoceros. It became the first work in her trilogy *Heroes and Saints and Other Plays* (1994). Sandoval-Sánchez and Saporta Sternbach (2001, 77) believe that it is one of the "foundational" plays for Latina playwrights. Jorge Huerta (2000,

161) identifies the play as "the first play about lesbian desire, written by a [Latina] lesbian, to be produced and published," although Portillo-Trambley's *Day of the Swallows* did predate it in addressing lesbian themes.

Giving Up the Ghost has three characters: Marisa, Corky, and Amalia, Marisa's lover. Marisa and Amalia must first overcome the "ghosts" within them before becoming conscious of why and how they love each other. The play is a series of long monologues by each of the three characters, and each monologue contains a flashback to a rape scene, an event around which are clustered a complex nexus of "ghosts" that are eventually surfaced and dealt with as the play develops. Corky speaks of struggling as a girl and young woman to shed the constraints of her culture's mandatory heterosexuality along with its gendered strictures regarding dress and behavior; her lesbian desire eventually emerges. Corky and Marisa embrace their sexual feelings toward other women and bear no shame. Amalia, an older Mexican woman, is more ambivalent about her sexual feelings.

A second much praised play by Moraga is *Heroes and Saints*, which premiered in 1992 in San Francisco. The play is an expression of the playwright's moral outrage over a grave social injustice: the use of toxic pesticides in California's agricultural fields despite the repeated attempts of the United Farm Workers Union to ban them. The play is divided into two acts with sixteen scenes in the first and thirteen in the second. The play is strung together in a cinematic, episodic montage of scenes and monologues. Moraga's central figure is Cerezita, a precocious young woman who is born without a body; during the entire play it is only her head the audience sees. Cerezita's condition is linked to the excessive and indiscriminate use of pesticides as well as the dangers of toxic waste. Unsuccessful in their repeated attempts to obtain federal subsidies to underwrite their relocation to a cleaner site, the townspeople take matters into their own hands and torch the fields.

Denise Chávez

Denise Chávez is best known as a narrative fiction writer (see chapter 5), but she also holds a prominent place in contemporary Chicana/o theater as one of the earliest playwrights to produce individually written plays. She has written more than twenty plays although only one has been published. Chávez was born in Las Cruces, New Mexico, in 1948; she received an MFA from Trinity University in San Antonio and an MA in creative writing from the University of New Mexico. Chávez was instrumental in creating and serving as artistic director for the Border Book Festival, which has been held annually in Las Cruces since 1994.

Chávez is best known for her *Novenas narrativas y ofrendas nuevomexicanas* (also titled *Women in the State of Grace*, 1988), which has been produced numerous times. A novena is a Catholic prayer that is said on nine successive days. The play has nine women characters who appear one by one: María Isabel Gonzales, a writer and the play's main character; Jesusita Rael, a spinster who owns a small store; Esperanza Gonzales, the wife of a Chicano Vietnam veteran; Minda Mirabal, a foster child; Magdalena Telles, a mother of a large family of seven children; Tomasa Pacheco, who lives in a nursing home; Juana Martínez, a factory worker; Pauline Mendoza, a teenager; and Corrine "La Cory" Delgado, a bag lady. The play is a mixture of lightly humorous and deadly serious moments as the women introduce themselves and their individual circumstances. Its theme is that women across generations and from different walks of life and different classes are all united by a common history of patience, forbearance, suffering, and ultimately love. Regardless of their personal circumstances, women need to support each other through life's difficulties, many of which are caused by men or the alien culture in which they live.

Edit Villarreal

Edit Villarreal was born in 1944 in Brownsville, Texas. She was cared for by her maternal grandmother, Marta Garza, upon whom the Marta Grande character in her play *My Visits with MGM* is based. Villarreal's family moved to the Los Angeles area in the 1960s. She received an MFA in playwriting at Yale University in 1986.

Villarreal has written a handful of plays; the best-known and most frequently produced work by far is *My Visits with MGM* (1992). Marta Grande, the play's main character, is characterized as a strong, pragmatic, and kind matriarch. The entire play is presented as a memory, so the transformation in the characters' ages and the work's multiple settings require close attention on the part of the audience. Villarreal explores the relationship between Marta Grande and Marta Feliz, her granddaughter. The play's other characters, who span three generations of a Chicana family, are Florinda, Marta Grande's sister; Marta Chica, her daughter and Marta Feliz's mother; and two male characters, the grandfather Juan and a young Chicano priest, Father Ernesto. As the play begins, Marta Grande and her sister, Florinda, have died in a house fire in Texas and Marta Feliz has returned to Texas from California to settle their affairs. Her grandmother, grandfather, grandaunt, mother, and best friend appear as ghosts. They give form to Marta Feliz's rush of conflicting feelings as she recalls her younger years in Texas living with them. In both life and death, Marta Grande serves as a source of emotional strength and spiritual guidance for Marta Feliz as the younger woman struggles to find (and eventually succeeds in finding) a sense of her own destiny.

Josefina López

Josefina López was born in Mexico in 1969, was raised in East Los Angeles where she attended public schools, and became a temporary resident under the 1987 Amnesty Program. She has commented that she did not become a Chicana until she was twenty. In 1989, López started her formal university studies in theater as an undergraduate at the University of California, San Diego. Her interest in theater began early; she recalls writing plays in fifth grade and being fascinated by the magic of theater. She studied acting in high school and from 1985 to 1988 she participated in the Los Angeles Theatre Center's Young Playwrights Lab.

López's career as a playwright began in 1988 when her first play, *Simply María, or the American Dream*, was produced as part of the California Young Playwrights' Contest in San Diego. In this play, López is harshly critical of the Catholic Church and its complicity in perpetuating patriarchal attitudes and practices in Mexican and Chicana/o culture. She confronts a whole set of implicit and explicit expectations that her culture imposes on both men and women but that disproportionately affect women in very negative and lasting ways. In 1988, López participated in a theater workshop in New York City where she wrote a draft of her best-known play, *Real Women Have Curves*, which premiered in 1990. It was very well received and since has been produced many times. *Real Women Have Curves* can best be described as a Chicana bildungsroman; Ana, a young Chicana and the main character, struggles to liberate herself from the strictures that her patriarchal culture imposes on all women, thereby limiting their potential. The play, which is set in a small sewing factory somewhere in East Los Angeles, takes place over a period of five days. A group of women of various ages, including Ana and Estela, her sister, who owns the factory, struggles to fill a large order of dresses. The women banter about several topics, including their boyfriends and husbands. The sizes of the dresses they are sewing prompt their discussions about the play's central theme, the female body, as they reveal their attitudes about whether fat, plump, large, and voluptuous bodies are acceptable in their culture and in Anglo culture in general. Ana comes to realize that from the time she was a child the men in her family, in Chicano culture, and in the wider circle of society have very narrowly proscribed women's attitudes, behaviors, decisions, and roles. The underlying message is that women must accept the norms and expectations that men (and even other women) impose on them from the time they are children. Women should remain virginal until they marry and raise a family, and assume and be content with subservient positions as nurturers and caretakers. Ana comes to realize that these expectations are completely unrealistic and unattainable.

Elaine Romero

Elaine Romero, a prolific playwright of more than thirty plays, has received wide recognition, including several prestigious awards. She holds an MFA in playwriting from the University of California, Irvine. Her best-known and most frequently produced play, *The Fat-Free Chicana and the Snow-Cap Queen*, focuses on the complex meanings that food takes on within Chicana/o culture and how its treatment is sometimes a cause of intergenerational conflict. The play's main characters are Amy, a Chicana college student majoring in dietetics; and the Snow-Cap Queen, a Mexican trickster figure known as Lard Lady who also appears as the Good Witch of the North/Doña Norte and La Crítica, a restaurant critic.

Having been alerted by the Good Witch of the North about serious but unspecified trouble at home somewhere in the Southwest, Amy has returned home to help her family advance their restaurant business. As a young college-educated Chicana with knowledge about food—especially the unhealthy practice of cooking with artery-clogging, heart-stopping lard, a staple of traditional Mexican cooking—and a range of other subjects, Amy confronts her family's eating habits. She also confronts their cultural expectations which dictate that women must accept the norms and expectations that are imposed on them from the time they are children. Not unlike thousands of other Chicanas/os who leave home to pursue higher education, Amy becomes aware of the widening gap that is developing between her traditional family and their friends and the educated person she is becoming. In leaving behind her traditional culture to enter a new, Anglo-dominated culture, she has at least momentarily forgotten the positive aspects of the former in favor of both the positive and negative aspects of the latter. Part of her negotiation to arrive at a compromise between the two extremes is learning how to cook in the traditional Mexican way but substituting a healthier ingredient for lard. The role of the Snow-Cap Queen in her various identities is both interesting as a theatrical device and also crucial to Amy's process of self-discovery and self-identity.

Alicia Mena

Alicia Mena was for many years very active in the Houston theater community before moving to San Antonio in 1993 to work with the Guadalupe Cultural Arts Center as playwright, director, and actor. Like Romero's *Fat-Free Chicana and the Snow-Cap Queen*, Alicia Mena's widely produced one-act play *Las nuevas tamaleras* (The New Tamale Makers) deals with food as a site of conflict, self-awareness, and self-identity. The play's characters are Doña Mercedes, described in the stage directions as "a woman in her sixties, very severe, old-guard type"; Doña Juanita, a fifty-year-old woman who is described as "tenderhearted"; Silvia, "a very bossy and methodical woman in her twenties or thirties"; Josie, "a very malleable, mediating woman" of the same age as Silvia; and Patsy, a "very anglicized" younger woman who is dressed inappropriately for the tamalada (tamale-making session).

The first scene takes place in heaven, where Doña Mercedes and Doña Juanita comment on a variety of topics but most importantly their memories of the frequent tamaladas where women of all ages would gather to produce mouth-watering tamales from scratch. Doña Mercedes recalls that the men would kill a fat pig and the pig's lard would be integral to the recipe. The scenes that follow take place in Silvia's kitchen, where she and her friends have gathered to make Christmas tamales. Doña Mercedes and Doña Juanita, who are present as invisible spirits, comment on what they consider to be the tamalada farce because the younger, contemporary Chicanas use prepared, refined, and store-bought *masa* (fine cornmeal) and a pork roast, and cooking instruments that differ from those used in traditional tamaladas. Finally, the tamales are cooked and Josie and her friends celebrate their success as nuevas tamaleras and drink a toast to their foremothers, including Doña Mercedes and Doña Juanita, who passed on the tradition to them. Despite the changes in the ingredients and the process, the ritual aspect of making tamales has survived from one generation to another as the younger women experience a kind of collective coming into a state of self-identity and self-actualization.

■ Gay/Lesbian Theater

Although less so today than forty years ago, male and female homosexuality is a taboo subject for many Chicana/o families because it is a sin according to traditional Mexican and Chicana/o values. Gay and lesbian themes did not begin to emerge in Chicana/o narrative nonfiction, narrative fiction, and poetry with any regularity until the 1980s and 1990s (see chapters 4, 5, and 7). With the exception of Estela Portillo-Trambley, Cherríe Moraga, and Alfonso Hernández (discussed below), contemporary Chicana/o playwrights have been even slower to deal openly with homosexuality in their works. Jorge Huerta has commented on this trend, "It is one thing to read about forbidden topics without intervention, in the privacy of your home, but quite another to attend a play that exposes your community's worst fears" (Huerta 2000, 141).

After Portillo-Trambley's play *Day of the Swallows*, dealing with Josefa, a "closeted" lesbian, was produced in the early 1970s, only a smattering of plays with gay or lesbian characters and themes appeared in the next twenty-five years. These include Teatro Campesino's 1975 version of *Fin del mundo* (The End of the World); Alfonso Hernández's *Every Family Has One* (1979); Cherríe Moraga's *Giving Up the Ghost* whose theme is lesbian desire; Josefina López's *Food for the Dead* (1989), in which a gay Chicano is included but not featured; several plays with gay or lesbian characters by Chilean-born playwright Guillermo Reyes, such as *Men on the Verge of a His-panic Breakdown* (1994); Moraga's *Shadow of a Man* (1990 premier), which deals with a Chicana/o family's problems including the father's repressed homosexuality and a daughter's budding lesbianism, and *Heroes and Saints* (1992 premier), which portrays the homosexual desire of a secondary character; Oliver Mayer's *Blade to the Heat*, which premiered in 1994 at the prestigious Joseph Papp Theater in New York City; and Moraga's play *Watsonville* (1996 premier). I have already discussed several of the plays by Chicanas; here I briefly review the works of Alfonso Hernández and Oliver Mayer.

Alfonso C. Hernández

Alfonso Hernández is one of the most artistically innovative of contemporary Chicana/o playwrights. His early works are a harmonious combination of music, dance, film, and pantomime. Stage directions and settings are elaborate. There is little dialogue as the playwright attempts to engage his audience through movement and light. Erotic scenes are common on stage. Hernandez's later plays retain many of these elements in more fully developed form. *The False Advent of Mary's Child* (1979) deals with the general state of decadence in traditional Hispanic culture, particularly its hypocritical attitude toward male-female sexuality and the hierarchical relationship between the classes. *Every Family Has One*, a play in six scenes, deals broadly with the theme of exploitation and inhumanity in social interactions, which Hernández highlights within the context of homosexual relationships. Most of the dialogue deals explicitly and openly with homosexuality. Hernández demonstrates his skill by creating a work of complex human emotions in which sexual orientation is heavily influenced by class, social, and racial differences. The tragic finale to the play, a suicide, points to the social predicament of people who choose to live outside of the norm.

Oliver Mayer

Oliver Mayer is, along with Portillo-Trambley, Hernández, and Moraga, one of the first Chicana/o playwrights to focus on homosexuality as a main theme. His play *Blade to the Heat* deals with homoeroticism in professional boxing. Mayer was born in Hollywood in 1965. He received a BA from Cornell University, attended Oxford University in England for a year, and then completed an MFA in the Program in Playwrighting at Columbia University in 1989. He served as associate literary manager at the Mark Taper Forum until 1997, where he wrote plays, read other playwrights' manuscripts, and learned the business of nonprofit theater.

Mayer already was familiar with some of the positive and negative aspects of boxing and its history before he set out to write *Blade to the Heat*. Boxing has historically been associated with a man's physical power and unambiguous heterosexuality. The play has four main characters: Pedro Quinn, an Irish-Mexican boxer; Mantequilla Décima, an Afro-Cuban boxer who is the world champion in his weight class until Quinn defeats him; Wilfred Vinal, a Puerto Rican boxer; and Sarita, Mantequilla's girlfriend. At the beginning of the play, Vinal accuses both Décima and Quinn of being homosexuals (*maricones*), and this accusation sets in motion the confrontations with friends, trainers, boxers, Sarita, and other characters that take place on stage during the rest of the play. The two boxers are fixated on proving and demonstrating their heterosexuality (or at least covering their latent or active homosexuality) by, among other ways, flaunting a girlfriend. The play ends with a boxing match between Décima and Quinn; Quinn leaves Décima dying on the mat after Décima taunts him (Huerta 2000, 166–72).

The presentation of gay and lesbian themes is still viewed warily by Chicana/o playwrights and theater companies. Nonetheless, the future seems a little brighter than the past. In addition to the aforementioned well-known playwrights who have dealt with gay or lesbian themes, Jorge Huerta (2000, 179) cites several playwrights who are emerging and becoming better known: the performance artist Mónica Palacios whose one-woman show *Latin Lezbo Comic* has toured widely in the United States; Luis Alfaro, who performs a one-man show *O Solo Homo*; Ric Oquita; and visual artist David Zamora Casas and dancer-actor Paul Bonín-Rodríguez, who perform together.

Organized Chicana/o Theater Groups

Latins Anonymous

Latins Anonymous was founded in 1987 by a group of young Latina/o actors that reflected the diverse makeup of California's Latina/o community. It has a collective identity and its members work together to write and produce their plays. The group has performed its signature play, *Latins Anonymous*, and a second play, *The La La Awards*, all over the United States.

Latins Anonymous is a series of comedic playlets, each satirizing Anglo culture while providing observations in a humorous vein about different aspects of the Latina/o condition in the United States. One playlet, "Machos of Omaha," parodies machismo while another one, "Latin Denial," pokes fun at Latinas/os who would prefer to be identified as European. *The La La Awards* satirizes the scarce Latina/o presence in Hollywood as well as the award ceremonies (for example, the Academy Awards, the Tony Awards). It includes several characters based on Latina/o celebrities such as Cheech Marin County (Cheech Marín), Edward James Almost (Edward James Olmos), and Linda Roncha (Linda Ronstadt), as well as stereotypes such as Aztec Studs and Juan Valdez (the fictional Colombian coffee farmer featured in coffee advertisements).

Culture Clash

Culture Clash is another theater group that functions as a collective. It is made up of mainly northern California Latina/o actors and writers who came together around 1984 at the Galería de la Raza/Studio 24 in San Francisco to begin producing satirical theater. The group has written and produced several plays including *The Mission*, *A Bowl of Beings*, and *Radio Mambo: Culture Clash Invades Miami*. The name signifies for the group "the culture clash of Latinos against mainstream America, as well as the culture clash between the different Latino races" (*Culture Clash* 2003, 3). Prior to writing *The Mission*, the group performed cabaret-style without a narrative. Each actor would take his or her turn on stage performing individual material, although they did collaborate on sketches and play off each other's jokes. *The Mission* premiered in San Francisco in 1988 and has subsequently been performed at venues throughout the United States. *A Bowl of Beings*, which premiered in 1991 in Los Angeles, is the group's tribute to the legacy of the Chicano Movement and as such it is explicitly political in its content. It takes a broad sweep through the history of Hispanics in the United States from the time of the discovery of America forward. The play takes on a number of sacred cows, including the historical figures of Columbus, Che Guevara, Leon Trotsky, and Frida Kahlo; Chicana/o popular icons such as Edward James Olmos; and folk myths such as La Llorona. *Radio Mambo: Culture Clash Invades Miami* is unique in contemporary Chicana/o theater in that a Chicana/o theater group has written and performed a play that deals with Cuban, Haitian, African American, and Jewish themes within the distinctly non-Chicano city of Miami. The play premiered in Miami in 1994 to very positive reviews and enthusiastic audiences. It deals with a number of issues that both unite and separate different ethnic groups in the Miami area in an irreverent but humorous way.

■ Discussion Questions

1. Discuss the importance of theater projects and workshops in the development of contemporary Chicana/o playwrights.

2. What are the various themes that Chicana/o playwrights emphasize in their works?

3. Discuss the themes in contemporary Chicana/o theater that also appear in autobiographical and narrative fiction works.

4. How are Latins Anonymous and Culture Clash similar to and different from El Teatro Campesino?

■ Suggested Readings

Arrizón, Alicia. 1999. *Latina Performance: Traversing the Stage*. Bloomington: Indiana University Press.

Horno-Delgado, Asunción, et al. 1989. *Breaking Boundaries: Latina Writing and Critical Readings*. Amherst: University of Massachusetts Press.

Huerta, Jorge. 2000. *Chicano Drama: Performance, Society and Myth*. Cambridge: Cambridge University Press.

Sandoval-Sánchez, Alberto, and Nancy Saporta Sternbach. 2001. *Stages of Life: Transcultural Performance and Identity in Latina Theater*. Tucson: University of Arizona Press.

Yarbro-Bejarano, Yvonne. 1985. Chicanas' Experience in Collective Theater: Ideology and Form. *Women and Performance* 2: 45–48.

——. 1986. The Female Subject in Chicano Theater: Sexuality, "Race," and "Class." *Theatre Journal* 38 (4): 389–407.

7

Contemporary Chicana/o Poetry

Chicana/o poetry since the early 1970s has become progressively more sophisticated, nuanced, introspective, and varied than much of the poetry published during the height of the Chicano Movement (see chapter 3). Poets have become more interested and focused on the aesthetic dimensions of their craft without backing off from addressing the trenchant social issues of the past four decades, including continuing racism and discrimination, class stratification, sexism, and homophobia.

In her book *Chicano Poetry: A Critical Introduction* (1986), the Chicana literary scholar Cordelia Candelaria (see figure 30) provides a comprehensive, concise, and thoughtful examination of Chicana/o poetry from about 1965 to the mid-1980s. She divides the development of this body of poetry into distinct phases, with Chicano Movement poetry constituting the first phase. She characterizes the second phase as one during which poets strived for and developed a "poetics," or a composite of the formal and thematic aspects of writing. In the third phase, the movement away from the ideological poetry of the Chicano Movement continues, as poets begin to express more of their individual sentiments rather than speaking for Chicanas/os collectively. Because I have already discussed Chicano Movement poetry in chapter 3, I begin my discussion of contemporary Chicana/o poetry with what Candelaria has identified as second-phase poets. I continue with third-phase poets then summarize poets who have been active in the period since Candelaria wrote her book.

Second-Phase Poets

Although some critics would argue that Alurista should be considered as a poet representative of the Chicano Movement, I believe that Candelaria makes a strong and persuasive case that he is representative of second-phase poets. Candelaria illustrates the general characteristics of the second phase by concentrating on Alurista's earlier works. The poets Inés Tovar, Raúl Salinas, and Leo Romero are among Alurista's contemporaries who

■ 30. Cordelia Candelaria

continued the elements characteristic of his poetry while adding new thematic and formal elements to Chicana/o second-phase poetry (Candelaria 1986, 108–9).

Alurista (Alberto Baltazar Urista)

Alurista (see figure 31) is one of the most influential Chicana/o poets of the last forty years. He was born in 1947 in Mexico City and immigrated to San Diego with his family in 1961. He received a BA degree from San Diego State University in 1970 and MA (1978) and PhD (1983) degrees from the University of California, San Diego. He has taught at several universities.

Alurista became known in the late 1960s and early 1970s for his bold experiments with bilingualism and incorporation of indigenous themes in his work. He has been more successful than most other contemporary Chicana/o poets in combining standard American English, English slang (regional forms including Black English), standard Spanish, Spanish regional dialect forms, English-Spanish bilingualism, and an amalgam of ancient indigenous languages such as Nahua and Mayan (Candelaria 1986, 73). This linguistic experimentation adds an oral dimension to his poetry, one of its key traits, and it is in keeping with Alurista's view that the poet is a public rather than a private artist whose work should be communal in nature and carry a social message. Many of the poems in his first book, *Floricanto en Aztlán* (Flower and Song in Aztlán, 1971), provide excellent examples of his poetic experiments with language.

Candelaria and other scholars have identified categories of symbolism that characterize the second and later phases of Chicana/o poetry and that are present in Alurista's early works. These categories include symbolism from pre-Columbian indigenous mythology and cosmology; symbols of Indian and Spanish mestizo culture; symbolism based on the rhetoric and history of the Chicano

■ 31. Alurista (courtesy of Bilingual Review Press)

Movement (for example, *huelga* [strike], *¡sí se puede!* [you can do it!], UFW, Crystal City); and non-Chicana/o symbolism referring to the Establishment (for example, the Man, Coca-Cola, Them). Candelaria cites the poem, "What's Happening," from *Floricanto en Aztlán*, as an excellent example of the interplay and contrast of Establishment, indigenous, and Chicano Movement symbols.

The experimentation with language and symbolism characteristic of Alurista's first collection of poetry continues in his second book, *Nation-child Plumaroja* (Red Plume Nationchild, 1972), and his third book, *Timespace huracán: Poems, 1972–1975* (Timespace Hurricane, 1976). He went on to publish several additional books of poetry including *A'nque/Alurista* (1979), *Spik in Glyph?* (1981), *Return: Poems Collected and New* (1982), *Z Eros* (1995), *Et Tú . . . Raza?* (1996), and *As the Barrio Turns Who the Yoke B On* (2000).

Along with linguistic experimentation and complex and varied symbolism, ritual is another category that defines the second and later phases of Chicana/o poetry. Alurista epitomizes a strong ritualistic practice in the very frequent public performances he gave at political rallies, *festivales de flor y canto* (festivals celebrating Chicana/o culture through performances and song), college campuses, barrio community centers, and elsewhere during the late 1960s and early 1970s. I was fortunate to have been present at one of Alurista's performances at the University of New Mexico in the late 1960s. Alurista's singing, dancing, and chanting of his own poetry was mesmerizing and deeply moving. Ritualistic elements are also ample in the title of *Floricanto en Aztlán* and in the content of poems from it such as "My Raza," "Mi Pueblo" and "The People."

Inés Hernández Tovar

Inés Hernández Tovar has published only one book of poetry, *Con razón corazón* (Do It Right, Heart, 1977). As her work reflects, Tovar was greatly influenced by Alurista, especially by his style and the strong presence in his poetry of Mexican Indian culture as the roots of Chicanismo. She refers to him in her poem "Chicano-Hermano" (Chicano Brother) and, like Alurista, uses Spanish and bilingual idioms in her verse. In one notable way, Tovar's poetry is different from Alurista's: she explores more abstract meanings of love and other themes, such as the very nature of being, solitude, and the existence of a Mother Goddess (Candelaria 1986, 167).

Raúl Salinas

Raúl Salinas published two works based largely on the twenty years he spent in prison: a 1973 chapbook entitled *Viaje/Trip*; and a 1980 collection of new and previously published poetry titled *Un Trip through the Mind Jail y Otras Excursiones* (A Trip through the Mind Jail and Other Excursions). Like Alurista's poetry, Salinas's poetry is multilingual and ritualistic. Unlike the former poet, however, Salinas refers frequently to his experiences as a drug addict and a prisoner. The "trip" motif reflects not only drug-induced states of consciousness but also his journey through a life of crime and frequent periods of incarceration. Salinas ties his experiences to those of millions of other individuals who through their own failings combined with the very considerable societal obstacles they cannot overcome are enslaved victims.

Leo Romero

Leo Romero is a New Mexican poet who has published a chapbook, *During the Growing Season* (1978), and two collections of poetry, *Agua negra* (Black Water, 1981) and *Celso* (1985). *Agua negra* won the Pushcart Prize "Best of the Small Presses" competition. Romero uses his familiarity with his native state, especially its varied geography, as a background for his rich evocation of beauty and meaning. Candelaria (1986, 118–19) observes that many of Romero's earliest poems—originally published in local newspapers and avidly read in New Mexico and only later collected in his first book—are highly lyrical at a time when Chicana/o social protest poetry was far more common. She compares his pastoral subjects and themes to those in Rudolfo Anaya's *Bless Me, Ultima* (see chapter 3). Both New Mexican writers capture the nature and essence of the land as an essential and living aspect of nuevomexicana/o culture and a reflection of interior states of consciousness.

▊ Third-Phase Poets

Several scholars have noted that Chicana/o poetry of the mid-1970s and 1980s evolved away from the explicitly ideological, often confrontational and combative poetry of the Chicano Movement (Pérez-Torres 1995; Sánchez 1985; Shirley and Shirley 1988; Tatum 1982). This trend is already clear in the second-phase poets just discussed, but it becomes much stronger in the works of poets such as Bernice Zamora and Lorna Dee Cervantes.

Candelaria has identified this trend as constituting a third phase in Chicana/o poetry. Some of the characteristics she associates with this poetry are greater sophistication in style and technique, lyrical subtlety, individuality in the treatment of subject and theme, and mature skill and control of the craft of poetry. She contrasts the sociocultural polarities of the first phase with the tendency of third-phase poets to write as individuals who speak primarily for themselves rather than collectively or didactically on behalf of Chicanas/os. These many different individual perspectives necessarily result in a multiplicity of highly subjective, personal, and more private poetic voices and themes (Candelaria 1986, 137–38).

Also, unlike most of the poets of the first two phases, who learned their craft largely on their own without specific training as writers, many of the poets discussed in this and later sections studied poetry formally in university creative writing or literature programs and established poetry workshops. In this sense, they are similar to the Chicana/o playwrights who benefited immensely from university training and formal workshops (see chapter 6).

Bernice Zamora

Born in Colorado in 1938, Bernice Zamora was married young and later divorced, becoming a single parent of two children. She received her BA degree from Southern Colorado University at the age of thirty-one, followed by an MA degree from Colorado State University in 1972 and a PhD in English and American literature from Stanford University in 1984.

Zamora's sole book of poetry, *Restless Serpents* (1976) represents a decided shift away from the strong and uncompromising message and tone of the Chicano Movement toward a more introspective examination of self within a complex world of often competing gender roles and values. At the same time, her poetry continues to reflect a strong commitment to social justice for her people. The multiplicity of motifs and themes, ranging from some found in the poetry of Alurista and earlier Chicano Movement poets, to art, religion, and death is very much in keeping with the characteristics of the third phase of Chicana/o poetry. Candelaria observes that the intimacy of the poetic voice in Zamora's poetry is a combination of joy and confusion, of love and passion. Her sense of wonder over the complexities and paradoxes of life reflects these sentiments (Candelaria 1986, 147).

Several of the poems in *Restless Serpents* deal with the mythic origins of the Chicana/o people. Her best-known and most anthologized poem, "Restless Serpents," suggests on one level the socioeconomic divide between Chicanas/os and Anglos and on another level points toward less tangible concepts and cultural, spiritual, and archetypal currents underlying humankind in general. Her poetry also points toward the widening divide between male and female participants in the Chicano Movement and Chicanas' increasingly more insistent questioning of the powerful roles that Chicano males have insisted on maintaining. Like these women, Zamora explicitly condemns the exploitation of Chicanas by males within the family, within Chicana/o culture, and in society at large.

Lorna Dee Cervantes

Lorna Cervantes was born in 1954 in San Francisco. She received her BA degree at San Jose State University in 1984. She has published two books of poetry: *Emplumada* (the title has the double meaning of *feathered* and *pen*, 1981), winner of the prestigious University of Pittsburgh Poetry Series award and the Texas-based Before Columbus Foundation American Book Award (hereafter referred to as the American Book Award); and *From the Cables of Genocide: Poems on Love and Hunger* (1991). Cervantes is the founder of Mango Publications and the literary magazine *Red Dirt*.

Candelaria includes Cervantes among a small group of third-phase Chicana/o poets "because of the consistent fineness of her work and because the subject of her poetry is inclusive and wide-ranging" (Candelaria 1986, 156). *Emplumada* is a collection of bilingual and free-verse lyric poetry divided into three sections that foreground the poet's social environment along with its limitations and opportunities, her intimate and positive relationship with the natural world, and her joyful acceptance of dreams and hopes for her future. In the first section, Cervantes draws on childhood memories by calling forth persons and objects that she associates with her cultural ancestry and her sense of being rooted. In the second section, she moves out of childhood memory poems into ones that are descriptive of nature and the feelings and images that nature evokes for her. The third section contains several love poems tinged with regret and hope.

Cervantes displays her considerable talent for painting vivid and strong visual images and evoking different moods, such as mourning, despair, acceptance, hope, and renewal. As other 1970s and 1980s Chicana writers frequently do, Cervantes questions the static and subservient roles to which women in Chicana/a politics are relegated.

Cervantes's mother was brutally killed in 1982, and the trauma, confusion, and sadness the poet felt is reflected in her second book of poetry, *From the Cables of Genocide*. Cervantes also returns to the themes of love, nature, cultural ancestry, and the position of women in the male-dominated Chicano subculture, writing with an artistic self-assuredness and maturity that has reinforced a consensus among Chicana/o literary critics that Cervantes is one of the finest poets of the past thirty years. This consensus is all the more remarkable in view of her relatively modest production of two books.

Other Third-Phase Chicana Poets

Along with Bernice Zamora and Lorna Dee Cervantes, several other Chicana poets stand out in different ways during the third phase of Chicana/o poetry: Carmen Tafolla, Evangelina Vigil-Piñón, Alma Luz Villanueva, Lucha Corpi, and Sandra Cisneros.

CARMEN TAFOLLA In her two books of poetry, *Get Your Tortillas Together* (1976) and *Curandera* (1983), Carmen Tafolla demonstrates what the Chicano scholar Rafael Pérez-Torres (1995, 220) refers to as an "interlanguage," or a kind of linguistic mestizaje; that is, a combination of two distinct languages to create a unique third language. For example, in her 1983 poem "La Isabela de Guadalupe y el Apache Mio Cid," Tafolla appeals to prominent historical figures from disparate cultures (Isabela, the Spanish Queen of Castile who financed Christopher Columbus's journeys; Mio Cid, a medieval Spanish epic poetry hero; and el Apache, a brave Indian who resisted conquest by both Mexico and the United States). Like many Chicana poets and narrative fiction writers, Tafolla also reappropriates and redefines cultural figures such as la Virgen de Guadalupe.

EVANGELINA VIGIL-PIÑÓN   Evangelina Vigil-Piñón has published a chapbook of poems, *Nada y nadie* (Nothing and No One, 1978), and two collections of poetry: *Thirty an' Seen a Lot* (1982) and *The Computer Is Down* (1987). The poet acknowledges her literary relationship to Chicano intellectuals and poets such as Américo Paredes and José Montoya, but also speaks with the independent voice of a strong Chicana feminist who while recognizing the positive traits of family and culture, also boldly criticizes them. As the title indicates, *The Computer Is Down* takes the reader on a journey through a thoroughly modern but dehumanizing and alienating urban landscape. Vigil-Piñón conveys through her poetry that although her allegiance to her culture, its institutions, and its values cannot be unquestioning, in the end they constitute her moorings as she ventures forth into an often hostile Anglo world.

ALMA LUZ VILLANUEVA   Alma Luz Villanueva is not only a prolific novelist but a fine poet who has published several poetry collections: *Bloodroot* (1977), *Poems* (1977), *Mother, May I?* (1978), and *Life Span* (1985). Central to both her poetry and her narrative fiction is her concept of womanhood as a positive and affirming life force that is invigorated by passion—especially sexual passion—for natural love, the reproductive cycle, family, and her mixed German/Chicana ancestry. Like other Chicana feminists, she affirms the inherent value and strength of women and considers that the feminine individualism that springs from these qualities is key to overcoming male dominance, particularly within Chicana/o traditional culture.

LUCHA CORPI   Lucha Corpi also deals with sexual passion and male-female relationships within Chicana/o culture in her two bilingual books of poetry: *Palabras de mediodía/Noon Words* (1982); and *Variaciones sobre una tempestad/Variations on a Storm* (1990). Unlike many Chicana/o poets, who combine English, Spanish, and barrio slang, Corpi originally writes her poems in Spanish, then translates them into English; the two versions appear side by side in her books. Pérez-Torres (1995, 196–201) has observed that Corpi's first collection lacks the polemical tone of much other Chicana/o poetry. In the best tradition of lyrical poetry, Corpi's poetry is sensual and highly evocative of deep feelings ranging from love to betrayal. Many of her poems are short meditations on the pleasure of rain, the comfort of sweets, and other everyday experiences.

SANDRA CISNEROS   Although much better known as a writer of narrative fiction (see chapter 5), Sandra Cisneros also enjoys a solid reputation as a poet. She received her BA degree from Loyola University (1976) and her MFA degree in creative writing from the very prestigious University of Iowa/Iowa Writer's Workshop (1978). Although only one of her books, *Bad Boys* (1980), falls within the timeframe of the third phase of Chicana/o poetry, I include her in this section because *Bad Boys* is entirely consistent in theme and tone with her two subsequent books, *My Wicked, Wicked Ways* (1987) and *Loose Woman: Poems* (1994), which appeared several years later. Like the other Chicana poets discussed in this section, Cisneros deals frequently with gender relationships, but as the titles of her poetry collections reflect, she does so in a much more explicit way. Tey Diana Rebolledo (1995, 183) includes Cisneros among a group of Chicana writers she calls "mujeres andariegas" (women who wander and roam) and "mujeres callejeras" (street women) because they write about their heterosexual, bisexual, or lesbian sexuality in a bold and frank manner "as an important step towards healing the wounds of racism, homophobia, and marginalization." For Cisneros, "wickedness" means having transgressed or "sinned" against parental expectations, the church, and the very norms of society. Many of the poems in her three poetry collections illustrate her in-your-face stance as she expresses her sentiments about behaviors that "good" Chicanas would only imagine.

■ Chicana/o Poetry from the Mid-1980s Forward

This last section includes a discussion of two groups of Chicana/o poets. First are those who began publishing their work prior to the mid-1980s and have continued to be both productive and innovative in the practice of their craft through the 1990s and in some cases into the first decade of the twenty-first century. The poetry of poets like Gary Soto, Alberto Ríos, Jimmy Santiago Baca, Pat Mora, Ana Castillo, Juan Felipe Herrera, Francisco X. Alarcón, and Benjamin Alire Sáenz has at least some of the characteristics and traits of the third phase of Chicana/o poetry just discussed, but their poetry has evolved and changed. Second are those poets who began to publish their work more recently and who show great promise, poets like Ray Gonzalez, Demetria Martínez, Luis J. Rodríguez, and Luis Alberto Urrea.

Gary Soto

As mentioned in chapter 4, Gary Soto (see figure 32) was born in Fresno, California, in 1952. He has become one of the finest and most versatile writers of his generation. Soto received a BA degree from California State University, Fresno (1974). Crucial to his development as a poet was the mentoring he received from the critically acclaimed American poet Philip Levine, a creative writing professor at CSUF. He went on to earn an MFA in creative writing from the University of California, Irvine (1976). Soto has taught at several universities.

Soto has won numerous national literary awards and fellowships including the Discovery-Nation prize, 1975; the United States Award, International Poetry Forum, 1976, for his first book of poetry, *The Elements of San Joaquin*; the Bess Hokin Prize from *Poetry*, 1978; a Pulitzer Prize nomination, 1978; a Guggenheim Fellowship, 1979; several National Endowment for the Arts fellowships; and the Levison Award from *Poetry*, 1984.

The Elements of San Joaquin (1977) is perhaps Soto's signature book of poetry, at least until the publication, in 1995, of *New and Selected Poems*. *The Elements* is divided into three parts: the first section consists of six poems in which Soto presents images of Fresno in the 1950s; the second and longest section contains twenty poems in which he focuses on the hardscrabble life in the agricultural fields of the San Joaquin Valley; and the third section draws on his memories of childhood. The "elements" refer to earth, air, fire, and water. These elements are essential parts of the Fresno cityscape, the agricultural landscapes, and the fragments of a childhood existence affected deeply by the surrounding factories, streets, and fields populated by Chicanas/os and recently arrived immigrant Mexicans, Asians, and Anglos. In the second section, which gives the book its title, Soto gazes outward from Fresno's poor barrios of factory workers and farmworkers to the agricultural fields and rural areas that surround the city. Soto alternates between presenting the great beauty of nature and the misery of the workers and their families that it cradles. Dirt, wind, and heat all seem to conspire to wear down and defeat the farmworkers' bodies and spirits as they participate in a never-ending cycle of backbreaking work in the fields and packing sheds. The third section of the book is more directly autobiographical than the first two, as Soto draws on the positive and negative memories of his childhood and adolescence.

In his second book of poetry, *The Tale of Sunlight* (1978), Soto departs from the rural and city settings associated with the socioeconomic circumstances of a Chicano childhood.

■ 32. Gary Soto

The geographical and spatial context of this second book is much expanded to include Mexico and Latin America: Taxco, Panama, Colombia, Peru, Brazil, and the Orinoco River. Social criticism is not lacking in *Tale*, but Soto expresses it more subtly and in a more general way than he does in *Elements*. In *Where Sparrows Work Hard* (1981), Soto continues to render poetically the lives of the poor and downtrodden who, like the common and unnoticed birds of the title, struggle endlessly to survive in a world of physical hardship imposed by their social class and economic status. The lives of the factory and seasonal agricultural workers are bound together by friendships, family loyalties, and the very commonality of hard labor that contributes to their perseverance in a world beset by elemental issues of survival.

After *Where Sparrows Work Hard* Soto did not publish another book of poetry for four years. By the time *Black Hair* appeared in 1985, he had become more confident in his command of poetic diction, which had become more abstract, and in his philosophical exploration of themes such as childhood, relationships, and death. He published two books of poetry in rapid succession five and six years after *Black Hair: Who Will Know Us?* (1990) and *Home Course in Religion* (1991). Common images of a working people's California are distributed throughout his poems. The agricultural fields of the San Joaquin Valley dominant in his earlier poetry are again present but so are roadside cafes and diners, pets, cemeteries, trains in the distance, perfect houses behind white picket fences, small rural towns, radios blaring on a lazy summer afternoon, and feeding time at the local zoo. In *Home Course in Religion* Soto addresses the topic of religion more explicitly than in any previous book of poetry. He expresses nostalgia for some of the trappings of Catholicism and reflects on how the Catholic Church has changed since his childhood.

New and Selected Poems (1995) brought Soto well-deserved national recognition. This collection, consisting mainly of selections from all of his previously published books, was selected as a finalist for the National Book Award. Only the last section, "Super-Eight Movies," contains new poems. The new poems resonate with Soto's earlier poetry, foregrounding some of the same themes. In his next book of poetry, *Junior College* (1997), Soto alternates between serious, even somber, retrospective poems and lighter humorous poems that capture a young man's introduction to post–high school education. *A Natural Man* (1999) is Soto's most recently published collection of poetry. It picks up on some of the themes in *Junior College*, loops back to some themes in his earlier poetry, and reveals the poet in his mid-forties who is beginning to reflect in a more focused way on questions surrounding life's mysteries, including death itself.

Alberto Alvaro Ríos

Alberto Alvaro Ríos (see figure 33) whose autobiographical work *Capirotada* is discussed in chapter 4, is another outstanding Chicana/o writer of fiction, nonfiction, and poetry. He received both his BA (1973) and MFA (1979) degrees in creative writing from the University of Arizona. He is currently Regents Professor at Arizona State University. Like Soto, Ríos is best known as an award-winning poet. He took first place in the Academy of American Arts poetry contest in 1977 while he was still a graduate student. He received the very prestigious Walt Whitman Award from the National Academy of American Poets for his first book of poetry, *Whispering to Fool the Wind* (1982), and was one of five finalists for the 2002 National Book Award in the poetry category for *The Smallest Muscle in the Human Body* (2002). Between *Whispering to Fool the Wind* and *The Smallest Muscle in the Human Body*, Ríos published three other books of poetry: *Five Indiscretions* (1985), *The Lime Orchard Woman* (1988), and *Teodoro Luna's Two Kisses* (1990). Ríos's poetry has been widely anthologized.

As is true for numerous Chicana/o writers, Ríos's loss of his first language, Spanish, has profoundly influenced and informed all his work. Although he regrets not maintaining Spanish as a child and adolescent, he learned a valuable lesson from the loss. He learned what he calls a "third language of non-words," that is not English, Spanish, nor a hybrid of the two, but rather a language of the body that has served him well as a poet. The much anthologized poem "Nani," from *Whispering to Fool the Wind*, is an excellent example of how he uses this third language. The poem is about having lunch with his grandmother, a monolingual Spanish speaker, during which they "talk" almost completely nonverbally by means of the food, *albóndigas* (meatball) soup, that she tenderly and lovingly prepares for him. The food they share bridges both language and cultural barriers.

33. Alberto Alvaro Ríos

In *Five Indiscretions*, his second book of poetry, Ríos emphasizes the interrelated themes of desire, sexuality, and religion. The poems in the first part of the collection are written from a woman's perspective. They deal with the constraints that religion in general and Roman Catholicism in particular place on the expression of sexuality, especially for women. Some of the poems in this section also debunk the myth that rape is an expression of sexuality as opposed to an act of aggression and physical assault. In the second part, Ríos shifts to the masculine perspective of, in particular, the expression of sexuality and love. In the third part, he focuses on the sometimes painful courtship of young lovers who outgrow their awkwardness and discomfort and learn to relate to each other in tender and longing ways. In the fourth and final part, Ríos draws on his own family history.

In his latest book of poetry, *The Smallest Muscle in the Human Body*, Ríos expresses what he has called his mission as a poet: to nurture a keener sensitivity and sharper awareness about things, events, and feelings that exist beyond the areas (of, for example, the body or emotions) that are protected. He describes the poetry in this book, and in fact all of his poetry, as being guided by the "science of the single event" situated in different cultures and languages. Most of the poems in his recent book of poetry deal with such single events.

Jimmy Santiago Baca

Jimmy Santiago Baca recounts in his autobiography, *A Place to Stand: The Making of a Poet*, his remarkable development as a poet (see chapter 4). He has been prolific as a poet, having published more than nine books of poetry since 1977 when his first book, *Immigrants in Our Own Land*, appeared. Baca draws heavily on his own experiences in most of his poetry, especially in the first several books. His prison years, especially the brutality of prison life, figure prominently in *Immigrants*. Baca has won several prestigious literary prizes, including a National Endowment of Poetry Award, a Vogelstein Foundation Award, a National Hispanic Heritage Award, a Berkeley Regents Award, a Pushcart Prize, and an American Book Award. He also was a guest writer at Yale University, where he held the Wallace Stevens Chair.

The first poem in *Immigrants*, "The Sun on Those," highlights the dramatic loss of freedom and legal rights that occurs when one crosses the threshold into a prison facility. Baca contrasts this lack of freedom to the birds flying overhead that he glimpses from the prison yard, as well as to the trees and animals that he can see at a distance through the prison bars. At the same time, he foregrounds very graphic images of prison brutality between the prisoners themselves and by prison guards, who beat the prisoners in the name of keeping order. The entire book, the publication of which coincided with his release from prison in 1979, reflects Baca's strong desire to regain a sense of self after the years of dehumanization, humiliation, and physical and emotional pain he underwent. In *What's Happening* (1982) Baca continues to pursue through poetry a sense of individual identity and self-worth by establishing a connection with the land that is such an integral aspect of his *nuevomexicano* ancestral roots. On a more abstract level, he also explores the redemptive power of human ties and long-term relationships.

Baca lived for a short time in the city of Albuquerque before moving with his family to a house on a piece of land in the city's South Valley. *Poems Taken from My Yard* (1986) focuses on Baca's deep feelings of tenderness as a father and his connection to his firstborn child during the winter of his birth, when Baca was rebuilding an adobe house for his family. In *Martín and Meditations on the South Valley* (1987), best described as a long narrative poem, Baca continues to explore his role as husband and father, but mainly he takes the reader back to the very painful and traumatic years of his childhood and adolescence.

In *Black Mesa Poems* (1989), Baca's poetic vision expands to encompass the Chicana/o people who come from Indian, Spanish, and Mexican forebears. Martín, the "speaker" in his previous book of poetry, continues in this book to be Baca's thinly disguised autobiographical voice. Baca also explores more broadly the complex historical dynamics that have played out in the Southwest since Anglos arrived and began to interact politically and socially with the peoples that had preceded them. The poet seems keen to find a sense of balance and harmony from the clash of diverse cultures that has brought so much strife and suffering.

Baca has published several books since *Black Mesa Poems*, including *Healing Earthquakes: A Love Story in Poems* (2001), *C-train (Dream Boy's Story), and Thirteen Mexicans: Poems* (2002), and *Winter Poems along the Rio Grande* (2004). *Healing Earthquakes* is very long for a collection of poetry. It consists of five parts, or "books," each of which focuses on different stages of a man and woman's relationship from its tentative beginning to bittersweet end. In *C-train* we follow a young Chicano's difficult journey to kick a serious cocaine addiction—the *C* in the title—with the support of a loving and understanding community of families. Baca makes his connection with nature more explicit in *Winter Poems along the Rio Grande* than in his previously published works. A connection to and within nature is a part of Baca's belief in a Creator to whom he can pray for guidance, wisdom, and forgiveness.

Pat Mora

Pat Mora (see figure 34) was born in 1942 in El Paso, Texas. She received BA (1963) and MA (1967) degrees from the University of Texas, El Paso. Mora has published several collections of poetry in addition to works of nonfiction narrative and children's literature (see chapter 5). Among the recognitions she has received for her creative writing are a Southwest Book Award for *Chants* (1984), her first book of poetry; a Southwest Book Award for *Borders* (1986), her second book of poetry; and a National Endowment for the Arts fellowship in creative writing. Her third book of poetry is entitled *Communion* (1991).

In her poetry, Mora draws heavily on her experiences of growing up as a bilingual, bicultural Chicana on the U.S.–Mexico border in the midst of the Chihuahuan Desert. In fact, in many of her poems, she metaphorically links women to the positive aspects of the desert such as its beauty and the ability of its flora and fauna to survive and even thrive under harsh condi-

34. Pat Mora (photo by Cheron Bayna)

tions. She believes that women like herself who grow up in the desert acquire some of its resilience and strength.

As the title of *Borders* indicates, borders also play a very important metaphorical role in her poetry. She often portrays the dual character of borders: on one hand, border dwellers have the advantage of having a broad perspective of two cultures and their respective languages, values, and other characteristics; on the other hand, Chicanas/os are often made to feel like outsiders. They are not fully accepted as citizens on the U.S. side of the border nor are they accepted as authentic Mexicans on the Mexican side. Mora sees the border in terms of social class and racism, not just as a philosophical construct for writers to contemplate, debate, and write about.

Ana Castillo

Ana Castillo is better known as a writer of narrative fiction and nonfiction, but she is also a respected poet. Born in Chicago in 1953, she received BA (1975), and MA (1977) degrees from the University of Chicago, and a PhD in American studies from the University of Bremen, Germany (1991). She currently teaches at DePaul University in Chicago.

Much of Castillo's poetry is confrontational and provides a vehicle for social protest. She has published three collections: *Women Are Not Roses* (1984), *My Father Was a Toltec: Poems* (1988; republished as *My Father Was a Toltec and Selected Poems, 1973–1988*), and *I Ask the Impossible: Poems* (2001). Like the poetry of some of the third-phase and later Chicana/o poets, many of Castillo's poems are expressions of romantic love; for her, love constitutes an important element of women's strength and resistance in the face of patriarchal attitudes and practices. She departs from much of male lyric poetry, which tends to romanticize and idealize the female object of desire as being devoid of the capacity to feel and return love.

Alongside the more personal, lyrical strain in Castillo's poetry is one which is denunciatory of the injustices and racist practices that she perceives the dominant Anglo society to have perpetrated on Chicanas/os as well as on other historically oppressed groups. From her earliest poetry she has dealt with issues of the day such as the United Farm Workers Union campaigns against exploitative growers in California, active Chicana/o resistance against violent and discriminatory police behavior in the barrio, oppressive military regimes in Latin America, and the horrible mistreatment of innocent children.

Juan Felipe Herrera

Juan Felipe Herrera (see figure 35) was born in California in 1948. He received a BA degree from UCLA (1972), an MA from Stanford University (1980), and an MFA in creative writing from the University of Iowa/Iowa Writer's Workshop (1990). He currently teaches at California State University, Fresno.

Herrera is probably the most prolific of contemporary Chicana/o poets. His poetry is like a teleplay, with a highly innovative melding of standard verse, prose, journal entries, letters, and other genres. His poetry performances are very effective and popular with audiences, no doubt due to his extensive experience in theater during the 1970s and 1980s. He often disarms audiences with a combination of poetry, comedy, and music that leaves the impression he is a vato loco who has just walked onstage from the street.

Herrera's first book of poetry, *Rebozos of Love/We Have Woven/Sudor de Pueblos/On Our Back* (1974), is reflective of some of the themes and language use seen in Chicano Movement poetry, especially with regard to the prominent role indigenous cultures have played in the formation of the contemporary Chicana/o consciousness. Herrera then published several books of poetry in the 1980s: *Exiles of Desire* (1983), *Facegames* (1987), and *Akrilica* (1989). He has subsequently published more than a dozen collections of poetry: *Memorias from an Exile's Notebook of the Future* (1993), *The Roots of a Thousand Embraces: Dialogues* (1994), *Night Train to Tuxtla* (1994), *187 Reasons Why Mexicanos Can't Cross the Border* (1995), *Love after the Riots* (1996), *Mayan Drifter: Chicano Poet in the Lowlands of America* (1997), *Lotería Cards and Fortune Poems: A Book of Lives* (1999), *Border-Crosser with a Lamborghini Dream* (1999), *Thunderweavers/Tejedoras de rayos* (2000), *Giraffe on Fire* (2001), and *Notebooks of a Chile Verde Smuggler*

■ 35. Juan Felipe Herrera

(2002). Herrera has received a lot of recognition for his poetry, including awards from the National Endowment for the Arts; the Breadloaf Fellowship in Poetry (1990); the University of California, Berkeley, Regents' Fellowship (1997); and the Americas Award (2000).

Although it is difficult to describe adequately the wide variety of themes, images, and motifs in Herrera's extensive work over thirty years, the titles of many of his books suggest that movement, traveling, and journeys are important interrelated elements. In "Train Notes," the introduction to his 1994 book *Night Train to Tuxtla*, he credits his love for and philosophy of travel to his father: "My father had the quixotic belief that moving changed one's body cells and kept the world fresh" (Herrera 1994a, ix). In several poems in this collection, Herrera draws on his own travels and meanderings as a child and an adult. He attempts to create a sense of common historical and cultural identity and solidarity between U.S. Chicanas/os and their brothers and sisters in the United States and in Latin America. *Mayan Drifter* is situated in the Mayan region of southern Mexico. Herrera contrasts his own privileged position as a traveler from the United States to the poverty and struggles of the Lacandon peoples of Chiapas.

Herrera's poetry is also characterized by his experimental use of jarring imagery and abrupt juxtapositions of disparate elements, devices that have been compared to 1950s and 1960s Beat poetry, art, and jazz. These elements are already present in *Akrilica*, an early book in which, for example, he draws on the language of visual art for the title and in the organization of the work's six sections. He juxtaposes some visual elements with the written form as he asks us to see his poems as representing objects that might be hanging in an art gallery.

One of Herrera's recent books of poetry, *Notebooks of a Chile Verde Smuggler*, is a kind of poetic autobiography, but unlike most autobiographies, Herrera does not lay out his life chronologically; instead, he presents it in a fractured way, alternating back and forth among various moments and locations in his past. He presents a poetic overview of his rich but sometimes chaotic life, as well as some of the major themes in his poetry. As always, he is self-deprecating, mercilessly sharp in his criticism of individual behaviors and institutions, and cuttingly humorous in his satire. He will surely continue to publish at a steady pace in the future.

Francisco X. Alarcón

Francisco Alarcón was born in California in 1954. He received a BA degree from California State University, Long Beach (1977) and an MA degree from Stanford University (1979). Among his collections of poetry are *Tattoos* (1985), *Quake Poems* (1989), *Body in Flames/Cuerpo en llamas* (1990), *De amor Oscuro* (Of Dark Love, 1991), *Snake Poems* (1992), *No Golden Gate for Us* (1993), and *From the Other Side of Night: New and Selected Poems/Del otro lado de la noche* (2002). Alarcón generally writes in Spanish then translates his own poetry into English for publication, although others have translated his poetry as well. His has won many awards, including a Fulbright Fellowship and an American Book Award for *Snake Poems*. He currently teaches at the University of California, Santa Cruz.

Alarcón is an activist, performer, and professor. Although he is openly gay, most of his poetry does not directly reflect this. His first book, *Tattoos*, grew out of a very difficult personal situation when he was questioned by the police as a murder suspect. The poems in this volume are very short, almost abrupt, and evoke in their sharpness some of the psychological wounds he must have sustained seeing his name appear repeatedly in San Francisco Bay Area newspapers. The northern California earthquake of 1989 that created havoc and destruction in Santa Cruz, where he was teaching, inspired his second book of poetry, *Quake Poems*, in which he reflects on the human cost of the disaster and especially on the pettiness and greed exhibited by some who took advantage of others' misfortune and vulnerability.

Body in Flames/Cuerpo en llamas, a longer and more introspective collection than the first two, reflects Alarcón's maturation as a poet. He focuses on the mixed emotions he experienced as a child in a traditional Chicana/o family and his first experiences with racism and prejudice in school; adolescence and beginning to come to terms with his gayness in his own homophobic culture and in the wider society; acceptance of his sexuality; and reflection on death and loss that ends with his own epitaph. In this collection, he also reflects in a philosophical vein on the separation of body and spirit, using his own sexuality and how it is perceived by others as a case in point.

Snake Poems is subtitled *An Aztec Invocation* and indicates Alarcón's full and proud embrace of his own heritage. This is his first book of poems directed to young adults, especially Latinas/os but also those of other ethnic and racial groups who share a sense of confusion and anger at a society that does not acknowledge or value their culture, including the beauty and deep spirituality of the Aztecs. He implicitly invites his young readers to see that they are the inheritors of a rich and life-affirming cultural heritage.

Benjamin Alire Sáenz

Benjamin Alire Sáenz was born close to Las Cruces, New Mexico, in 1954. He received a BA degree from St. Thomas Seminary (1972), an MA degree from the University of Louvain in Belgium (1980), and an MA in creative writing from the University of Texas, El Paso (UTEP), in 1988. He attended Stanford University (1988–89) as a Stegner Fellow; he also received an equally prestigious Lannan Poetry Fellowship. Sáenz, who is respected for his narrative fiction, has published three books of poetry: *Calendar of Dust* (1991), for which he received an American Book Award; *Dark and Perfect Angels* (1995); and *Elegies in Blue* (2002). He currently is a faculty member at UTEP.

In *Calendar of Dust*, Sáenz celebrates the indigenous peoples of the Southwest as well as those who migrated to its lands (Spanish, Mexican, Anglo, and Asian). He also recognizes the hardships of those who have suffered from racism and other travesties and laments the destruction of some of the region's beauty and spirituality (for example, the explosion of the first atomic bomb at Trinity Site in New Mexico in 1945) as well as the unjust exile of whole groups of people from the region (for example, the deportation of Mexicans) and the exile of peoples to it (for example, undocumented workers from Mexico). The final poems are more hopeful as the poet reminds us that, as the title suggests, we can resurrect ourselves from despair and hopelessness.

Dark and Perfect Angels is a kind of eulogy for the ancestors, family, and friends who have despaired or have passed on. At the same time, Sáenz celebrates their triumphs over despair, trauma, and unspeakable suffering and the inspiration and joy that their triumphs, love, and caring have had on his own life. *Elegies in Blue* consists of a series of long prose poems about human conflicts, especially those that occur repeatedly along the U.S.–Mexico border. Sáenz also addresses the complexities that result when peoples from disparate cultural traditions and histories meet and try to reckon with each other. He ends the book on a tenuous note of vowing to redeem himself, not in a narrowly religious way, but in a more secularly spiritual way through drawing strength from his human and natural surroundings.

Leroy Quintana

Leroy Quintana was born in New Mexico in 1944. He received a BA degree from the University of New Mexico (1971) and two MA degrees from, respectively, New Mexico State University (1974) and Western New Mexico University (1984). He currently teaches at San Diego Mesa College. He has published several books of poetry including *Hijo del pueblo: New Mexico Poems* (Son of the People, 1976); *Sangre* (Blood, 1981), for which he won an American Book Award; *Interrogations* (1992); *The History of Home* (1993); *My Hair Turning Grey among Strangers* (1996); and *The Great Whirl of Exile* (1999). He has also published several collections of short narrative fiction.

In several collections of his poetry—especially in *Hijo del Pueblo*, *Sangre*, and *History of Home*—Quintana draws heavily from his New Mexico cultural roots, including the strong oral tradition that persists among nuevomexicanas/os and the lives of *los ancianas/os* (the old ones), who still cling to their traditional religious and secular values and customs. His view of this rich tradition is not nostalgic, but rather he sees it as the source of truths that have sustained him throughout his life and have helped him through difficult periods, such as his tour of duty in Vietnam (1967–69) at the height of U.S. involvement, when casualties among soldiers and civilians were mounting at an alarming rate. Quintana laments that ancient nuevomexicana/o traditions are fast disappearing, threatened increasingly by the bureaucratic and indifferent world of the city that is spreading to rural areas. In *My Hair Turning Gray among Strangers*, he expresses a longing to reconnect with what age and distance have taken from him: the emotional comfort and spirituality of his New Mexico childhood within the bosom of life in traditional communities.

In *Interrogations*, Quintana deals with the trauma of his Vietnam War experiences, focusing on his own hardships, loss of trust, and the psychological distance he felt from family and friends back home. He also laments the human toll suffered by both Americans and Vietnamese in the face of a dehumanized war machine. The images of war from the poetry in this collection are spare, stark, and graphic in their evocation of the dehumanizing effects of such conflicts on the active participants and innocent victims. Quintana recognizes that he has become the invader just like the Anglos who invaded the land of his ancestors.

Other Chicana/o Poets

Included in this section are poets whose published works have appeared over the past twenty years but who have not been as extensively recognized as the poets discussed in the previous section. These poets are Ray Gonzalez, Demetria Martínez, Luis J. Rodríguez, and Luis Alberto Urrea.

Known mostly for his narrative nonfiction, Ray Gonzalez has published several books of poetry including *From the Restless Roots* (1986), *Twilights and Chants: Poems* (1987), *The Heat of Arrivals* (1996), *Cabato Sentora* (1998), *Turtle Pictures* (2000), *The Hawk Temple at Tierra Grande* (2002), and *The Religion of Hands* (2005). His poetic language is at once accessible and striking for its purity and starkness. As with his autobiographical works (see chapter 4), Gonzalez's poetry is imbued with imagery of the Southwest in general and the Chihuahuan Desert in particular, including numerous references to its native peoples and its flora and fauna, such as cacti, creosote, snakes, scorpions, and lizards. The U.S.–Mexico border also plays a prominent role in his poetry, as it does in his narrative nonfiction works.

Known best for her short novel *Mother Tongue*, Demetria Martínez (see figure 36) has published two books of poetry, *Breathing between the Lines* (1997) and *The Devil's Workshop* (2002). She was one of three Chicana poets included in *Three Times a Woman: Chicana Poetry* (Gaspar de Alba, Herrera-Sobek, and Martínez 1989). As in her novel, Martínez draws extensively on her personal experiences of growing up Chicana in a patriarchal culture. She also refers to her intense involvement in the events surrounding the 1980s Sanctuary Movement, in which Chicano Movement activists brought thousands of Central Americans across the U.S.–Mexico border and harbored them in their homes and churches. The thematic threads that run through her poetry can be clustered around the broad themes of love, religion, war, U.S. foreign policy, and feminism. Her poems are almost always simple and direct, seemingly distilled down to the very basic essence of a feeling, an observation, a startling image, or a wry comment.

Luis J. Rodríguez is known best for his award-winning autobiography, *Always Running* (see chapter 4) and his narrative fiction (see chapter 5). He has recently published a very favorably reviewed novel, *Music of the Mill* (2005) about union organizing (and union busting) in the Los Angeles steel industry from the 1960s through the 1980s, when steel companies and other heavy industries closed their doors and moved to other locales in the United States and to foreign countries where they could pay far, far lower wages than they could in California. In addition to these literary accomplishments, Rodríguez is also an award-winning poet with two collections of poetry: *The Concrete River* (1991), which received the PEN Oakland Josephine Miles Award; and *Trochemoche* (Helter-Skelter, 1998).

36. Demetria Martínez
(photo by Douglas Kent Hall)

Reviewers have cited his poetry's lyrical beauty, exacting images, and artful use of street talk. As in Rodríguez's autobiography and narrative fiction, the mean streets of the barrio inhabited by violent gangs; drug pushers; and abusers, pimps, and prostitutes are found on practically every page of his poetry. He also raises some of the causes of these social problems, in particular the social and economic stratification and the racism that exist in society in general as well as in the barrio itself. At the same time, he finds personal redemption possible in ancestral religious practices, personal will and choice, and love and positive modeling from parents, family, and true friends.

Like Rodríguez, Luis Alberto Urrea is prolific and highly recognized for his narrative nonfiction and fiction. He has recently published a very long novel, *The Hummingbird's Daughter* (2005), based on the life of the Mexican folk saint Teresita de Urrea, a distant relative, who came into prominence in northwest Mexico during and after the Mexican Revolution. And again, like Rodríguez, Urrea is an award-winning poet. His collection *The Fever of Being* (1994), won a Western States Book Award in 1994. His poetry explores some of the same rich thematic veins that run through the rest of his work, most notably the very significant problems of border populations and their dignity and forbearance in the face of daunting socioeconomic obstacles.

The future bodes well for Chicana/o poetry. Like narrative nonfiction, fiction, and theater, it is thriving as more and more young and emerging poets—many of them graduates of some of the finest U.S. creative writing programs—begin to publish in prestigious poetry magazines and journals as well as with highly respected small and university presses. Although I have not reviewed them in my discussion of contemporary Chicana/o poets, several young poets show great promise and are just beginning to become better known. These poets include Sarah Cortez, David Domínguez, Diana García, Rigoberto González, Valerie Martínez, Naomí Helena Quiñónez, Renato Rosaldo, and Dixie Salazar. Undoubtedly, I have left out other poets whose work has not come to my attention. I regret these omissions.

◼ Discussion Questions

1. Discuss the general characteristics of second-phase poetry and how it differs from the poetry of the Chicano Movement.

2. How does the poetry of Alurista reflect the general characteristics of second-phase poetry?

3. Discuss how the characteristics of third-phase poetry are found in poets such as Gary Soto, Alberto Alvaro Ríos, and Jimmy Santiago Baca.

4. What are some of the common themes in the poetry of Chicana poets over the past thirty years?

◼ Suggested Readings

Arteaga, Alfred. 1997. *Chicano Poetics: Heterotexts and Hybridities.* Cambridge: Cambridge University Press.

Bruce-Novoa, Juan. 1982. *Chicano Poetry: A Response to Chaos.* Austin: University of Texas Press.

Candelaria, Cordelia. 1986. *Chicano Poetry: A Critical Introduction.* Westport, CT: Greenwood Press.

Hancock, Joel. 1973. The Emergence of Chicano Poetry: A Survey of Sources, Themes, and Techniques. *Arizona Quarterly* 29 (1): 57–73.

Olguín, B. V. 2004. Jimmy Santiago Baca. In *Latino and Latina Writers*, ed. Alan West-Durán, 161–71. New York: Charles Scribner's Sons.

Pérez-Torres, Rafael. 1995. *Movements in Chicano Poetry.* Cambridge: Cambridge University Press.

Saldívar, José David. 1986. Towards a Chicano Poetics: The Making of the Chicano-Chicana Subject. *Confluencia* 1 (2): 10–17.

Sánchez, Marta Ester. 1985. *Contemporary Chicana Poetry: A Critical Approach to an Emerging Literature.* Berkeley and Los Angeles: University of California Press.

Wooten, Leslie A. 2003. Interview with Alberto Alvaro Ríos. *World Literature Today* 77: 57–60.

Conclusion

I hope that this book has led you to appreciate and understand the variety, dynamism, complexity, and evolution of Chicana/o literature over the centuries and particularly during the past several decades. And perhaps as important, I hope that you have become sufficiently interested in and curious about Chicana/o literature to develop a much deeper knowledge of the authors and their works to which I have briefly introduced you. After all, there is no meaningful substitute for your reading the texts themselves; no description of a poem, a theater piece, a novel, or other work can adequately capture or convey the eloquence, emotional impact, or intellectual stimulation that can result from your direct encounter with the work.

Chicana/o literature will in the future play an increasingly more important and prominent role within the larger context of U.S. literature. At the same time that publishing enterprises such as Arte Público Press and Bilingual Review Press will continue to be essential outlets for Chicana/o authors, especially those who are largely unknown, university and mainstream commercial presses are increasingly becoming more receptive to publishing the works of both established and new writers. A sure sign of the vitality of Chicana/o literature is that limitations of space and time have necessarily resulted in my exclusion from this book of many worthy authors. Another indicator of its vitality is that this book, like any introduction to contemporary literature, is out of date as soon as it is published.

As I have emphasized throughout this book, Chicana/o literature provides a window through which to view the historical, political, cultural, and social aspects of a segment of U.S. society that is rapidly growing and is already by far the largest component of the total population of Latinas/os in this country. From the earliest, sixteenth-century chronicles of the Spanish period, through the poetry and narrative fiction of the second half of the nineteenth century and the first half of the twentieth century, and the flowering of all literary genres in the post–Chicano Movement years, Chicana/o literature amply reflects the hopes and aspirations as well as the frustrations and disillusionments of an often marginalized population. If for no other reason than this, a familiarity with the broad sweep of Chicana/o literature can lead us to better understand today's Americans of Mexican descent.

■ PHOTO CREDITS

■ WORKS CONSULTED

Acosta, Oscar "Zeta." 1989a. *The Autobiography of a Brown Buffalo.* New York: Vintage Books. (Originally published in 1972)

——. 1989b. *The Revolt of the Cockroach People.* New York: Vintage Books. (Originally published in 1973)

Acuña, Rodolfo. 2000. *Occupied America: A History of Chicanos.* New York: Longman.

Alarcón, Francisco X. 1985. *Tattoos.* Oakland: n.p.

——. 1989. *Quake Poems.* Santa Cruz, CA: We Press.

——. 1990. *Body in Flames/Cuerpo en llamas.* San Francisco: Chronicle Books.

——. 1991. *De amor oscuro/Of Dark Love.* Santa Cruz, CA: Moving Parts Press.

——. 1992. *Snake Poems: An Aztec Invocation.* San Francisco: Chronicle Books.

——. 1993. *No Golden Gate for Us.* Santa Fe: Pennywhistle Press.

——. 2002. *From the Other Side of Night: /Del otro lado de la noche: New and Selected Poems.* Tucson: University of Arizona Press.

Alcalá, Kathleen. 1992. *Mrs. Vargas and the Dead Naturalist.* Corvallis, OR: Calyx Books.

Almaguer, Tomás. 1993. Chicano Men: A Cartography of Homosexual Identity and Behavior. In *The Lesbian and Gay Studies Reader,* eds. Henry Abelove, Michèle Aina Barale, and David M. Halperin, 255–73. New York: Routledge.

Alurista. 1971. *Floricanto en Aztlán.* Los Angeles: UCLA Chicano Studies Center.

——. 1972. *Nationchild Plumaroja.* San Diego: Toltecas en Aztlán Publications.

——. 1976. *Timespace Huracán: Poems, 1972–1975.* Albuquerque: Pajarito Publications.

——. 1979. *A'nque/Alurista.* San Diego, CA: Maize Publications.

——. 1981. *Spik in glyph?* Houston: Arte Público Press.

——. 1982. *Return: Poems Collected and New.* Ypsilanti, MI: Bilingual Review/Press.

——. 1995. *Z Eros.* Tempe, AZ: Bilingual Press/Editorial Bilingüe.

——. 1996. *Et tú . . . Raza?.* Tempe, AZ: Bilingual Press/Editorial Bilingüe

——. 2000. *As the Barrio Turns Who the Yoke B On?* San Diego: Calaca Press.

Anaya, Rudolfo A. 1972. *Bless Me, Ultima.* Berkeley: Quinto Sol Publications.

——. 1992. *Alburquerque.* New York: Warner Books.

——. 1995. *Zia Summer.* New York: Warner Books.

——. 1996a. *Maya's Children: The Story of La Llorona.* New York: Hyperion.

——. 1996b. *Rio Grande Fall.* New York: Warner Books.

——. 1998. *Farolitas for Abuela.* New York: Hyperion.

——. 1999a. *My Land Sings: Stories from the Rio Grande.* New York: Morrow.

——. 1999b. *Shaman Winter.* New York: Warner Books.

——. 2000. *Roadrunner's Dance.* New York: Hyperion.

——. 2004. *Serafina's Stories.* Albuquerque: University of New Mexico Press.

——. 2005. *Jemez Spring*. Albuquerque: University of New Mexico Press.

Anzaldúa, Gloria. 1987. *Borderlands/La frontera: The New Mestiza*. San Francisco: Spinsters/Aunt Lute Books.

Arellano, Anselmo, ed. 1976. *Los pobladores nuevo mexicanos y su poesía, 1889–1950*. Albuquerque: Pajarito Publications.

Arias, Ron. 1992. *The Road to Tamazunchale*. Tempe, AZ: Bilingual Review/Press.

Arizemendi, Yarelí. 2000. Nostalgia Maldita: 1-900-Mexico. In *Puro teatro: An Anthology of Latina Playwrights, Performance and Testimonios,* eds. Alberto Sandoval-Sánchez and Nancy Saporta Sternbach, 228–38. Tucson: University of Arizona Press.

Avendaño, Fausto. 1979. *El corrido de California: A Three-Act Play*. Berkeley: Editorial Justa.

Baca, Jimmy Santiago. 1977. *Immigrants in Our Own Land and Selected Early Poems*. New York: New Directions Books.

——. 1982. *What's Happening*. Willimantic, CT: Curbstone Press.

——. 1986. *Poems Taken from My Yard*. Fulton, MO: Timberline Press.

——. 1987. *Martín and Meditations on the South Valley*. New York: New Directions Books.

——. 1989. *Black Mesa Poems*. New York: New Directions.

——. 2001a. *Healing Earthquake: A Love Story in Poems*. New York: Grove Press.

——. 2001b. *A Place to Stand: The Making of a Poet*. New York: Grove Press.

——. 2002. *C-train (Dream Boy's Story), and Thirteen Mexicans: Poems*. New York: Grove Press.

——. 2004. *Winter Poems along the Rio Grande*. New York: New Directions Books.

Bertens, Hans. 2001. Literary Theory: The Basics. New York: Routledge.

Boscana, Gerónimo. 1846. Chinigchinich. In *Life in California during a Residence of Several Years in That Territory,* ed. Alfred Robinson. New York: Wiley and Putnam.

Brito, Aristeo. 1976. *El diablo en Texas*. Tucson: Editorial Peregrinos. (Translation, 1990. *The Devil in Texas*. Tempe: Bilingual Press/Editorial Bilingüe.)

Broadway Publishing. 2000. *Latino Plays from South Coast Repertory: Hispanic Playwrights Project Anthology*. New York: Broadway Publishing.

Brown, Monica. 2002. *Gang Nation: Delinquent Citizens in Puerto Rican, Chicano, and Chicana Narratives*. Minneapolis: University of Minnesota Press.

Broyles-González, Yolanda. 1994. *El Teatro Campesino: Theater in the Chicano Movement*. Austin: University of Texas Press.

Bruce-Novoa, Juan. 1980. *Chicano Authors: Inquiry by Interview*. Austin: University of Texas Press.

——. 1982. *Chicano Poetry: A Response to Chaos*. Austin: University of Texas Press.

——. 1990. *RetroSpace: Collected Essays on Chicano Literature*. Houston: Arte Público Press.

Burruel, Francisco. 1970. The Dialogue of Cuco Rocha. *El Grito* 3 (4): 37–45.

Cabeza de Baca, Fabiola. 1954. *We Fed Them Cactus.* Albuquerque: University of New Mexico Press.

Cabeza de Vaca, Alvar Núñez. 1962. *Adventures in the Unknown Interior of America.* New York: Collier Books.

Candelaria, Cordelia. 1986. *Chicano Poetry: A Critical Introduction.* Westport, CT: Greenwood Press.

Candelaria, Nash. 1977. *Memories of the Alhambra.* Palo Alto, CA: Cíbola Press.

——. 1982. *Not by the Sword.* Binghamton, NY: Bilingual Press/Editorial Bilingüe.

——. 1985. *Inheritance of Strangers.* Binghamton, NY: Bilingual Review/Press.

——. 1991. *Leonor Park.* Tempe, AZ: Bilingual Press/Editorial Bilingüe.

Cano, Daniel. 1995. *Shifting Loyalties.* Houston: Arte Público Press.

Cantú, Norma. 1995. *Canícula: Snapshots of a Girlhood en la Frontera.* Albuquerque: University of New Mexico Press.

Casares, Oscar. 2003. *Brownsville.* Boston: Little, Brown.

Castillo, Ana. 1984. *Women Are Not Roses.* Houston: Arte Público Press.

——. 1986. *The Mixquiahuala Letters.* Binghamton: Bilingual Press/Editorial Bilingüe.

——. 1988. *My Father Was a Toltec and Selected Poems, 1973–1988.* Albuquerque: West End Press.

——. 1990. *Sapogonia: An Anti-Romance in 3/8 Meter.* Tempe, AZ: Bilingual Press/Editorial Bilingüe.

——. 1993. *So Far from God.* New York and London: W. W. Norton.

——. 1995. *Massacre of the Dreamers: Essays on Xicanismo.* New York: Plume.

——. 1996. *Loverboys: Stories.* New York and London: W. W. Norton.

——. 1999. *Peel My Love Like an Onion.* New York: Anchor Books.

——. 2001. *I Ask the Impossible: Poems.* New York: Anchor Books.

Cervantes, Lorna Dee. 1981. *Emplumada.* Pittsburgh: University of Pittsburgh Press.

——. 1991. *From the Cables of Genocide: Poems on Love and Hunger.* Houston: Arte Público Press.

Chávez, Denise. 1986. *The Last of the Menu Girls.* Houston: Arte Público Press.

——. 1988. Novenas narrativas y ofrendas nuevomexicanas. In *Chicana Creativity and Criticism. Charting New Frontiers in American Literature,* eds. María Herrera-Sobek and Helena María Viramontes, 85–100. Houston: Arte Público Press.

——. 1994. *Face of an Angel.* New York: Warner Brothers.

——. 2001. *Loving Pedro Infante.* New York: Washington Square Press.

Chávez, Fray Angélico. 1957. *From an Altar Screen; El Retablo: Tales from New Mexico.* New York: Farrar, Straus and Cudahy.

——. 1974. *My Penitente Land: Reflections on Spanish New Mexico.* Albuquerque: University of New Mexico Press.

——. 1976. *New Mexico Triptych.* Santa Fe, NM: William Gannon. (Originally published 1940)

Cisneros, Sandra. 1980. *Bad Boys.* Houston: Arte Público Press.

———. 1984. *The House on Mango Street.* Houston: Arte Público Press.

———. 1987. *My Wicked, Wicked Ways.* Berkeley: Third Woman Press.

———. 1991. *Woman Hollering Creek and Other Stories.* New York: Vintage Books.

———. 1994. *Loose Woman.* New York: Alfred Knopf.

———. 2002. *Caramelo.* New York: Vintage Books.

Corpi, Lucha. 1982. *Palabras de mediodía/Noon Words.* Berkeley: El Fuego de Aztlán Publications.

———. 1989. *Delia's Song.* Houston: Arte Público Press.

———. 1990. *Variaciones sobre una tempestad/Variations on a Storm.* Berkeley: Third Woman Press.

———. 1992. *Eulogy for a Brown Angel.* Houston: Arte Público Press.

———. 1995. *Cactus Blood.* Houston: Arte Público Press.

———. 1999. *Black Widow's Wardrobe.* Houston: Arte Público Press.

Cota Cárdenas, Margarita. 2000. *Puppet: A Chicano Novella.* Albuquerque: University of New Mexico Press. (Originally published in 1985.)

———. 2005. *Santuarios del corazón/Sanctuaries of the Heart.* Tucson: University of Arizona Press.

Culture Clash: Life, Death, and Revolutionary Comedy. 1998. New York: Theatre Communications Group.

de León, Nephtali. 1972. *Five Plays.* Denver: Totinem Publications.

de Niza, Fray Marcos. 1926. Fray Marcos de Niza and His Discovery of the Seven Cities of Cibola. *New Mexico Historical Review* 1: 193–223.

Delgado, Abelardo. 1969. *Chicano: 25 Pieces of a Chicano Mind.* Denver: Barrio Publications.

———. 1973. *Bajo el sol de Aztlán: 25 soles de Abelardo.* El Paso: Barrio Publications.

———. 1974. *It's Cold: 52 Cold Thought-Poems of Abelardo.* Salt Lake: Barrio Publications.

Durán, Javier. 2004. Alejandro Morales. In *Latino and Latina Writers,* ed. Alan West-Durán, 383–404. New York: Charles Scribner's Sons.

Durán, Miguel. 1991. *Don't Spit on My Corner.* Houston: Arte Público Press.

Eagleton, Terry. 2003. *Literary Theory: An Introduction.* Minneapolis: University of Minnesota Press.

Elizondo, Sergio. 1972. *Perros y antiperros: Una épica Chicana.* Berkeley: Quinto Sol.

———. 1977. *Libro para batos y chavalas chicanas.* Berkeley: Editorial Justa.

Esparza, Laura. 2000. Battle-Worn. In *Puro teatro: A Latina Anthology of Playwrights, Performance and Testimonios,* eds. Alberto Sandoval-Sánchez and Nancy Saporta Sternbach, 287–99. Tucson: University of Arizona Press.

Esturoy, Annie O. 1996. *Daughters of Self-Creation: The Contemporary Chicana Novel.* Albuquerque: University of New Mexico Press.

Feyder, Linda, and Denise Chávez, eds. 1992. *Shattering the Myth: Plays by Hispanic Women.* Houston: Arte Público Press.

Fregoso, Rosa Linda, and Angie Chabram. 1990. Chicana/o Cultural Representations: Reframing Alternative Critical Discourses. *Cultural Studies* 4: 203–12.

Galarza, Ernesto. 1971. *Barrio Boy: The Story of a Boy's Acculturation.* Notre Dame and London: University of Notre Dame Press.

Gamio, Manuel. 1931. *The Mexican Immigrant: His Life Story.* Chicago: University of Chicago Press.

García, Nasario, ed. 1997. *Comadres: Hispanic Women of the Río Puerco Valley.* Albuquerque: University of New Mexico Press.

Garza, Robert J., ed. 1976. *Contemporary Chicano Theater.* Notre Dame and London: University of Notre Dame Press.

Gaspar de Alba, Alicia. 1993. *The Mystery of Survival and Other Stories.* Tempe, AZ: Bilingual Press/Editorial Bilingüe.

——. 1999. *Sor Juana's Second Dream.* Albuquerque: University of New Mexico Press.

——. 2005. *Desert Blood: The Juárez Murders.* Houston: Arte Público Press.

Gaspar de Alba, Alicia, María Herrera-Sobek, and Demetria Martínez, eds. 1989. *Three Times a Woman: Chicana Poetry.* Tempe, AZ: Bilingual Press/Editorial Bilingüe.

Gonzales, Rodolfo. 1967. *I Am Joaquín/Yo soy Joaquín.* New York: Bantam Books.

Gonzales-Berry, Erlinda. 1991. *Paletitas de guayaba.* Albuquerque: El Norte Publications.

González, Alicia. 1996. *Alicia in Wonder Tierra (or I Can't Eat Goat Head).* Woodstock, IL: Dramatic Publishing Group.

Gonzalez, Ray. 1986. *From the Restless Roots.* Houston: Arte Público Press.

——. 1987. *Twilights and Chants: Poems.* Golden, CO: J. Andrews.

——. 1993. *Memory Fever: A Journey beyond El Paso del Norte.*

——. 1996. *The Heat of Arrivals.* Brockport, NY: BOA Editions.

——. 1998. *Cabato Sentora.* Brockport, NY: BOA Editions.

——. 2000a. *Turtle Pictures.* Tucson: University of Arizona Press.

——. 2000b. *The Woman Who Lost Her Soul.* Houston: Arte Público Press.

——. 2002a. *The Hawk Temple at Tierra Grande: Poems.* Rochester, NY: BOA Editions.

——. 2002b. *The Underground Heart: A Return to a Hidden Landscape.* Tucson: University of Arizona Press.

——. 2005. *The Religion of Hands: Prose Poems and Flash Fictions.* Tucson: University of Arizona Press.

González, Rigoberto. 2003. *Crossing Vines.* Norman: University of Oklahoma Press.

Grajeda, Ralph F. 1979. Tomás Rivera's . . . *Y no se lo tragó la tierra:* Discovery and Appropriation of the Chicano Past. *Hispania* 62: 71–81.

Griswold del Castillo, Richard. 1984. *La Familia: Chicano Families in the Urban Southwest, 1848 to Present.* Notre Dame: University of Notre Dame Press.

Gutiérrez, Ramón. 1993. The Politics of Theater in Colonial New Mexico: Drama and the Rhetoric of Conquest. In *Reconstructing a Chicano/a Literary Heritage: Hispanic Colonial Literature of the Southwest,* ed. María Herrera-Sobek, 49–67. Tucson: University of Arizona Press.

Hernández, Alfonso. 1979. *The False Advent of Mary's Child and Other Plays.* Berkeley: Editorial Justa.

Hernández Tovar, Inés. 1977. *Con razón, corazón.* San Antonio: Caracol.

Herrera, Juan Felipe. 1974. *Rebozos of Love/We Have Woven/Sudor de Pueblos/On Our Back.* San Diego: Toltecas de Aztlán.

——. 1985. *Exiles of Desire.* Houston: Arte Público Press. (Originally published in 1983)

——. 1987. *Facegames: Poems.* San Francisco: As Is/So & So Press.

——. 1989. *Akrilica.* Santa Cruz, CA: Alcatraz Editions.

——. 1993. *Memorias from an Exile's Notebook of the Future.* Santa Monica, CA: Santa Monica College Press.

——. 1994a. *Night Train to Tuxtla.* Tucson: University of Arizona Press.

——. 1994b. *The Roots of a Thousand Embraces: Dialogues.* San Francisco: Manic D. Press.

——. 1996. *Love after the Riots.* Willimantic, CT: Curbstone Press.

——. 1997. *Mayan Drifter: Chicano Poet in the Lowlands of America.* Philadelphia: Temple University Press.

——. 1999a. *Border-Crosser with a Lamborghini Dream: Poems.* Tucson: University of Arizona Press.

——. 1999b. *Lotería Cards and Fortune Poems: A Book of Lives.* San Francisco: City Lights Books.

——. 2000. *Thunderweavers/Tejedoras de rayos.* Tucson: University of Arizona Press.

——. 2001. *Giraffe on Fire.* Tucson: University of Arizona Press.

——. 2002. *Notebooks of a Chile Verde Smuggler.* Tucson: University of Arizona Press.

Herrera-Sobek, María. 1990. *The Mexican Corrido: A Feminist Analysis.* Bloomington: Indiana University Press.

Hinojosa, Rolando. 1973. *Estampas del Valle y otras obras.* Berkeley: Quinto Sol Publications.

——. 1976. *Klail City y sus alrededores.* Havana: Casa de las Américas.

——. 1980. *Korean Love Songs from Klail City Death Trip.* Berkeley: Editorial Justa.

——. 1982. *Rites and Witnesses.* Houston: Arte Público Press.

——. 1983. *The Valley.* Ypsilanti, MI: Bilingual Press/Editorial Bilingüe.

——. 1985a. *Dear Rafe.* Houston: Arte Público Press.

——. 1985b. *Partners in Crime: A Rafe Buenrostro Mystery.* Houston: Arte Público Press.

——. 1986. *Claros varones de Belken/Fair Gentlemen of Belken County.* Tempe, AZ: Bilingual Press/Editorial Bilingüe.

———. 1987. *Klail City: A Novel.* Houston: Arte Público Press.

———. 1990. *Becky and Her Friends.* Houston: Arte Público Press.

———. 1993. *The Useless Servants.* Houston: Arte Público Press.

———. 1998. *Ask a Policeman.* Houston: Arte Público Press.

Hoyos, Angela de. 1975a. *Arise, Chicano! And Other Poems.* Bloomington, IN: Backstage Books.

———. 1975b. *Chicano Poems for the Barrio.* Bloomington, IN: Backstage Books.

Huerta, Jorge. 1989. *Necessary Theater: Six Plays about the Chicano Experience.* Houston: Arte Público Press.

———. 2000. *Chicano Drama: Performance, Society and Myth.* Cambridge: Cambridge University Press.

Islas, Arturo. 1984. *The Rain God: A Desert Tale.* Palo Alto, CA: Alexandria Press.

———. 1990. *Migrant Souls.* New York: William Morrow and Co.

Jaramillo, Cleofas. 2000. *Romance of a Little Village Girl.* Albuquerque: University of New Mexico Press. (Originally published in 1955)

Jiménez, Francisco. 1997. *The Circuit: Stories from the Life of a Migrant Child.* Albuquerque: University of New Mexico Press.

———. 2001. *Breaking Through.* Boston: Houghton Mifflin Co.

Kanellos, Nicolás. 1993. A Socio-Historic Study of Hispanic Newspapers in the United States. In *Recovering the U.S. Hispanic Literary Heritage,* eds. Ramón Gutiérrez and Genaro Padilla, 107–28. Houston: Arte Público Press.

Kanellos, Nicolás, and Jorge Huerta, eds. 1979. *Nuevos pasos: Chicano and Puerto Rican Drama.* Houston: Arte Público Press.

Limón, Graciela. 1990. *María de Belén: The Autobiography of an Indian Woman.* New York: Vintage Books.

———. 1993. *In Search of Bernabé.* Houston: Arte Público Press.

———. 1994. *The Memories of Ana Calderón.* Houston: Arte Público Press.

———. 1996. *Song of the Hummingbird.* Houston: Arte Público Press.

———. 1999. *The Day of the Moon.* Houston: Arte Público Press.

Lomas, Clara. 1978. Resistencia cultural o apropiación ideológica. *Revista Chicano-Riqueña* 6 (4): 48–57.

Lomelí, Francisco A. 2004. Discussion and Analysis. In *Chicano Sketches: Short Stories by Mario Suárez,* eds. Francisco A. Lomelí, Cecilia Cota-Robles, and Juan José Casillas-Núñez, 146–79. Tucson: University of Arizona Press.

López, Josefina. 1992. Simply María, or the American Dream. In *Shattering the Myth: Plays by Hispanic Women,* eds. Linda Feyder and Denise Chávez, 113–41. Houston: Arte Público Press.

———. 1996. *Real Women Have Curves.* Woodstock, IL: Dramatic Publishing Group.

López-Stafford, Gloria. 1996. *A Place in El Paso: A Mexican American Childhood.* Albuquerque: University of New Mexico Press.

Macey, David. 2000. *The Penguin Dictionary of Critical Theory.* New York: Penguin Books.

Macías, Ysidro R. 1976a. Mártir Montezuma. In *Contemporary Chicano Theatre,* ed. Roberto J. Garza, 165–90. Notre Dame: University of Notre Dame Press.

——. 1976b. The Ultima Pendejada. In *Contemporary Chicano Theatre,* ed. Roberto J. Garza, 135–64. Notre Dame: University of Notre Dame Press.

Madsen, Deborah L. 2000. *Understanding Contemporary Chicana Literature.* Columbia: University of South Carolina Press.

Mariscal, George, ed. 1999. *Aztlán and Vietnam: Chicano and Chicana Experiences of the War.* Berkeley: University of California Press.

Mariscal, Jorge. 2000. Reading Chicano/a Writing about the American War in Vietnam. *Aztlán* 25 (2): 13–49.

Martin, Patricia Preciado. 1983. *Images and Conversations: Mexican Americans Recall a Southwestern Past.* Tucson: University of Arizona Press.

——. 1992. *Songs My Mother Sang to Me: An Oral History of Mexican American Women.* Tucson: University of Arizona Press.

——. 2004. *Beloved Land: An Oral History of Mexican Americans in Southern Arizona.* Tucson: University of Arizona Press.

Martín-Rodriguez, Manuel M. 2003. *Life in Search of Readers. Reading (in) Chicano/a Literature.* Albuquerque: University of New Mexico Press.

Martínez, Demetria. 1994. *Mother Tongue.* Tempe, AZ: Bilingual Review/Press.

——. 1997. *Breathing between the Lines.* Tucson: University of Arizona Press.

——. 2002. *The Devil's Workshop.* Tucson: University of Arizona Press.

Martínez, Eliud. 1977. Ron Arias's *Road to Tamazunchale:* A Chicano Novel of the New Reality. *Latin American Literary Review* 5 (10): 51–63.

Mayer, Oliver. 1996. *Blade to the Heat.* New York: Dramatists Play Service.

Meléndez, A. Gabriel. 1997. *So All Is Not Lost: The Poetics of Print in Nuevomexicano Communities, 1834–1958.* Albuquerque: University of New Mexico Press.

Mena, Alicia. 2000. Las nuevas tamaleras. In *Puro teatro: A Latina Anthology,* eds. Alberto Sandoval-Sánchez and Nancy Saporta Sternbach 149–75. Tucson: University of Arizona Press.

Méndez, Miguel M. 1986. *El sueño de Santa María de las Piedras.* Guadalajara: Universidad de Guadalajara.

——. 1991. David W. Foster, trans. *The Dream of Santa María de las Piedras.* Tempe, AZ: Bilingual Review/Press.

——. 1992. *Pilgrims in Aztlán.* Trans. David W. Foster. Tempe, AZ: Bilingual Press/Editorial Bilingüe.

Miller, Elaine K. 1973. *Mexican Folk Narrative from the Los Angeles Area.* Austin: University of Texas Press.

Montoya, José. 1972. *El sol y los de abajo.* San Francisco: Ediciones Pocho-Ché.

Montoya, Richard, Ricardo Salinas, and Herbert Siguenza. 1999. *Culture Clash: Life, Death and Revolutionary Comedy.* New York: Theatre Communications Group.

Mora, Pat. 1984. *Chants.* Houston: Arte Público Press.

206   Works Consulted

——. 1986. *Borders.* Houston: Arte Público Press.

——. 1991. *Communion.* Houston: Arte Público Press.

——. 1994. *Listen to the Desert: Oye al desierto.* New York: Clarion Books.

——. 1995. *Agua santa/Holy Water.* Boston: Beacon Press.

——. 1997. *Aunt Carmen's Book of Practical Saints.* Boston: Beacon Press.

——. 1998. *Delicious Hullabaloo: Pachanga deliciosa.* Houston: Arte Público Press.

——. 2001. *The Bakery Lady: La señora de la panadería.* Houston: Arte Público Press.

——. 2005. *Doña Flor: A Tall Tale about a Giant Woman with a Great Big Heart.* New York: Knopf.

Moraga, Cherríe. 1983. *Loving in the War Years: lo que nunca pasó por sus labios.* Cambridge: South End Press.

——. 1986. *Giving Up the Ghost.* Los Angeles: West End Press.

——. 1994. *Heroes and Saints and Other Plays.* Albuquerque: West End Press.

——. 2001. *The Hungry Woman: A Mexican Medea. Heart of the Earth: A Popul Vuh Story.* Albuquerque: West End Press.

——. 2002. *Watsonville/Circle in the Dirt: Some Place Not Here/El Pueblo de East Palo Alto.* Albuquerque: University of New Mexico Press.

Moraga, Cherríe, and Gloria Anzaldúa, eds. 1981. *This Bridge Called My Back: Writings by Radical Women of Color.* Watertown, MA: Persephone Press.

Morales, Alejandro. 1975. *Caras viejas y vino nuevo.* México, DF: Joaquín Mortiz. (Translation, 1981. *Old Faces and New Wine.* San Diego: Maize Press.)

——. 1979. *La verdad sin voz.* México, DF: Joaquín Mortiz.

——. 1992. *The Rag Doll Plagues.* Houston: Arte Público Press.

Morton, Carlos. 1983. *The Many Deaths of Danny Rosales and Other Plays.* Houston: Arte Público Press (Includes *Rancho Hollywood*).

——. 1991. *Johnny Tenorio and Other Plays.* Houston: Arte Público Press.

——. 2000. *Rancho Hollywood y otras obras del teatro chicano.* Houston: Arte Público Press.

Moya, Paula M. L. 2002. *Learning from Experience: Minority Identities, Multicultural Struggles.* Berkeley: University of California Press.

Murray, Yxta Maya. 1997. *Locas.* New York: Grove Press.

——. 1999. *What It Takes to Get to Vegas.* New York: Grove Press.

——. 2002. *The Conquest.* New York: HarperCollins.

Nava, Michael. 1986. *The Little Death.* Boston: Alyson Publications.

——. 1990. *How Town.* New York: Ballantine Books.

——. 1992. *The Hidden Law.* New York: Ballantine Books.

——. 1996a. *The Death of Friends.* New York: G. P. Putnam's Sons.

——. 1996b. *Goldenboy: A Mystery.* New York: Ballantine Books.

——. 1999. *The Burning Plain.* New York: Bantam Books.

——. 2001. *Rag and Bone.* New York: Berkley Prime Crime.

Neate, Wilson. 1998. *Tolerating Ambiguity: Ethnicity and Community in Chicano/a Writing.* New York: Peter Lang.

Nelson, Eugene, comp. 1975. *Pablo Cruz and the American Dream: The Experiences of an Undocumented Immigrant from Mexico.* Salt Lake City: Peregrine Smith.

Niggli, Josefina. 1945. *Mexican Village.* Chapel Hill: University of North Carolina Press.

———. 1947. *Step Down, Elder Brother.* New York: Rinehart.

Olney, James, ed. 1980. *Autobiography: Essays Theoretical and Critical.* Princeton: Princeton University Press.

Ortiz Taylor, Sheila. 1982. *Faultline.* Tallahassee: Naiad Press.

Osborn, M. Elizabeth, ed. 1987. *On New Ground: Contemporary Hispanic-American Plays.* New York: Theatre Communications Group.

Otero-Warren, Nina. 1936. *Old Spain in the Southwest.* New York: Harcourt Brace and Co.

Padilla, Genaro M. 1993. *My History, Not Yours: The Formation of Mexican American Autobiography.* Madison: University of Wisconsin Press.

———, ed. 1987. *The Short Stories of Fray Angélico Chávez.* Albuquerque: University of New Mexico Press.

Palacios, Mónica. 2000. Latin Lesbo Comic: A Performance about Happiness, Challenges, and Tacos. In *Latinas on Stage,* eds. Alicia Arrizón and Lillian Manzor, 90–116. Berkeley: Third Woman Press.

Paredes, Américo. 1958. *With a Pistol in His Hand: A Border Ballad and Its Hero.* Austin: University of Texas Press.

———. 1963. The Hammon and the Beans. *Texas Observer,* April 18, pp. 42–49.

———. 1990. *George Washington Gómez.* Houston: Arte Público Press.

Peña, Manuel. 1992–1996. Música fronteriza/Border Music. *Aztlán* 21 (1–2): 191–225. Available online at http:/www.lib.utexas.edu/benson/border/pena/.

Peña, Terri de la. 1992. *Margins.* Seattle: Seal Press.

———. 1994. *Latin Satins: A Novel.* Seattle: Seal Press.

Pérez, Emma. 1996. *Gulf Dreams.* Berkeley: Third Woman Press.

Pérez, Judith, and Severo Pérez. 1989. *Necessary Theater: Six Plays about the Chicano Experience,* ed. Jorge Huerta, 20–75. Houston: Arte Público Press.

Pérez, Ramón "Tianguis." 1991. *Diary of an Undocumented Immigrant.* Houston: Arte Público Press.

———. 1999. *Diary of a Guerrilla.* Houston: Arte Público Press.

Pérez de Villagrá, Gaspar. 1900. *Historia de la Nueva México.* México, DF: Imprenta del Museo Nacional.

Pérez-Torres, Rafael. 1995. *Movements in Chicano Poetry.* Berkeley: University of California Press.

Perkins, Kathy A., and Roberta Uno, eds. 1996. *Contemporary Plays by Women of Color.* New York: Routledge.

Pimentel, Ricardo. 1997. *House with Two Doors.* Tempe, AZ: Bilingual Review/Press.

———. 2001. *Voices from the River.* Tempe, AZ: Bilingual Review/Press.

Piñeda, Cecile. 1992. *The Love Queen of the Amazon.* Boston: Little, Brown.

Ponce, Mary Helen. 1989. *The Wedding.* Arte Público Press.

———. 1993. *Hoyt Street: An Autobiography.* Albuquerque: University of New Mexico Press.

Portillo Trambley, Estela. 1975. *Rain of Scorpions and Other Writings.* Berkeley: Tonatiuh International.

———. 1976. The Day of the Swallows. In *Contemporary Chicano Theater,* ed. Roberto J. Garza, 205–45. Notre Dame: University of Notre Dame Press.

———. 1983. *Sor Juana and Other Plays.* Ypsilanti, MI: Bilingual Review/Press.

———. 1986. *Trini.* Houston: Arte Público Press.

Preciado Martin, Patricia. 1983. *Images and Conversations: Mexican Americans Recall a Southwestern Past.* Tucson: University of Arizona Press.

———. 1992. *Song My Mother Sang to Me: An Oral History of Mexican American Women.* Tucson: University of Arizona Press.

———. 2004. *Beloved Land: An Oral History of the Mexican Americans in Southern Arizona.* Tucson: University of Arizona Press.

Quiñónez, Naomi Helena. 1998. *The Smoking Mirror.* Albuquerque: West End Press.

Quintana, Leroy V. 1976. *Hijo del Pueblo: New Mexico Poems.* Las Cruces, NM: Puerto del Sol Press.

———. 1981. *Sangre.* Las Cruces, NM: Prima Agua Press.

———. 1992. *Interrogations.* Tempe, AZ: Bilingual Review/Press.

———. 1993. *The History of Home.* Tempe, AZ: Bilingual Review/Press.

———. 1996. *My Hair Turning Gray among Strangers.* Tempe, AZ: Bilingual Review/Press.

———. 1999. *The Great Whirl of Exile.* Willimantic, CT: Curbstone Press.

———. 2002. *La Promesa and Other Stories.* Norman: University of Oklahoma Press.

Rael, Juan B. 1977. *Cuentos populares de Colorado y Nuevo México.* 2d ed. 2 vols. Santa Fe: Museum of New Mexico Press.

Ramírez, Juan. 1999. *A Patriot after All: The Story of a Chicano Vietnam Vet.* Albuquerque: University of New Mexico Press.

Ramos, Manuel. 1993. *The Ballad of Rocky Ruiz.* New York: St. Martin's Press.

———. 1994. *The Ballad of Gato Guerrero.* New York: St. Martin's Press.

———. 1996. *The Last Client of Luis Montez.* New York St. Martin's Press.

———. 1997. *Blues for the Buffalo.* New York: St. Martin's Press.

———. 2002. *Moony's Road to Hell.* Albuquerque: University of New Mexico Press.

———. 2003. *Brown-on-Brown.* Albuquerque: University of New Mexico Press.

Rebolledo, Tey Diana. 1995. *Women Singing in the Snow: A Cultural Analysis of Chicana Literature.* Tucson: University of Arizona Press.

Rebolledo, Tey Diana, Erlinda Gonzales-Berry, and Teresa Márquez. 1988. *Las mujeres hablan: An Anthology of Nuevo Mexicana Writers.* Albuquerque: El Norte Publications.

Rebolledo, Tey Diana, and María Teresa Márquez, eds. 2000. *Women's Tales from the New Mexico WPA: La diabla a pie.* Houston: Arte Público Press.

Works Consulted   209

Rebolledo, Tey Diana, and Eliana S. Rivero. 1993. *Infinite Divisions: An Anthology of Chicana Literature.* Tucson: University of Arizona Press.

Rechy, John. 1969. *This Day's Death.* New York: Grove Press.

——. 1984. *City of Night.* New York: Grove Press.

Ríos, Alberto Alvaro. 1982. *Whispering to Fool the Wind.* New York: Sheep Meadow Press.

——. 1984. *The Iguana Killer.* Lewiston, ID: Blue Moon and Confluence Press.

——. 1985. *Five Indiscretions.* New York: Sheep Meadow Press.

——. 1988. *The Lime Orchard Woman.* New York: Sheep Meadow Press.

——. 1990. *Teodoro Luna's Two Kisses.* New York: W. W. Norton.

——. 1995. *Pig Cookies.* San Francisco: Chronicle Books.

——. 1999a. *Capirotada: A Nogales Memoir.* Albuquerque: University of New Mexico Press.

——. 1999b. *The Curtain of Trees: Stories.* Albuquerque: University of New Mexico Press.

——. 2002. *The Smallest Muscle in the Human Body.* Port Townsend, WA: Copper Canyon Press.

Ríos, Isabella (Diana López). 1976. *Victuum.* Ventura: Diana-Etna.

Rivera, Tomás. 1971. *. . . Y no se lo tragó la tierra/ . . . And the Earth Did Not Part.* Berkeley: Quinto Sol Publications.

Rodríguez, Joe. 1989. *Oddsplayer.* Houston: Arte Público Press.

Rodríguez, Luis J. 1989. *Poems across the Pavement.* Chicago: Tía Chucha Press.

——. 1991. *The Concrete River.* Willimantic, CT: Curbstone Press.

——. 1993. *América Is Her Name.* Willimantic, CT: Curbstone Press.

——. 1994. *Always Running: La vida loca, Gang Days in L.A.* New York: Simon and Schuster. (Originally published 1993 by Curbstone Press)

——. 1998. *Trochemoche.* Willimantic, CT: Curbstone Press.

——. 2002. *The Republic of East L.A.: Stories.* New York: HarperCollins.

——. 2005. *Music of the Mill.* New York: HarperCollins.

Rodríguez, Ralph E. 2005. *Brown Gumshoes: Detective Fiction and the Search for Chicana/o Identity.* Austin: University of Texas Press.

Rodríguez, Richard. 1982. *Hunger of Memory: The Education of Richard Rodríguez: An Autobiography.* Boston: David Godine.

——. 1992. *Days of Obligation: An Argument with My Mexican Father.* New York: Penguin Books.

——. 2002. *Brown: The Last Discovery of America.* New York: Penguin.

Romero, Elaine. 2000. The Fat-Free Chicana and the Snow Cap Queen. In *Puro teatro: A Latina Anthology of Playwrights, Performance and Testimonios,* eds. Alberto Sandoval-Sánchez and Nancy Saporta Sternbach, 89–144. Tucson: University of Arizona Press.

Romero, Leo. 1978. *During the Growing Season.* Tucson: Maguey Press.

——. 1981. *Agua negra*. Boise: Ahsahra Press.

——. 1985. *Celso*. Houston: Arte Público Press.

Rosales, F. Arturo. 1996. *Chicano! The History of the Mexican American Civil Rights Movement*. Houston: Arte Público Press.

Rosaldo, Renato. 2003. *Prayer to Spider Woman: Rezo de la mujer arena*. Saltillo, Coahuila: Instituto Coahuilense de Cultura.

Ruiz de Burton, María Amparo. 1992. *The Squatter and the Don*. Houston: Arte Público Press.

——. 1995. *Who Would Have Thought It?* Houston: Arte Público Press.

Sáenz, Benjamin Alire. 1991. *Calendar of Dust*. Seattle: Broken Moon Press.

——. 1992. *Flowers for the Broken*. Seattle: Broken Moon Press.

——. 1995a. *Carry Me Like Water*. New York: Hyperion.

——. 1995b. *Dark and Perfect Angels*. El Paso: Cinco Puntos Press.

——. 2002. *Elegies in Blue*. El Paso: Cinco Puntos Press.

——. 2004. *Sammy and Juliana in Hollywood*. El Paso: Cinco Puntos Press.

Saldívar, José David. 1986. Towards a Chicano Poetics: The Making of the Chicano-Chicana Subject. *Confluencia* 1 (2): 10–17.

——. 1997. *Border Matters: Remapping American Cultural Studies*. Berkeley: University of California Press.

Saldívar, Ramón. 1979. A Dialectic of Difference: Towards a Theory of the Chicano Novel. *MELUS* (Fall): 73–92.

——. 1990. *Chicano Narrative: The Dialectics of Difference*. Madison: University of Wisconsin Press.

Salinas, Luis Omar. 1970. *Crazy Gypsy: Poems*. Fresno: Orígenes Publications.

——. 1987. *The Sadness of Days: Selected and New Poems*. Houston: Arte Público Press.

Salinas, Raúl. 1973. *Viaje/Trip*. Providence, RI: Hellcoal Press.

——. 1980. *Un Trip through the Mind Jail y Otras Excursiones*. San Francisco: Editorial Pocho-Ché.

Sánchez, Marta Ester. 1985. *Contemporary Chicana Poetry: A Critical Approach to an Emerging Literature*. Berkeley and Los Angeles: University of California Press.

Sánchez, Ricardo. 1971. *Canto y grito mi liberación*. El Paso: Mictla Publications.

——. *HechizoSpells*. Los Angeles: UCLA Chicano Studies Center Publications.

Sánchez, Rosaura. 1987. Postmodernism and Chicano Literature. *Aztlán* 18: 1–14.

——. 2004. Rolando Hinojosa. In *Latino and Latina Writers,* ed. Alan West-Durán, 299–318. New York: Charles Scribner's Sons.

Sandoval, Chela. 2000. *Methodology of the Oppressed*. Minneapolis: University of Minnesota Press.

Sandoval-Sánchez, Alberto, and Nancy Saporta Sternbach. 2001. *Stages of Life: Transcultural Performance and Identity in Latina Theater*. Tucson: University of Arizona Press.

——, eds. 2000. *Puro teatro: A Latina Anthology*. Tucson: University of Arizona Press.

Santana, Patricia. 2002. *Motorcycle Ride on the Sea of Tranquility.* Albuquerque: University of New Mexico Press.

Shirley, Carl R., and Paula W. Shirley. 1988. *Understanding Chicano Literature.* Columbia: University of South Carolina Press.

Sierra, Rubén. 1976a. Manolo. *Contemporary Chicano Theatre,* ed. Roberto J. Garza, 65–109. Notre Dame: University of Notre Dame Press.

——. 1976b. La Raza Pura, or Racial, Racial. In *Contemporary Chicano Theatre,* ed. Roberto J. Garza, 39–64. Notre Dame: University of Notre Dame Press.

Solís, Octavio. 1998. *Man of the Flesh: Plays from the South Coast Repertory.* Vol. 2. New York: Broadway Play Publishing.

Sommers, Joseph. 1977. From the Critical Premise to the Product: Critical Modes and Their Application to a Chicano Literary Text. *New Scholar* 6: 51–80.

Sommers, Joseph, and Tomás Ybarra-Frausto, eds. 1979. *Modern Chicano Writers: A Collection of Critical Essays.* Englewood Cliffs, NJ: Prentice Hall.

Soto, Gary. 1977. *The Elements of San Joaquin.* Pittsburgh: University of Pittsburgh Press

——. 1978. *The Tale of Sunlight.* Pittsburgh: University of Pittsburgh Press.

——. 1980. *Father Is a Pillow Tied to a Broom.* Pittsburgh: Slow Loris.

——. 1981. *Where Sparrows Work Hard.* Pittsburgh: University of Pittsburgh Press.

——. 1985a. *Black Hair.* Pittsburgh: University of Pittsburgh Press.

——. 1985b. *Living up the Street: Narrative Recollections.* San Francisco: Strawberry Hill.

——. 1986. *Small Faces.* Houston: Arte Público Press.

——. 1988. *Lesser Evils: Ten Quartets.* Houston: Arte Público Press.

——. 1990a. *Baseball in April.* New York: Harcourt Brace Jovanovich.

——. 1990b. *Who Will Know Us?* San Francisco: Chronicle Books.

——. 1991a. *Home Course in Religion.* San Francisco: Chronicle Books.

——. 1991b. *Taking Sides.* San Diego: Harcourt Brace Jovanovich.

——. 1993a. *Pieces of the Heart: New Chicano Fiction.* San Francisco: Chronicle Books.

——. 1993b. *The Pool Party.* New York: Delacorte Press.

——. 1995a. *Boys at Work.* New York: Delacorte Press.

——. 1995b. *New and Selected Poems.* San Francisco: Chronicle Books.

——. 1997. *Junior College.* San Francisco: Chronicle Books.

——. 1999. *A Natural Man.* San Francisco: Chronicle Books.

——. 2000. *The Effects of Knut Hamsun on a Fresno Boy: Recollections and Short Essays.* New York: Persea Books.

——. 2002. *If the Shoe Fits.* New York: G. P. Putnam's Sons.

Suárez, Mario. 2004. *Chicano Sketches: Short Stories by Mario Suárez,* eds. Francisco A. Lomelí, Cecilia Cota-Robles, and Juan José Casillas Núñez. Tucson: University of Arizona Press.

Svich, Caridad, and María Teresa Marrero, eds. 2000. *Out of the Fringe: Contemporary Latina/Latino Theatre and Performance.* New York: Theatre Communications Group.

Tafolla, Carmen. 1976. *Get Your Tortillas Together.* N.p.

——. 1983. *Curandera.* San Antonio: M & A Editions.

Tatum, Charles M. 1982. *Chicano Literature.* Boston: G. K. Hall and Co.

——, ed. 1990. *Mexican American Literature.* Orlando: Harcourt Brace Jovanovich.

——, ed. 1992a. *New Chicana/Chicano Writing I.* Tucson: University of Arizona Press.

——, ed. 1992b. *New Chicana/Chicano Writing II.* Tucson: University of Arizona Press.

——, ed. 1993. *New Chicana/Chicano Writing III.* Tucson: University of Arizona Press.

Treviño Hart, Elva. 1999. *Barefoot Heart: Stories of a Migrant Child.* Tempe, AZ: Bilingual Review/Press.

Trujillo, Carla. 2003. *What Night Brings.* Willimantic, CT: Curbstone Press.

——. 1998. *Living Chicana Theory.* Berkeley: Third Woman Press.

——, ed. 1991. *Chicana Lesbians: The Girls Our Mothers Warned Us About.* Berkeley: Third Woman Press.

Ulibarrí, Sabine. 1971. *Tierra Amarilla: Stories of New Mexico/Cuentos de Nuevo México.* Albuquerque: University of New Mexico Press.

——. 1997. *Mayhem Was Our Business: Memorias de un veterano.* Tempe, AZ: Bilingual Press/Editorial Bilingüe.

Urrea, Luis Alberto. 1993. *Across the Wire: Life and Hard Times on the Mexican Border.* New York: Anchor Books.

——. 1994a. *The Fever of Being.* Albuquerque: West End Press.

——. 1994b. *In Search of Snow.* New York: HarperCollins.

——. 1996. *By the Lake of Sleeping Children: The Secret Life of the Mexican Border.* New York: Anchor Books.

——. 1998. *Nobody's Son: Notes from an American Life.* Tucson: University of Arizona Press.

——. 2004. *The Devil's Highway.* Boston: Little, Brown.

——. 2005. *The Hummingbird's Daughter.* Boston: Little, Brown.

Valdez, Luis. 1989a. *Actos and pensamiento serpentino.* Houston: Arte Público Press.

——, ed. 1989b. *Necessary Theater: Six Plays About the Chicano Experience.* Houston: Arte Público Press.

——. 1990. *Early Works.* Houston: Arte Público Press.

——. 1992. *Zoot Suit and Other Plays.* Houston: Arte Público Press.

Valdez, Luis, and Stan Steiner, eds. 1972. *Aztlán: An Anthology of Mexican American Literature.* New York: Vantage.

Véa, Alfredo, Jr. 1993. *La Maravilla.* New York: Plume.

——. 1996. *The Silver Cloud Cafe.* New York: Dutton.

——. 1999. *Gods Go Begging.* New York: Plume.

Venegas, Daniel. 1999. *Las aventuras de don Chipote o, cuando los pericos mamen.* Houston: Arte Público Press. (Originally published in 1928)

Vigil-Piñón, Evangelina. 1978. *Nada y nadie*. San Antonio: M & A Editions.

———. 1982. *Thirty an' Seen a Lot*. Houston: Arte Público Press.

———. 1987. *The Computer Is Down*. Houston: Arte Público Press.

Villanueva, Alma Luz. 1977. *Bloodroot*. Austin: Place of the Heron Press.

———. 1985. *Lifespan*. Austin: Place of the Heron Press.

———. 1993. *Planet, with Mother, May I?* Tempe, AZ: Bilingual Press/Editorial Bilingüe.

———. 1994a. *Naked Ladies*. Tempe, AZ: Bilingual Press/Editorial Bilingüe.

———. 1994b. *Weeping Woman: La Llorona and Other Stories*. Tempe, AZ: B Bilingual Press/Editorial Bilingüe.

Villanueva, Tino. 1972. *Hay otra voz: Poems (1969–1971)*. Staten Island: Editorial Mensaje.

———. 1984. *Shaking Off the Dark*. Houston: Arte Público Press.

———. 1994. *Crónica de mis años peores/Chronicle of My Worst Years*. Evanston, IL: TriQuarterly Books.

Villarreal, Edit. 1992. My Visits with MGM (My Grandmother Marta). In *Shattering the Myth: Plays by Hispanic Women of Color,* eds. Linda Feyder and Denise Chávez, 143–208. Houston: Arte Público Press.

Villarreal, José Antonio. 1959. *Pocho*. New York: Doubleday.

Villegas de Magnón, Leonor. 1994. *The Rebel*. Houston: Arte Público Press.

Viramontes, Helena María. 1985. *The Moths and Other Stories*. Houston: Arte Público Press.

———. 1995. *Under the Feet of Jesus*. New York: Dutton.

The WPA Guide to 1930s New Mexico. 1989. Tucson: University of Arizona Press.

Yáñez, Richard. 2003. *El Paso del Norte: Stories on the Border.* Las Vegas and Reno: University of Nevada Press.

Yarbro-Bejarano, Yvonne. 1983. Teatropoesía in the Bay Area: Tongues of Fire. In *Mexican American Theatre Then and Now,* ed. Nicolás Kanellos. 78–94. Houston: Arte Público Press.

Zamora, Bernice. 1976. *Restless Serpents*. Menlo Park: Diseños Literarios.

INDEX

ABOUT THE AUTHOR

CHARLES TATUM is professor of Spanish and dean of the College of Humanities at the University of Arizona. He was born in El Paso, Texas, and raised in Parral, Chihuahua, Mexico. His mother, Eloísa Aínsa, a Mexican American, was born and raised in El Paso. Tatum received his BA from the University of Notre Dame, his MA from Stanford University, and his PhD from the University of New Mexico.

Tatum is the author of a monographic study *Chicano Literature* (1982)—published in translation in Mexico in 1986—and coauthor of *Not Just for Children: The Mexican Comic Book in the Late 1960s and 1970s* (1992). He is cofounder and coeditor of the journal *Studies in Latin American Popular Culture*. He is editor of three volumes of *New Chicana/Chicano Writing* (1991–1993) for the University of Arizona Press and coeditor of a volume of essays, *Recovering the U.S. Hispanic Literary Heritage, Vol. II*. His most recent publication is a book, *Chicano Popular Culture* (University of Arizona Press, 2001). It was selected as a "Best of the Best of the University Presses" book by the American Association of American Presses. His published book chapters and articles include studies on Latin American prose fiction, Chicana/o literature, and Mexican popular culture.

Tatum serves on the advisory board of the Recovering the U.S. Hispanic Literary Heritage Project. He is a member of an editorial group that produced *Herencia*, an anthology of U.S. Hispanic literature that was published in 2001 by Oxford University Press and of a Spanish-language anthology, *En otra voz. Antología de la literatura hispana en los Estados Unidos* (Arte Público Press, 2002). Most recently, he has published a study of the Chicano poet Gary Soto in Scribner's *Encyclopedia of Latino/a Writers* (2004).

Tatum has been very active in advancing diversity issues at the University of Arizona, where he is a member of the Diversity Coalition and various committees and task forces that deal with diversity issues. He has advanced the College of Humanities as a model for recruiting and retaining a diverse faculty as well as undergraduate and graduate students.

Chicano and Chicana Literature is a volume in the series The Mexican American Experience, a cluster of modular texts designed to provide greater flexibility in undergraduate education. Each book deals with a single topic concerning the Mexican American population. Instructors can create a semester-length course from any combination of volumes, or may choose to use one or two volumes to complement other texts.

Additional volumes deal with the following subjects:

Mexican Americans and Health
Adela de la Torre and Antonio Estrada

Chicano Popular Culture
Charles M. Tatum

Mexican Americans and the U.S. Economy
Arturo González

Mexican Americans and the Law
Reynaldo Anaya Valencia, Sonia R. García, Henry Flores, and José Roberto Juárez Jr.

Chicana/o Identity in a Changing U.S. Society
Aída Hurtado and Patricia Gurin

Mexican Americans and the Environment
Devon G. Peña

Mexican Americans and the Politics of Diversity
Lisa Magaña

Mexican Americans and Language
Glenn A. Martínez

For more information, please visit
www.uapress.arizona.edu/textbooks/latino.htm